CANTINA

Recipes from a

MEXICAN KITCHEN

CANTINA

Recipes from a

MEXICAN KITCHEN

×

PAUL WILSON

hardie grant books

MELBOURNE · LONDON

INTRODUCTION

I left the United Kingdom many years ago, a classically trained chef setting out on a culinary adventure to Australia. Never did I think it would lead to an unrelenting enthusiasm for discovering more about our gastronomic universe.

Living in Australia I've realised we are blessed with so many food cultures that have formed a natural part of our life and make up our national cuisine. So it's no wonder that now Latin and, in particular, Mexican foods are increasingly establishing themselves as yet another important and popular food genre. However, this is no trending fusion cuisine. The new wave of popularity is simply timely recognition for an ancient and intellectual food culture, about which we have much to learn.

I have travelled and studied this interesting and evolving cuisine and have come to realise that we owe so much to the ancient cultures of the pre-Columbian Americas. The Spanish conquistadores were introduced to an array of foods that we simply couldn't live without today: from tomatoes, corn, avocados, beans, squash, capsicums (bell peppers) and chillies, potatoes and peanuts, to vanilla, strawberries, pineapple and chocolate, to name just a few.

The tomato, as we know it, came from Yucatán, where the Maya cultivated it long before the Spanish conquest. It made its first appearance in Europe in the mid-16th century and today it seems unthinkable for Italy to be without their much-loved napoletana sauce!

Corn is said to be attributed to humankind's very existence. This domesticated strain of wild grass was originally cultivated by the Mayans as early as 2500 BC and is now one of the most important crops in the modern Americas.

Avocados originated in southern Mexico, where they were used as an aphrodisiac. The excitement about this fruit spread to the Rio Grande and central Peru, way before the Europeans learned about it. In the United Kingdom and Australia, the avocado didn't really become popular until the 1960s, but since then we have truly embraced it.

Archaeological digs show that the cultivation of the black bean originated in southern Mexico and Central America more than 7000 years ago. It's now widely used as a staple throughout Latin America, the Caribbean, the United States and Asia.

Capsicums (bell peppers) and chillies have also been cultivated in the Americas for more than 6000 years. Today the *Capsicum annuum* species, with its many strains, has spread far and wide, and is crucial to nearly every fiery dish of the world's many cuisines.

Vanilla, the elixir from a unique species of orchid, originally flavoured Mayan drinks. The jungle of southern Mexico is still the only place that this orchid grows wild, pollinated by native stingless bees that produce Mayan honey.

But perhaps the one ingredient we are most grateful for is chocolate. This Mayan 'food of the gods', made from the toasted, fermented seeds of the cacao tree, is arguably the New World's greatest gift to world cuisines. It was so highly prized that, as well as eating it, the Aztecs and the Maya used cacao beans as currency.

All these ingredients are well documented but one thing my travels have taught me is that there are undoubtedly many more exciting ingredients awaiting discovery. The only problem is that there is not enough time to try them all!

This book is the culmination of my culinary journeys. Please look past the cheesy burrito and realise that there is so much more to discover about Mexican everyday cooking. I have done my best to introduce you to the real flavours of Mexico and Latin America. Many distinct regional and ancient recipes await you, with simply mind-blowing flavours, from magical moles and barbecoa, to cebiches, masa and the delectable wonders of Mexican street food.

While I've tried to stay true to my belief that there are no shortcuts to great complex flavours, I am sympathetic to the constraints of the home cook. I have included a useful chapter of recipes that represent the building blocks of Mexican cuisine. Here you will find out how to make amazing stocks, sauces, rubs, relishes, doughs and more. You will use these as the base of many of the other recipes in this book. If you want authentic flavour, then you should embrace these basic recipes. However, where appropriate I have suggested shortcuts. Some of the ingredients may sound unusual, but you should be able to find them in Spanish grocers and gourmet food stores. The glossary at the back of the book will give you further information on the more exotic items.

Not taking food too seriously, and having fun in the kitchen has always been a successful approach for me, so I hope you enjoy discovering the vibrant, complex, smoky and mysterious flavours of the cantina. Buen apetito!

PAUL WILSON

01

MEXI-MART
BUILDING
BLOCKS
&
USEFUL RECIPES

There are so many useful
recipes in this chapter that
capture the flavours of Mexico and
South America. They will help give
your Latin cooking the edge.

~~~~~~~~~

As with all great cuisines, to achieve Mexican and South American
flavours you need to know the basic recipes and building blocks.
In this chapter I have included all my restaurant kitchen's useful
recipes to get you started. Always remember to use seasonal, fresh
and local ingredients where possible. Don't be puzzled by the
exotic items required in this chapter and throughout the book;
you will find they are available at gourmet food stores and
Spanish grocers. The key marinades and sauces can be
prepared in advance and then simply refrigerated
or frozen, ready for when you need them.

CHIPOTLE CHICKEN STOCK

～～～～～～

+ 1 onion
+ 1 garlic bulb
+ 2 green jalapeños
+ 1.5 litres (51 fl oz/6 cups) chicken stock
+ 1 kg (2 lb 3 oz) chicken wings
+ 150 g (5½ oz) chipotle in adobo sauce (see Glossary)

+ 50 g (1¾ oz) achiote paste (see Glossary) or a large pinch of saffron threads
+ 2 cinnamon sticks
+ 2½ tablespoons ground cumin
+ 2½ tablespoons smoked paprika
+ 1 tablespoon salt

MAKES 1 LITRE (34 FL OZ/4 CUPS)

This smoky and spicy chicken stock is the foundation of many sauces and is a feature of everyday Latin cooking. It is fantastically fragrant and provides a great depth of flavour. It is wonderful as a base for flavoured rice, pozole, slow-cooked meats and for cooking shellfish.

Preheat an overhead grill (broiler) to high.

Cut the onion and garlic in half crossways. Arrange the onion, garlic and jalapeños on a grill tray and grill (broil) for 10 minutes, or until caramelised and charred.

Combine the onion, garlic and jalapeños with all the remaining ingredients, except the saffron (if using), in a large saucepan and bring to the boil over medium–high heat. Reduce the heat and simmer for 15 minutes, skimming away any impurities that rise to the surface. Add the saffron, if using, and gently simmer for a further 30 minutes.

Remove from the heat and set aside to cool slightly. Strain into an airtight container. Store in the refrigerator for up to 1 week, or freeze for up to 1 month.

PAUL'S TIP The left-over chicken wings can be re-used for a great snack or for another recipe.

ADOBO SAUCE

~~~~~~~~~~~~~~~~~

- + 3 large red capsicums (bell peppers), halved lengthways
- + 1 red onion, quartered
- + 1 garlic bulb, peeled
- + 3 long green chillies
- + 2 dried guajillo chillies (see Glossary)
- + 75 g (2¾ oz) (about 4) dried chipotle chillies (see Glossary)
- + 80 ml (2½ fl oz/⅓ cup) olive oil
- + large handful of oregano leaves

- + 2 tablespoons smoked paprika
- + 3 teaspoons Mexican spice blend (page 30)
- + 115 g (4 oz/½ cup) caster (superfine) sugar
- + 125 ml (4 fl oz/½ cup) sherry vinegar
- + 1 litre (34 fl oz/4 cups) Chipotle chicken stock (opposite page) or chicken stock
- + sea salt to taste

MAKES 500 ML (17 FL OZ/2 CUPS)

If you only make one sauce then this should be it. Its flavour is so intriguing when used in a myriad of savoury and meat applications. It's truly the taste of Latin food that we all love. You can also add it to mayonnaise or a tomato sauce to create new sauces to enjoy at home.

Preheat an overhead grill (broiler) to high.

Place the capsicum, onion, garlic and fresh chillies on a grill tray and grill (broil), turning occasionally, for 10–15 minutes, until soft and charred black. Allow to cool slightly then roughly chop.

Remove the stalks and roughly chop the guajillo and chipotle chillies, retaining the seeds.

Heat the oil in a medium heavy-based saucepan over low heat. Gently fry the dried chillies for 2–3 minutes, until they begin to colour. Add the charred vegetable mixture, oregano and spices and cook for a further 2 minutes, or until fragrant. Add the sugar and sherry and cook until the liquid reduces to a syrup.

Pour in the stock and bring to the boil. Reduce the heat and simmer gently for 45 minutes, or until reduced to a thick sauce.

Transfer the mixture to a food processor or blender and process, gradually adding a little water if required, to make a smooth sauce. Strain through a fine-mesh sieve, pressing and rubbing with the back of a spoon to ensure all of the sauce passes through. Season with salt.

Store in an airtight container in the refrigerator for up to 1 week, or freeze for up to 3 months.

RED MOLE

~~~~~~~~~~~~~~~~~~~~~

+ 250 g (9 oz) tinned or fresh tomatillos, drained if tinned or outside leaves removed if fresh (see Glossary)
+ 4 garlic cloves
+ 50 g (1¾ oz/⅓ cup) sesame seeds
+ 50 g (1¾ oz/⅓ cup) blanched almonds
+ 35 g (1¼ oz) (about 3) dried mulato chillies (see Glossary)
+ 35 g (1¼ oz) (about 3) dried ancho chillies (see Glossary)
+ 35 g (1¼ oz) (about 7) dried pasilla chillies (see Glossary)
+ 35 g (1¼ oz) fresh or dried jalapeño or poblano chillies (see Glossary)
+ 80 ml (2½ fl oz/⅓ cup) vegetable oil
+ 85 g (3 oz/⅔ cup) raisins
+ 1 tablespoon Mexican spice blend (page 30)
+ 1.25 litres (42 fl oz/5 cups) chicken stock
+ 1 thick slice day-old, crusty white bread
+ 50 g (1¾ oz) dark bitter chocolate, minimum 50% cocoa solids, roughly chopped
+ 50 ml (1¾ fl oz) agave syrup (see Glossary)
+ 50 ml (1¾ fl oz) sherry vinegar
+ sea salt to taste
+ hot sauce, if you like your mole extra-hot

MAKES 750 ML (25½ FL OZ/3 CUPS)

Mole (pronounced mo-lay, and meaning sauce) is the unique culinary symbol of Mexico. It comes in various colours and flavours and is often spiced with exotic chillies, chocolate, nuts, fruits and spices. Mole originates from two main areas of Mexico – Oaxaca and Puebla. I am a big mole fan. It may seem like a daunting sauce because of the unusual ingredients, but it's really a one-pot dish. Once you've mastered the sauce you can use it for a myriad of dishes, simple or complicated. This mole has a more complex and deeper flavour than the quick red mole, which follows. The main difference is the inclusion of the mulato, ancho and pasilla chillies, known as the 'holy trinity' by passionate Mexican cooks. The dried chillies are important to the authentic flavours of Mexican food.

Preheat an overhead grill (broiler) to high.

Place the tomatillos and garlic on a grill tray and grill (broil), turning occasionally, for 10–15 minutes, until soft and charred black. Transfer to a large bowl.

Dry-fry the sesame seeds in a medium frying pan over medium heat, stirring occasionally, for 3 minutes or until golden. Repeat with the almonds. Combine with the tomatillos and garlic.

Remove the stalks and roughly chop the chillies, retaining the seeds.

Heat the oil in a medium heavy-based saucepan over low heat. Gently fry the chillies for 2–3 minutes, until they begin to colour. Add the raisins and spice blend and cook until fragrant. Pour in 1 litre (34 fl oz/4 cups) of the stock, add the charred tomatillos, garlic, sesame seeds and almonds, bread and chocolate. Gently simmer for 45 minutes, or until reduced to a thick sauce.

Transfer the mixture to a food processor or blender and process, gradually adding the remaining stock, to make a smooth sauce. Strain through a fine-mesh sieve, pressing and rubbing with the back of a spoon to ensure all of the sauce passes through.

Combine the agave syrup and vinegar in a small saucepan. Simmer over medium-low heat, until reduced to a caramel. Add the caramel to the sauce and stir to combine. Season with salt. If you prefer your mole hotter, adjust with hot sauce.

Store in an airtight container in the refrigerator for up to 1 week, or freeze for up to 3 months.

QUICK RED MOLE

~~~~~~~~~~~~~~~~~

+ 250 g (9 oz) tinned or fresh
  tomatillos, drained if tinned,
  outside leaves removed if fresh
  (see Glossary)
+ 2 garlic cloves
+ 100 g (3½ oz/⅔ cup) sesame
  seeds
+ 40 g (1½ oz/¼ cup) blanched
  almonds
+ 75 g (2¾ oz) (about 6) dried
  mulato chillies (see Glossary)
+ 30 g (1 oz) (about 6) dried
  pasilla chillies (see Glossary)
+ 2 tablespoons vegetable oil
+ 40 g (1½ oz/⅓ cup) raisins
+ ½ cinnamon stick, broken
  into pieces

+ 2 teaspoons black peppercorns
+ ½ star anise
+ 2 whole cloves
+ 1 teaspoon cumin seeds
+ 1 litre (34 fl oz/4 cups) chicken
  stock
+ 1 thick slice day-old, crusty
  white bread
+ 15 g (½ oz) dark bitter
  chocolate, minimum 50% cocoa
  solids, roughly chopped
+ 1 large handful of oregano
  leaves
+ 1½ tablespoons sherry vinegar
+ 1½ tablespoons sugar
+ sea salt to taste

MAKES 500 ML (17 FL OZ/2 CUPS)

This is one of my favourite moles because it's so versatile. Carefully grilling (broiling) to almost burn your ingredients is a must, as you're not really cooking mole unless you're roasting, charring and caramelising. I always have this mole in my refrigerator and so should you. The vinegar and sugar caramel is known as a gastrique; it adds balance and harmonises the flavours of the chocolate, spices and chillies in the mole.

Preheat an overhead grill (broiler) to high.

Place the tomatillos and garlic cloves on a grill tray and grill (broil), turning occasionally, for 10–15 minutes, until soft and charred black. Transfer to a large bowl.

Dry-fry the sesame seeds in a medium frying pan over medium heat, stirring occasionally, for 3 minutes or until golden. Repeat with the almonds. Combine with the tomatillos and garlic.

Remove the stalks and roughly chop the chillies, retaining the seeds.

Heat the oil in a medium heavy-based saucepan over low heat. Gently fry the chillies for 2–3 minutes, until they begin to colour. Add the raisins and spices and cook until fragrant. Pour in 750 ml (25½ fl oz/3 cups) of the stock, add the charred tomatillos, garlic, sesame seeds, almonds, bread, chocolate and oregano. Gently simmer for 45 minutes, or until reduced to a thick sauce.

Transfer the mixture to a food processor or blender and process, gradually adding the remaining stock, to make a smooth sauce. Strain through a fine-mesh sieve, pressing and rubbing with the back of a spoon to ensure all of the sauce passes through.

Combine the vinegar and sugar in a small saucepan. Simmer over medium–low heat, until reduced to a caramel. Add the caramel to the sauce and stir to combine. Season with salt.

Store in an airtight container in the refrigerator for up to 1 week, or freeze for up to 3 months.

BLACK MOLE

~~~~~~~~~~~~~~~~~~~~

- + 1 cinnamon stick
- + 1 star anise
- + 1 teaspoon black peppercorns
- + 1 whole clove
- + 35 g (1¼ oz) (about 3) dried mulato chillies (see Glossary)
- + 25 g (1 oz) (about 5) dried guajillo chillies (see Glossary)
- + 20 g (¾ oz) (about 3) dried pasilla chillies (see Glossary)
- + 125 ml (4 fl oz/½ cup) olive oil
- + ½ teaspoon ground allspice

- + 750 ml (25½ fl oz/3 cups) chicken stock
- + ½ small white onion, quartered
- + 50 g (1¾ oz) field mushrooms
- + 4 garlic cloves
- + ½ large plantain or ripe banana
- + 25 g (1 oz) prunes, pitted
- + 1 large handful of tarragon or oregano leaves, roughly chopped
- + 125 ml (4 fl oz/½ cup) Red mole (page 16)

- + 100 g (3½ oz) freshly cooked black beans, cooking liquid reserved
- + 75 g (2¾ oz) dark bitter chocolate, minimum 50% cocoa solids, roughly chopped
- + ½ slice day-old white bread
- + 50 g (1¾ oz) unsalted butter, cubed
- + lime juice to taste
- + sugar to taste
- + sea salt to taste

> MAKES 750 ML (25½ FL OZ/3 CUPS)

The tall, dark and handsome mole. With rich coffee and chocolate overtones, describing this mole feels like describing a complex red wine. With its layered flavour profile, serve it with kangaroo, duck or venison to truly appreciate its complexity and depth of flavour.

Soak the cinnamon stick, star anise, peppercorns and clove in water for 15 minutes. Drain.

Remove the stalks and roughly chop the chillies, retaining the seeds.

Heat 1 tablespoon of the oil in a medium frying pan over low heat. Gently fry the chillies, the whole spices and the allspice for 2–3 minutes, until fragrant and beginning to colour. Pour in 500 ml (17 fl oz/2 cups) of the stock and bring to the boil. Remove from the heat and set aside.

Heat 1 tablespoon of the oil in a medium heavy-based saucepan over low heat. Cook the onion, mushroom and garlic, until softened. Add the plantain, prunes and herbs and cook for 2 minutes, until caramelised. Add the chilli and spiced stock mixture, red mole sauce and black beans and their cooking liquid and gently simmer for 25–30 minutes, until thick.

Add the chocolate and bread and cook, stirring occasionally, for a further 10–15 minutes, until reduced to a thick sauce.

Add the remaining oil and the butter and stir to combine.

Transfer the mixture to a food processor or blender and process, gradually adding the remaining stock, to make a smooth sauce. Strain through a fine-mesh sieve, pressing and rubbing with the back of a spoon to ensure all of the sauce passes through.

Season with lime juice, sugar and salt.

Store in an airtight container in the refrigerator for up to 1 week, or freeze for up to 3 months.

MEXICAN SALSA VERDE

~~~~~~~~~~~~~

+ 1 jalapeño
+ 2 small garlic cloves
+ 25 g (1 oz) (about 5) pasilla chillies (see Glossary)
+ 125 ml (4 fl oz/1/2 cup) extra-virgin olive oil
+ 60 ml (2 fl oz/1/4 cup) lemon juice
+ 1 tablespoon dijon mustard
+ 1 tablespoon cider vinegar
+ 1 tablespoon raisins
+ 15 g (1/2 oz) capers, rinsed
+ 1 large handful of flat-leaf parsley
+ 1 small handful of mint leaves
+ 1 small handful of chocolate mint leaves
+ 1 small handful of coriander (cilantro) leaves
+ 1 small handful of sweet basil leaves
+ 1 small handful of oregano leaves
+ 100 g (3 1/2 oz) cooked English spinach
+ sea salt to taste
+ habanero sauce to taste

MAKES 400 ML (13 1/2 FL OZ)

The charring of the garlic and chillies and the use of chocolate mint give this famous Latin sauce its Mexican accent. The deep flavour achieved here is lovely with the subtle sweetness of the raisins. It's a lovely, complex sauce with a rich smokiness and a beautiful, deep red colour. It makes a great addition to any barbecued meat.

Preheat an overhead grill (broiler) to high heat.

Place the jalapeño and garlic on a small tray and grill (broil), turning occasionally, for 10 minutes, until soft, caramelised and charred black.

Remove the stems from the pasilla chillies and roughly chop, retaining the seeds. Place in a small heatproof bowl, cover with boiling water and set aside for 10 minutes, to rehydrate. Reserve the liquid.

Combine the olive oil, lemon juice, mustard, vinegar, raisins, capers, charred chilli and garlic in a food processor or blender and process until emulsified.

Gradually add the herbs, spinach and some of the reserved chilli soaking liquid, as required, to make a fine sauce.

Season with salt and habanero sauce.

Transfer to a bowl and set over a larger bowl filled with iced water to rapidly chill.

Store in an airtight container in the refrigerator for up to 1 week.

PAUL'S TIP If the herb chocolate mint is hard to find, substitute 10 g (1/4 oz) dark bitter chocolate, minimum 50% cocoa solids.

TOMATILLO VERDE

- 250 g (9 oz) tinned or fresh tomatillos, drained if tinned or outside leaves removed if fresh (see Glossary)
- 1 red onion, thickly sliced into rounds
- 2 green jalapeños
- 3 garlic cloves
- 125 g (4½ oz) cherry tomatoes
- 60 ml (2 fl oz/¼ cup) chicken or vegetable stock
- juice of 3 limes
- 1 large handful of coriander (cilantro) leaves
- 1 small handful of oregano leaves
- 2 teaspoons ground cumin
- sugar to taste
- sea salt to taste

MAKES 400 ML (13½ FL OZ)

This is a favourite sauce of mine for white meats, fish and vegetables. Tomatillos are similar to green tomatoes or gooseberries. The tinned varieties are excellent and are available from Latin and gourmet food stores. This sauce refreshes the palate with its layers of flavour and hit of chilli.

Preheat an overhead grill (broiler) to high heat.

Place the tomatillos, onion, jalapeños and garlic on a grill tray and grill (broil), turning occasionally, for 10–15 minutes, until soft, caramelised and charred black. Allow to cool slightly then roughly chop.

Place the charred vegetable mixture into a food processor or blender. Add the tomatoes, stock, lime juice, coriander, oregano and cumin and process to make a smooth sauce. Season with sugar and salt.

Depending on how thick you like your sauce, either strain through a fine-mesh sieve for a thin sauce or leave as is if you prefer a thicker sauce.

Store in an airtight container in the refrigerator for up to 1 week.

NEW-STYLE CHIMICHURRI

~~~~~~~~~~~~~~~~

+ 250 ml (8½ fl oz/1 cup) extra-virgin olive oil
+ 3 large handfuls of flat-leaf parsley
+ 3 large handfuls of oregano leaves
+ 1½ large handfuls of tarragon leaves
+ 2 garlic cloves, smashed
+ 1 green jalapeño
+ 1 tablespoon dijon mustard
+ 1 tablespoon sherry vinegar
+ juice of ½ lime
+ sea salt and freshly ground black pepper

GARNISH

+ 1 green jalapeño, finely chopped
+ 1 eschalot, finely chopped

> MAKES 250 ML (8½ FL OZ/1 CUP)

This table sauce from Argentina is often used to slather onto grilled meats. There are many versions using dried herbs, chilli flakes, coriander (cilantro) or parsley. It's really up to you and what you like on your meats from the grill. My modernisation here is to blend and emulsify the herbs with the oil and vinegar. Before serving you simply add finely chopped jalapeño and eschalots. My chefs at Cantina call it 'Latin béarnaise'.

Combine all of the ingredients in a food processor or blender and process to make a smooth sauce. Season with salt and pepper.

Transfer to a serving bowl and sprinkle with the finely chopped jalapeño and eschalot to garnish.

Store in an airtight container in the refrigerator for up to 1 week.

PAUL'S TIP Add this sauce to mayonnaise for a fragrant herb aïoli.

POMEGRANATE MOJO

~~~~~~~~~~~~~~~~

+ 1½ tablespoons cumin seeds
+ 2 garlic cloves, crushed
+ 100 ml (3½ fl oz) sherry vinegar
+ 125 ml (4 fl oz/½ cup) olive oil
+ 200 ml (7 fl oz) pomegranate juice or molasses
+ 2 tablespoons sugar
+ 40 g (1½ oz/¼ cup) sesame seeds, toasted
+ sea salt and freshly ground black pepper

> MAKES 500 ML (17 FL OZ/2 CUPS)

This is a signature sauce of Latin cooking, said to be the condiment of the Portuguese explorers who left their garlic scent throughout their travels. So many nations have now added their own accents and that's the charm of this popular sauce. The sourness that interplays with the garlic is the key and I choose to add pomegranate for its striking and full zesty zing. This sauce can be used to dress raw sashimi-grade fish or to invigorate barbecued meats, soups or stews.

Place the cumin seeds in a small, dry frying pan and sprinkle with water to moisten. Cook over low heat, until the water evaporates and the seeds begin to dry-fry and become fragrant.

Add the garlic and vinegar and cook for 30 seconds. Add 1½ tablespoons of the oil and gently warm over low heat for 2 minutes, or until the garlic is cooked.

Transfer to a blender and process, gradually adding the remaining oil, the pomegranate juice or molasses and sugar. Stir in the sesame seeds. Season with salt and pepper.

Store in an airtight container in the refrigerator for up to 1 week.

WATERMELON ROJO

~~~~~~~~~~

+ 500 g (1 lb 2 oz) seedless watermelon, peeled and diced
+ 3 serrano chillies, roughly chopped (see Glossary)
+ 1 small handful of basil leaves
+ zest and juice of 2 limes
+ 1 tablespoon sherry vinegar
+ 1/2 small garlic clove
+ sea salt and freshly ground black pepper to taste
+ sugar to taste
+ 1 small red onion, finely diced
+ 1 small handful of mint leaves, finely chopped
+ 1 small handful of coriander (cilantro) leaves, finely chopped
+ habanero hot sauce to taste (optional)

MAKES 500 ML (17 FL OZ/2 CUPS)

Rojo (red) sauce is generally a table sauce, made with red chillies, and used like a condiment. It usually contains very ripe tomatoes but here I have used watermelon for a very different flavour. I like to use watermelon for various salsas to dress seafood, and this one is the perfect sauce for briny oysters.

Combine the melon, chilli, basil, lime zest and juice, vinegar and garlic in a blender and process until smooth. Season with salt and pepper and sugar if you feel it needs more sweetness. Refrigerate until required.

Just before serving, add the onion, mint and coriander. If you like your rojo hotter, add a little habanero sauce.

Store in an airtight container in the refrigerator for up to 1 week.

SMOKY ROJO SAUCE

~~~~~~~~~~

+ 1/2 red capsicum (bell pepper)
+ 1 red jalapeño or long red serrano chilli (see Glossary)
+ 4 garlic cloves
+ 100 ml (3 1/2 fl oz) extra-virgin olive oil
+ 50 ml (1 3/4 fl oz) pomegranate molasses
+ juice of 2 limes
+ 1 small handful of basil or oregano leaves
+ 25 g (1 oz) chipotle in adobo sauce (see Glossary)
+ 1 teaspoon smoked paprika
+ 1/2 teaspoon ground cumin
+ sea salt to taste

MAKES 300 ML (10 FL OZ)

This is a smoky rojo sauce using red capsicum (bell pepper). The grilled and charred capsicum and chilli, plus the chipotle and paprika, add a lovely smoky flavour, creating a richly spiced sauce suited to meats and vegetables.

Preheat an overhead grill (broiler) to high heat.

Place the capsicum, jalapeño and garlic on a grill tray and grill (broil), turning occasionally, for 10 minutes, until soft, caramelised and charred black.

Place the capsicum and chilli in a bowl, cover with plastic wrap and set aside to sweat and cool.

Peel and seed the capsicum and chilli.

Combine the capsicum, chilli and garlic with the remaining ingredients in a food processor or blender and process to make a smooth sauce. Season with salt.

Store in an airtight container in the refrigerator for up to 1 week.

PASILLA CHILLI RELISH

~~~~~~~~~~~

+ 50 g (1³/₄ oz) (about 8) dried pasilla chillies (see Glossary)
+ 60 ml (2 fl oz/¼ cup) extra-virgin olive oil
+ 6 garlic cloves
+ 1 large handful of oregano leaves
+ 2 teaspoons ground cumin
+ 1 teaspoon freshly ground black pepper
+ 1½ tablespoons honey
+ 1½ tablespoons merlot or sherry vinegar
+ sea salt to taste

MAKES 250 ML (8½ FL OZ/1 CUP)

Pasilla means raisin-like. Pasilla is a sweet and savoury chilli that is very popular in the food of Oaxaca, one of my favorite parts of Mexico. I like to think of this sauce as the Mexican mint sauce, as it goes so well with lamb and makes a great condiment for other meats too. Its fantastic bronze colour reflects a marinade full of complex flavour.

Remove the stalks and roughly chop the pasilla chillies, retaining the seeds.

Heat 1½ tablespoons of the oil in a medium frying pan set over medium–low heat. Fry the chillies for 2–3 minutes, until they begin to colour. Pour in enough boiling water to cover and set aside for 10 minutes to rehydrate.

Meanwhile, heat an overhead grill (broiler) to high heat.

Place the garlic on a small tray and grill (broil), turning occasionally, for 5–7 minutes, until caramelised and dark golden brown.

Drain the rehydrated chillies, reserving the liquid.

Combine the chillies, remaining oil, garlic, oregano, cumin and pepper in a food processor or blender and process to make a coarse purée. Continue blending, gradually adding enough of the reserved liquid to make a smooth, thick purée.

Combine the honey and vinegar in a small saucepan and simmer over low heat, until reduced by half, to make a light caramel. Add to the chilli mixture and blend to combine. Gradually add a little more of the reserved liquid, blending to make a smooth relish. Season with salt. Set aside to cool.

Store in an airtight container in the refrigerator for up to 1 week or freeze for up to 3 months.

PERUVIAN SALSA CRIOLLA

~~~~~~~~~~

+ 250 g (9 oz) sugar
+ 250 ml (8 1/2 fl oz/1 cup) cider vinegar
+ 2 red or white onions
+ 80 g (2 3/4 oz) sea salt
+ 1 small bulb fennel
+ 2 jalapeños or amarillo chillies (see Glossary)

+ 1–2 red or white banana or bullhorn chillies (see Glossary)
+ 1 small handful of tarragon leaves, roughly chopped
+ 1 small handful of flat-leaf parsley or coriander (cilantro) leaves, roughly chopped
+ grated zest and juice of 4 limes

MAKES 750 G (1 LB 11 OZ/3 CUPS)

This red and white, sweet and sour Peruvian onion salsa is simple and delicious. Peruvians are very fussy about the treatment of onions and soak them to mellow their harshness, giving a more harmonious flavour that does not overwhelm other ingredients. This process also helps to prevent heartburn. Salsa criolla can be made using red or white onion. The red onion version is great with grilled spiced skirt (flank) steak, while the white onion version is better matched with sashimi or cured, smoked, roasted or barbecued oily fish such as tuna, swordfish or salmon. For a more authentic preparation, cut the onions into thin half-moons. This method is known as 'a la pluma', as the onions are said to look like feathers.

Combine the sugar and vinegar in a medium saucepan and gently simmer over low heat, stirring occasionally, until the sugar dissolves. Set aside to cool.

Cut the cheeks off the onions and slice very thinly. Place the onion in a medium bowl, sprinkle with the salt and cover with hot water. Stand for 5 minutes then drain.

Slice the fennel and chillies into thin strips the same size as the onion.

Place the onion, fennel, chillies and herbs in a medium bowl and combine.

Add the lime zest and juice to the cooled vinegar liquid and pour over the onion mixture.

Store in an airtight container in the refrigerator for up to 1 week.

PAUL'S TIP To make a red salsa criolla, instead of the fennel, substitute 1 cooked heirloom beetroot (beet), such as watermelon or target beetroot.

NUT-FREE ROMESCO

~~~~~~~~

+ 500 g (1 lb 2 oz) tomatoes
+ 250 ml (8$\frac{1}{2}$ fl oz/1 cup) olive oil
+ 2 red capsicums (bell peppers)
+ 80 g (2$\frac{3}{4}$ oz/$\frac{1}{2}$ cup) sesame seeds, toasted
+ 2 long red chillies, roughly chopped
+ 2 bird's eye chillies, roughly chopped
+ 2 garlic cloves
+ 1 small handful of mint leaves
+ 1 small handful of basil leaves

+ 2 tablespoons ground cumin
+ 1$\frac{1}{2}$ tablespoons smoked paprika
+ 60 ml (2 fl oz/$\frac{1}{4}$ cup) Pedro Ximénez sherry
+ 1$\frac{1}{2}$ tablespoons freshly squeezed lemon juice
+ 1 tablespoon cabernet or sherry vinegar
+ 50 g (1$\frac{3}{4}$ oz) baguette slices, lightly fried then torn into pieces
+ sea salt to taste

MAKES 750 ML (25$\frac{1}{2}$ FL OZ/3 CUPS)

The Spanish would be horrified by a romesco without almonds, but I've done it anyway. Sesame works equally well so, because many people have nut allergies, I decided to create this version. It can also be used as a great dip and relish for fried foods.

Preheat the oven to 150°C (300°F).

Cut the tomatoes in half crossways and place on a roasting tray. Drizzle with a little of the oil and cook for 1½–2 hours, until collapsed and a deep red colour.

Preheat an overhead grill (broiler) to high.

Place the capsicums on a grill tray and grill (broil), turning occasionally, for 10 minutes, until charred black and collapsing.

Place the capsicums in a bowl, cover with plastic wrap and set aside to sweat and cool.

Peel and seed the capsicums and roughly chop.

Place the roasted tomatoes and capsicum in a food processor or blender. Add the sesame seeds, chillies, garlic, herbs, spices, sherry, lemon juice and vinegar and process, gradually adding the remaining oil, to combine. Add the bread and blend to make a smooth sauce. Season with salt.

Store in an airtight container in the refrigerator for up to 1 week.

AÏOLI

〜〜〜〜〜〜〜〜

+ 3 large egg yolks
+ 2 teaspoons Champagne vinegar
+ 3 garlic cloves, grated
+ 2 teaspoons dijon mustard
+ 200 ml (7 fl oz) vegetable oil
+ 125 ml (4 fl oz/½ cup) peanut oil
+ juice of ½ lemon
+ 2 teaspoons sea salt
+ warm water if needed

MAKES 400 ML (13½ FL OZ)

A garlic-flavoured mayonnaise, this is a good base for several of the recipes used throughout this book, but it's also great on its own. You can add chilli or lime, or combine it with other sauces, such as adobo, for a creamy spiced sauce – a perfect accompaniment to tacos or quesadillas.

Whisk the yolks, vinegar, garlic and mustard together in a medium bowl using an electric mixer, until smooth and creamy.

Continuously whisking, gradually pour in the oils, one at a time, in thin streams, until they are fully incorporated and the sauce is smooth and thick. Add the lemon juice and season with the salt.

If the sauce is too thick, add a little warm water to achieve the desired consistency.

BLACK GARLIC SAUCE

〜〜〜〜〜〜〜〜

+ 50 ml (1¾ fl oz) olive oil
+ 2 eschalots, finely chopped
+ 6 black garlic cloves (see Glossary)
+ 50 ml (1¾ fl oz) balsamic vinegar
+ 30 g (1 oz) sugar
+ 50 ml (1¾ fl oz) squid ink
+ 25 g (1 oz) chipotle in adobo sauce (see Glossary)
+ 300 ml (10 fl oz) Aïoli (see left)
+ sea salt to taste

MAKES 450 ML (15 FL OZ)

This creamy sauce blends the taste of balsamic vinegar with tangy, licorice-like black garlic and sea-flavoured black squid ink. It pairs beautifully with Black bean bocoles with seared scallops (page 98), but marries well with any seafood.

Heat the olive oil in a small saucepan over low heat. Cook the eschalot and garlic until softened. Add the balsamic vinegar and sugar and simmer until reduced to a syrup. Add the squid ink and chipotle and simmer for 1 minute, or until reduced to a thick sauce. Set aside to cool.

Combine the cooled black sauce with the aïoli in a food processor or blender and process until smooth. Strain through a fine-mesh sieve. Season with salt.

Store in an airtight container in the refrigerator for up to 1 week.

BRAZILIAN PEANUT SAUCE

~~~~~~~~~~~~~~~~

+ 1 red onion, roughly chopped
+ 125 g (4½ oz) tinned or fresh tomatillos, drained if tinned and outer leaves removed if fresh, roughly chopped (see Glossary)
+ 3 garlic cloves, roughly chopped
+ 1 teaspoon ground cinnamon
+ 1 teaspoon ground allspice

+ 1 teaspoon ground coriander
+ 3 dried pasilla chillies (see Glossary)
+ 1 tablespoon peanut oil
+ 240 g (8½ oz/1½ cups) roasted peanuts, ground
+ 750 ml (25½ fl oz/3 cups) chicken stock
+ 100 g (3½ oz) chipotle in adobo sauce (see Glossary)

+ 50 g (1¾ oz) dark bitter chocolate, minimum 50% cocoa solids, roughly chopped
+ 50 g (1¾ oz) day-old bread
+ 55 g (2 oz/¼ cup) sugar
+ 50 ml (1¾ fl oz) cider vinegar
+ lime juice to taste
+ sea salt to taste

MAKES 750 ML (25½ FL OZ/3 CUPS)

We are so used to seeing peanuts in Thai and Malaysian cooking but peanuts and peanut-based sauces are used all over Latin America too, mostly for braising exotic meats like goat. In Brazil they make a light peanut sauce for fish stews and the Peruvians use a peanut sauce for coating cooked potatoes. This sauce has a Mexican accent and in the restaurant we use it for many tacos, tamales and bocoles. I like the way the sweet peanut sauce interplays with salty masa and corn.

Combine the onion, tomatillos, garlic and spices in a food processor and blend to make a paste.

Remove the stalks and roughly chop the chillies, retaining the seeds.

Heat the oil in a medium heavy-based saucepan over low heat. Gently fry the chilli for 2–3 minutes, until it begins to colour. Add the onion mixture, increase the heat to medium–low and fry for 4 minutes, or until fragrant. Add the peanuts and fry for a further 5 minutes. Pour in 625 ml (21 fl oz/2½ cups) of the stock. Add the chipotle, chocolate and bread and gently simmer for 30 minutes, or until reduced to a thick sauce.

Transfer the mixture to a food processor or blender and process, gradually adding the remaining stock, to make a smooth sauce. Strain through a fine-mesh sieve, pressing and rubbing with the back of a spoon to ensure all of the sauce passes through.

Combine the sugar and vinegar in a small saucepan. Simmer over medium–low heat, until reduced to a caramel. Add the caramel to the sauce and stir to combine. Season with lime juice and salt.

Store in an airtight container in the refrigerator for up to 1 week, or freeze for up to 3 months.

LATIN SPICE RUB

~~~~~~~~~~~~

+ 50 g (1¾ oz) finely chopped rosemary
+ 2 tablespoons smoked paprika
+ 1 tablespoon ground cumin
+ 1 tablespoon ground fennel
+ 1 tablespoon chilli powder
+ 1 tablespoon garlic powder
+ 1 tablespoon caster (superfine) sugar
+ 1 tablespoon sea salt
+ 2 teaspoons cayenne pepper

MAKES 150 G (5½ OZ)

A Latin spice rub ideal for grilled meats. With the addition of rosemary it is especially good with lamb. This is great to make in advance as it stores well.

Combine all the ingredients and store in an airtight container for up to 1 month.

MEXICAN SPICE BLEND

~~~~~~~~~~~~

+ 1 tablespoon ground cinnamon
+ 1 tablespoon ground cumin
+ 1 tablespoon smoked paprika
+ 2 teaspoons ground allspice
+ 2 teaspoons freshly ground black pepper
+ 2 teaspoons ground star anise
+ 1 teaspoon ground cloves

MAKES 50 G (1¾ OZ)

Another spice blend, this time with a Mexican flavour. The cinnamon, star anise and cloves add a lovely deep note reminiscent of the classic Mexican hot chocolate. Smoked paprika and cumin give this spice blend a more savoury twist.

Combine the spices and store in an airtight container for up to 1 month.

SESAME PIPIAN

~~~~~~~~~~

+ 50 g (1³/₄ oz/¹/₃ cup) sesame seeds
+ 180 ml (6 fl oz) Tomatillo verde (page 21)
+ 65 g (2¹/₄ oz/¹/₄ cup) tahini
+ 25 g (1 oz) chipotle in adobo sauce (see Glossary)
+ 60 ml (2 fl oz/¹/₄ cup) chicken or vegetable stock, boiling
+ sugar to taste
+ sea salt to taste
+ habanero sauce to taste (optional)

MAKES 200 ML (7 FL OZ)

This is a wonderfully subtle and mysterious sauce influenced by the Moors of medieval Spain. Traditionally made using tomatillo verde, red mole and adobo sauce, my chefs whip this up in minutes with a well-stocked refrigerator of Latin building blocks. Here I have created a simpler version so you don't need to make all three sauces, just the vibrant tomatillo verde. Sesame pipian can be used as a sauce for a myriad of vegetables - wild mushrooms, roasted root vegetables, snow peas (mangetout), asparagus and padrón peppers, to name just a few.

Place the sesame seeds in a small frying pan and toast over medium-low heat, until golden brown.

Combine the sesame seeds, tomatillo verde, tahini and chipotle in a food processor or blender and process to make a smooth paste.

Gradually add the hot stock, blending to make a smooth sauce.

Strain through a fine-mesh sieve. Season with sugar and salt. Add habanero sauce to taste, if desired.

Store in an airtight container in the refrigerator for up to 1 week, or freeze for up to 3 months.

DARK BEER GASTRIQUE

~~~~~~~~~~

+ 125 ml (4 fl oz/¹/₂ cup) dark beer
+ 125 ml (4 fl oz/¹/₂ cup) sherry vinegar
+ 115 g (4 oz/¹/₂ cup) caster (superfine) sugar

MAKES 250 ML (8¹/₂ FL OZ/1 CUP)

Beer is commonly used to braise meats and offal (variety meats). Here, beer is simmered with sherry vinegar and sugar to create a rich caramel gastrique, which can be used to refresh and rejuvenate a dull-tasting sauce. I also like to use this to caramelise red fruits such as figs, plums and cherries to serve with roast duck. Figs caramelised this way also make a great addition to empanadas.

Combine the beer, vinegar and sugar in a medium saucepan and simmer over low heat, stirring until the sugar dissolves. Increase the heat and bring to the boil. Reduce the heat to low and gently simmer until reduced to a caramel that just coats the back of a spoon. Set aside to cool.

Store in an airtight container in the refrigerator for up to 3 months.

ACHIOTE RELISH

~~~~~~~~~~

+ 2 jalapeños
+ 6 garlic cloves
+ 50 g (1¾ oz) achiote paste (see Glossary)
+ 1 large handful of oregano leaves
+ 60 ml (2 fl oz/¼ cup) chardonnay vinegar or best-quality white wine vinegar
+ 2 teaspoons ground allspice
+ 1 teaspoon ground fennel
+ 1 teaspoon smoked paprika
+ 1 teaspoon sea salt
+ ½ teaspoon freshly ground black pepper
+ 80 ml (2½ fl oz/⅓ cup) fruity olive oil

MAKES 250 ML (8½ FL OZ/1 CUP)

Perfect for seafood, pork and chicken, the rusty-coloured annatto seed is harvested from the annatto shrub to produce achiote spice. Most commonly available in paste form, achiote is sometimes called the 'saffron of Mexico'. It adds a unique, addictive, earthy and mineral flavour to dishes, especially those from the Yucatán region of Mexico.

Preheat an overhead grill (broiler) to high heat.

Place the jalapeños and garlic on a small tray and grill (broil), turning occasionally, for 10 minutes, until soft, caramelised and charred black.

Combine the charred jalapeños and garlic with the achiote paste, oregano leaves, vinegar, spices, salt and pepper in a small food processor and blend to make a coarse paste. Gradually pour in the oil, blending to make a smooth sauce.

Store in an airtight container in the refrigerator for up to 1 week.

AL PASTOR MARINADE

- + 3 garlic cloves
- + 1 jalapeño
- + 60 ml (2 fl oz/¼ cup) olive oil
- + 100 g (3½ oz) pineapple, finely chopped
- + 2 teaspoons ground cumin
- + 1 teaspoon ground fennel
- + 1 teaspoon freshly ground black pepper
- + 1 teaspoon smoked paprika
- + 1 teaspoon dried chilli flakes
- + 25 g (1 oz) achiote paste (see Glossary)
- + 1 small handful of oregano leaves, roughly chopped
- + 250 ml (8½ fl oz/1 cup) pineapple juice
- + sea salt to taste

MAKES 250 ML (8½ FL OZ/1 CUP)

If you've been to Mexico City you would have had a taco al pastor or two! These 'shepherd's style' tacos are said to be inspired by the Lebanese shawarma. Slices of pork are marinated and skewered then cooked on a vertical spit. Pineapple plays a key role as a tenderising agent with this spice paste, and tacos al pastor are always served with a chunky pineapple salsa. This marinade is wonderful with any robust fish like mackerel or tuna steaks.

Preheat an overhead grill (broiler) to high.

Place the garlic and jalapeño on a small tray and grill (broil), turning occasionally, for 10 minutes, until soft, caramelised and charred black.

Heat 1 tablespoon of the oil in a saucepan over medium–low heat. Cook the pineapple and spices for 1 minute, or until fragrant. Add the charred garlic and jalapeño, achiote paste and oregano and cook for a further minute. Pour in the pineapple juice and simmer for 10 minutes, or until reduced by half.

Transfer to a food processor and blend, gradually adding the oil, to make a smooth paste. Season with salt.

Store in an airtight container in the refrigerator for up to 1 week.

MEXICAN BEER BATTER

～～～～～～～

+ 10 g (¼ oz) fresh yeast
+ 250 ml (8½ fl oz/1 cup) pale ale
+ ½ teaspoon white vinegar
+ 150 g (5½ oz/1 cup) plain
  (all-purpose) flour
+ pinch of sea salt
+ pinch of sugar
+ pinch of saffron powder

MAKES 500 ML (17 FL OZ/2 CUPS)

This batter is perfect for coating fish for tacos, where the crunch of the batter is essential. This recipe is terrific because it can be prepared in advance and doesn't lose its stability or frying ability.

Crumble the fresh yeast into a small bowl. Pour in the ale and vinegar and stir to dissolve the yeast.

Sift the flour, salt, sugar and saffron powder together into a medium bowl. Make a well in the centre and pour in the yeast mixture. Whisk well to combine.

Strain through a fine-mesh sieve. Cover with a clean tea towel (dish towel) and set aside in a warm place for 10 minutes, or until the batter is aerated and increased in size.

Whisk the batter once more before using.

Mexican beer batter can be made in advance and stored in the refrigerator in an airtight container for up to 2–3 days.

SALSA MEXICANA

~~~~~~~~~~~~~~~

+ 1 red onion, finely diced
+ 6 cherry tomatoes, quartered
+ 150 g (5¹/₂ oz) jicama, finely diced (see Glossary)
+ 2 jalapeños, seeded and thinly sliced
+ 1 habanero chilli, seeded and thinly sliced (see Glossary)
+ 4 large handfuls of coriander (cilantro) leaves, roughly chopped
+ 150 ml (5 fl oz) Zesty lime dressing (opposite page) or lime juice
+ sea salt to taste

MAKES 750 G (1 LB 11 OZ/3 CUPS)

A fresh salsa and probably my favourite, as it was in this recipe that I first used the refreshing jicama, which I now can't live without. Seasonal elements can also be added to this classic salsa, like grilled pineapple or diced citrus fruit. It is also amazing with miniature Australian finger limes, which are the size of pea eggplants (aubergines). Ideally salsa should be consumed the day you make it.

Combine the onion, tomato, jicama, jalapeño, habanero and coriander in a medium bowl. Just before serving, add the lime dressing or juice and toss to combine. Season with salt.

PAUL'S TIP If jicama is hard to find, use breakfast radish or daikon (white radish).

LATIN VINAIGRETTE

~~~~~~~~~~~~~~~

+ 80 ml (2¹/₂ fl oz/¹/₃ cup) sweet sherry, or reposado tequila (see Glossary)
+ 60 ml (2 fl oz/¹/₄ cup) sherry vinegar
+ 1 teaspoon ground cumin
+ 1 teaspoon smoked paprika
+ ¹/₂ teaspoon chilli powder
+ freshly ground black pepper to taste
+ 150 ml (5 fl oz) extra-virgin olive oil
+ 80 ml (2¹/₂ fl oz/¹/₃ cup) sesame oil
+ 1 large handful of oregano leaves, finely chopped
+ 1 teaspoon sea salt

MAKES 400 ML (13¹/₂ FL OZ)

This is a great all-rounder for leafy salads, vegetables and pulses. Sherry can be substituted with tequila to make a dressing that packs more punch – it's used in Drunken bean salad (page 229) and gives the salad its name.

Combine the sherry or tequila, vinegar and spices in a small saucepan and bring to the boil. Pour into a medium bowl and set aside to cool.

Continuously whisking, gradually add the oils, one at a time, to the spiced vinegar mixture, until emulsified. Stir in the oregano leaves and season with salt.

Store in an airtight container in the refrigerator for up to 1 month.

ZESTY LIME DRESSING

〜〜〜〜〜〜〜〜

+ finely grated zest of 3 limes
+ 300 ml (10 fl oz) freshly squeezed lime juice
+ 115 g (4 oz/1/2 cup) caster (superfine) sugar
+ 325 ml (11 fl oz) extra-virgin olive oil
+ 2 teaspoons sea salt

MAKES 500 ML (17 FL OZ/2 CUPS)

We use this dressing for most of our dishes in the restaurant, as it is so fresh and uplifting. Boiling the zest really concentrates the flavour of the lime, which is so important in Latin cooking. This recipe makes more than you need for one recipe but it stores well and can be used in a wide range of salads and salsas.

Combine the lime zest, 100 ml (3½ fl oz) of the lime juice and the sugar in a small saucepan and simmer for 5 minutes, or until the zest is soft.

Transfer to a food processor or blender and process, gradually adding the olive oil and remaining juice, until emulsified. Season with salt.

Store in an airtight container in the refrigerator for up to 1 month.

JALAPEÑO & FINGER LIME CREMA

〜〜〜〜〜〜〜〜

+ 250 g (9 oz/1 cup) sour cream
+ 100 g (3½ oz) salted ricotta, finely grated
+ 2 green jalapeños, seeded and roughly chopped
+ finely grated zest and juice of 3 limes
+ 1 garlic clove, grated
+ pinch of ground cumin
+ 1 large handful of oregano leaves, finely chopped
+ 50 g (1¾ oz) finger lime flesh (see Glossary) or the zest and juice of 1 lime
+ sea salt to taste

MAKES 400 ML (13½ FL OZ)

There are a few crema recipes in this book and, though it might sound like a tricky name, it is simply a sauce made using sour cream. The addition of a crema helps cut through the heat of a dish. The jalapeño added here provides flavour but the sauce retains its purpose. This sauce is outrageously good spread on warm barbecued corn and sprinkled with smoked paprika and finely grated salted ricotta.

Combine the sour cream, salted ricotta, jalapeño, lime zest and juice, garlic and cumin in a bowl, and stir to make a smooth cream.

Stir in the oregano and finger lime flesh. Season with salt.

Store in an airtight container in the refrigerator for up to 1 week.

PAUL'S TIP This dressing is great for vegetables and salads. It works particularly well with small raw button mushrooms, grilled field mushrooms, baby beetroot (beets) and small waxy potatoes.

SWEETCORN CREMA

~~~~~~~~~~~~~~~~~~

+ 60 ml (2 fl oz/1/4 cup) rice bran oil
+ 1/2 white onion, finely chopped
+ 3 garlic cloves, sliced
+ 2 corn cobs, kernels removed, husks retained for stock,
+ 250 ml (81/2 fl oz/1 cup) chicken stock
+ 160 g (51/2 oz/2/3 cup) low-fat sour cream
+ 1 small handful of tarragon leaves, finely chopped
+ sea salt to taste

MAKES 500 ML (17 FL OZ/2 CUPS)

This crema makes a lovely, sweet creamy addition to many dishes. Used with Lobster tamales Veracruz-style (page 86) it adds moisture to the filling and dough. Like a Mexican creamed corn, this is a great sauce for cutting through the heat of many sauces.

Heat the oil in a medium saucepan over low heat. Cook the onion and garlic until softened. Add the corn kernels and cook for 2 minutes. Add the chicken stock and corn husks, increase the heat and bring to the boil. Turn down the heat and simmer until the stock reduces to just cover the corn. Discard the husks.

Transfer to a food processor or blender and process, gradually adding half of the sour cream, to make a smooth sauce.

Strain through a fine-mesh sieve and set aside to cool.

Stir in the remaining sour cream and the tarragon. Season to taste.

Store in an airtight container in the refrigerator for up to 1 week.

AVOCADO CREMA

~~~~~~~~~~~~~~~~~~

+ 3 overripe avocados
+ juice of 3 limes
+ 90 g (3 oz/1/3 cup) sour cream
+ 1 garlic clove, grated
+ 11/2 teaspoons ground cumin
+ 1 teaspoon smoked paprika
+ 1/4 teaspoon ground allspice
+ pinch of onion powder
+ pinch of ground coriander
+ sea salt to taste

MAKES 750 ML (251/2 FL OZ/3 CUPS)

A guacamole with the addition of sour cream makes it a crema. It is a great basic sauce to complement an array of dishes, such as lamb ribs, tacos or Mexican chicken, adding moisture, subtle flavour and helping to balance chilli heat. You can use left-over guacamole to make this recipe.

Halve the avocados lengthways, remove the stones and scoop out the flesh using a large spoon.

Combine the avocado, lime juice, sour cream, garlic and spices in a food processor and blend to make a smooth thick sauce. Season with salt.

Avocado crema is best used on the day it is made.

GREEN SALMOREJO

~~~~~~~~~~~~~

+ 225 ml (7¹/₂ fl oz) freshly squeezed lime juice
+ 25 ml (³/₄ fl oz) habanero sauce
+ 1¹/₂ garlic cloves
+ finely grated zest of 3 limes
+ 125 ml (4 fl oz/¹/₂ cup) extra-virgin olive oil
+ 1 large handful of coriander (cilantro) leaves
+ sea salt to taste

MAKES 400 ML (13¹/₂ FL OZ)

Salmorejo is very similar to the Spanish gazpacho. Traditionally thickened with bread, this sauce is referred to as 'cream of gazpacho'. Here I have given the sauce a Mexican accent and recreated it as a light green sauce that can be used for cebiche. If you prefer a more traditional salmorejo, simply add some crustless white bread and blend for a thick soup-like sauce.

Combine the lime juice, habanero sauce, garlic and lime zest in a food processor or blender and process, gradually adding the oil, until emulsified. Add the coriander and blend to make a silky sauce. Season with salt.

Store in an airtight container in the refrigerator for up to 1 week.

TARO CHIPS

~~~~~~~~~~~~~

+ 300 g (10¹/₂ oz) taro
+ sunflower oil for deep-frying
+ sea salt to taste

SERVES 4

This unusual root vegetable resembles an elephant's foot. Although it might already sound exotic and daunting, it is the best frying vegetable I've ever come across and you will find it in Asian supermarkets. It is really easy to use and these wafer-thin chips (crisps) are crunchy and delicious.

Peel and very thinly slice the taro using a mandoline.

Pour enough oil to half-fill a large heavy-based saucepan. Heat the oil to 140°C (275°F).

Fry the chips in batches, until golden. Remove from the oil using a slotted spoon and drain on paper towel.

Increase the oil temperature to 180°C (350°F). Fry the chips for a second time, until golden brown. Drain on paper towel.

Lightly season with salt before serving.

VERACRUZ SAUCE

~~~~~~~~~~

+ 500 g (1 lb 2 oz) tomatoes
+ 60 ml (2 fl oz/1/4 cup) olive oil
+ 1 onion, finely chopped
+ 3 garlic cloves, thinly sliced
+ 3 long red chillies, chopped
+ 2 tablespoons sugar
+ 1 tablespoon sherry vinegar
+ 1/2 teaspoon smoked paprika
+ 125 ml (4 fl oz/1/2 cup) white wine
+ 500 ml (17 fl oz/2 cups) chicken stock
+ 1 small handful of basil leaves, roughly chopped
+ 1 small handful of oregano leaves, roughly chopped
+ 50 g (1 3/4 oz/1/4 cup) baby capers in brine, drained
+ 25 g (1 oz) finely diced roasted capsicum (bell pepper)
+ 25 g (1 oz) finely chopped green olives
+ 25 g (1 oz) finely chopped pickled jalapeños
+ sea salt to taste

MAKES 500 G (1 LB 2 OZ/2 CUPS)

Veracruz is a major city on the Gulf of Mexico where the food is heavily influenced by Spain and the Caribbean. This spicy sauce is generally used for seafood. However, it also works particularly well as a base sauce to braise vegetables and delicate meats.

Preheat the oven to 150°C (300°F).

Cut the tomatoes in half crossways and place in a roasting tray. Drizzle with a little of the oil and cook for 1½–2 hours, until collapsed and a deep red colour.

Heat the remaining oil in a medium saucepan over low heat. Cook the onion and garlic until softened. Add the slow-roasted tomatoes, chilli, sugar, vinegar and paprika and cook until all the liquid has evaporated.

Add the wine and cook for a further 15 minutes, or until reduced to a rich compote. Add the stock and simmer for 20 minutes or until reduced to a thick sauce-like consistency.

Transfer to a food processor or blender and process to make a smooth sauce (or leave as is if you prefer it chunkier). Strain through a fine-mesh sieve into a medium saucepan and reheat. Add the herbs, capers, capsicum, olives and jalapeños and season with salt.

Store in an airtight container in the refrigerator for up to 1 week.

REFRIED BEANS

〰〰〰〰〰

+ 100 g (3½ oz/½ cup) dried borlotti (pinto) beans, soaked overnight in cold water
+ 1 large handful of oregano leaves
+ 3 garlic cloves, 1 whole, 2 of them thinly sliced
+ ½ teaspoon bicarbonate of soda (baking soda)
+ 80 ml (2½ fl oz/⅓ cup) extra-virgin olive oil
+ 1 avocado leaf or 1 star anise (optional)
+ 1 red onion, finely chopped
+ 1 jalapeño, thinly sliced
+ sea salt to taste

SERVES 4-6

It seems that refried beans, or frijoles, are served with almost every dish in Mexico, and why not? They are so delicious and comforting but not the most attractive of purées to plate, but I guarantee every scrap will be mopped up and adored. If you're lucky enough to have an avocado tree, you can use the avocado leaf to flavour the beans. Simply cut the leaf into small pieces and fry it for 2 minutes in a little olive oil until translucent. Add it to the pan with the beans and water for a subtle and authentic aniseed note.

Drain the beans and place them in a medium saucepan with half the oregano, the whole garlic clove and the bicarbonate of soda. Heat 1 tablespoon of the oil in a large frying pan and fry the avocado leaf or star anise, if using, until fragrant, and add it to the beans. Cover with 4 times the quantity of water and bring to the boil. Reduce the heat and simmer for 40 minutes, or until tender. Drain the beans, reserving any cooking liquid. Discard the garlic clove and avocado leaf or star anise.

Heat 2 tablespoons of the oil in the frying pan over low heat. Cook the sliced garlic, onion and jalapeño, until soft and caramelised. Add the beans and remaining oregano and cook for 2 minutes until soft and thickened. Transfer to a food processor and blend, adding a little of the reserved cooking liquid and remaining oil, to make a smooth purée. Season with salt and serve.

BRAISED BLACK BEANS

〰〰〰〰〰

+ 220 g (8 oz/1 cup) dried black beans, soaked overnight in cold water
+ 2 large handfuls of oregano leaves, roughly chopped
+ 6 garlic cloves, 3 whole, 3 roughly chopped
+ 1 cinnamon stick
+ 1 star anise
+ 1 teaspoon bicarbonate of soda (baking soda)
+ 125 ml (4 fl oz/½ cup) extra-virgin olive oil
+ 2 red onions, finely chopped
+ 2-3 jalapeños, depending on how hot you like it
+ sea salt and freshly ground black pepper to taste
+ lime juice to taste
+ 100 g (3½ oz) salted ricotta, grated

SERVES 4-6

This is a 'cheffier' version of refried beans. Retain the inky cooking liquid to further enhance the colour and flavour of the beans. Serve them with spicy foods and barbecued meats or just with corn (tortilla) chips.

Drain the beans and place them in a medium saucepan with a handful of the oregano, the 3 whole garlic cloves, the cinnamon stick, star anise and the bicarbonate of soda. Cover with 4 times the quantity of water and bring to the boil. Reduce the heat and simmer for 40 minutes, or until tender. Drain the beans, reserving any cooking liquid. Discard the garlic cloves, cinnamon stick and star anise.

Heat 60 ml (2 fl oz/¼ cup) of the oil in a large frying pan over low heat. Cook the chopped garlic, onion and jalapeños until soft and caramelised. Add three-quarters of the beans and 60 ml (2 fl oz/¼ cup) of the cooking water and cook for 2-4 minutes, until soft and thickened. Transfer to a food processor and blend, adding a little more of the oil and a little of the reserved cooking liquid to make a smooth purée. Return the purée to the pan. Add the remaining beans and oregano and reheat. Season with salt and pepper and a squeeze of lime.

Serve drizzled with oil and sprinkle with salted ricotta and the remaining oregano. Store in an airtight container in the refrigerator for up to 1 week, or freeze for up to 3 months.

HOMINY RICE

~~~~~~~~

+ 200 g (7 oz/1 cup) long-grain white rice
+ 75 g (2¾ oz) unsalted butter
+ 1 white onion, finely chopped
+ 1 x 4 cm (1½ in) piece of fresh ginger, grated
+ 3 garlic cloves, crushed

+ 250 g (9 oz) tin hominy corn kernels, drained, 200 ml (7 fl oz) of the liquid reserved (see Glossary)
+ 2 large handfuls of oregano leaves, roughly chopped
+ 1 tablespoon sea salt
+ 220 ml (7½ fl oz) chicken stock

SERVES 4

Hominy is a type of corn that has been treated with alkali in a process called nixtamalisation. Hominy is ground to make the flour known as masa harina, which is used to make tortillas. It is also treated to make grits, which are widely used in various parts of Africa and the Caribbean to make porridge-type dishes or soup. I like to use tinned hominy kernels to add interest to rice pilafs as well as to enrich stews. The water from the tin has a nice sweet and mysterious corn flavour, so use this for boiling rice too. To my mind, the flavour is the real taste of Mexico. If you can source epazote, use it instead of oregano for a more authentic version.

Place the rice in a fine-mesh sieve and rinse under cold running water, until the water runs clear. Drain.

Melt 50 g (1¾ oz) of the butter in a medium saucepan over low heat. Cook the onion, ginger and garlic, until softened. Add the hominy kernels and cook for a further minute. Add the rice, oregano and salt and stir to combine.

Pour in the reserved hominy corn liquid and the stock and bring to the boil. Reduce the heat to the lowest setting, cover and cook for 12 minutes. Remove from the heat and set aside with the lid on for 5–10 minutes to finish cooking.

Fluff the rice with a fork. Add the remaining butter and stir to combine. Adjust the seasoning with additional salt, if required, before serving.

SALT COD MIXTURE

~~~~~~~~~~~~~~~

+ 250 g (9 oz) salt cod or white fish, e.g. snapper, hapuka or ling, cured, see recipe, opposite
+ 400 ml (13½ fl oz) milk
+ 1 small handful of oregano leaves
+ 150 g (5½ oz) small floury potatoes, peeled and halved

+ 2 garlic cloves, grated
+ 80 ml (2½ fl oz/⅓ cup) olive oil
+ sea salt to taste

MAKES 450 G (1 LB)

Salt cod was brought to Mexico at the time of the Spanish conquests in the early 1500s. Adhering to the Spanish tradition, it is typically served in dishes at Christmas time in Mexico. Here I have combined salt cod with potato and garlic to make a creamy flavoursome paste, which can be used to stuff jalapeños and make fritters. Both are coated and fried, creating a delectable textural contrast.

If using pre-prepared salt cod, soak the fish in cold water for 24 hours, changing the water several times during this period. This will rehydrate as well as remove the excess saltiness from the fish. If preparing your own, prepare as on opposite page.

Place the fish in a medium saucepan, cover with milk, add the oregano and gently cook over low heat for 10 minutes, until tender. Drain, reserving 80 ml (2½ fl oz/⅓ cup) of the milk.

Boil the potato for 10 minutes or until tender. Drain. Return to the pan and cook over low heat until dry. While still warm, pass the potato through a mouli or potato ricer, if you have one, or finely grate onto a tray. Cover and set aside to cool.

Flake the fish, discarding any bones or skin.

Combine the fish, potato and garlic in an electric mixer fitted with a paddle attachment and mix to combine. Mixing continuously on low speed, gradually add the oil, and then the milk, to make a soft cake-like mixture. Season with salt. Refrigerate until required, or freeze for up to 48 hours.

LIME CURE FOR FISH

~~~~~~~~~~~~~~~

+ 500 g (1 lb 2 oz/2 cups) table
  salt
+ 250 g (9 oz) sugar
+ finely grated zest of 6 limes
+ firm white fish fillets for
  curing

MAKES 750 G (1 LB 11 OZ) CURING MIXTURE

Curing your own fish is a simple process. The fish is covered in a salt and sugar mixture then refrigerated to 'cold cook'. The cure mixture draws the moisture out of the fish, changing the texture to firm and compact rather than soft and flaky. Remember to soak and wash the cure mixture thoroughly off the fish before use.

To make the curing mixture, combine all of the ingredients, except the fish, in a medium bowl. Mix well.

Lay out a sheet of plastic wrap twice the length of the fish that you are curing. Place half of the curing mixture in the middle of the plastic. Spread out to make an even layer the length of the fish. Place the fish on top and cover with the remaining salt mixture. Wrap up tightly in the plastic wrap and refrigerate for 4 hours.

Soak the cured fish fillet in a bowl of cold water for 2 minutes. Rinse and repeat. Dry well on a clean tea towel (dish towel).

Trim and cut the cured fish fillet into equal-sized portions. Wrap up each piece and refrigerate or freeze until required.

Cured fish can be stored in an airtight container in the refrigerator for up to 3 days.

PAUL'S TIP The lime cure can be made in advance, 48 hours before use.

TORTILLA DOUGH

~~~~~~~~~~~~~

+ 300 g (10½ oz/3 cups) fine white masa harina flour (see Glossary)
+ 1 teaspoon sea salt
+ 450 ml (15 fl oz) water
+ 2 teaspoons vegetable oil

MAKES 750 G (1 LB 11 OZ)
(ENOUGH FOR TWENTY-FOUR 15 CM/6 IN
OR TWELVE 20 CM/8 IN TORTILLAS)

Tortillas are a staple on the Mexican table. The dough is simple to make using white masa harina flour and water, with a little salt and oil. Tortillas can be grilled for use as tacos or as an accompaniment to any meal. In addition they can be fried and used as tostadas or quesadillas or baked or fried and used as masa corn (tortilla) chips.

Combine the flour and salt using an electric mixer fitted with a dough hook.

Mixing at medium speed, gradually pour in the water and oil to make a dough. Work the dough until it comes away clean from the side of the bowl. Form a ball and press to flatten – when the dough is the right consistency it should not split at the sides. Add a little more water if necessary.

Shape the dough into 24 or 12 even-sized balls, depending on whether you are making small tortillas for tacos, or larger ones for quesadillas or tostadas.

Using a tortilla press, flatten the balls between 2 sheets of baking paper, creating thin discs. Alternatively, roll out between the baking paper using a rolling pin – but your discs will not be so perfectly round.

Ideally heat a cast-iron or non-stick frying pan over medium–high heat. Cook the tortillas for 1 minute on each side, until they are light golden.

FOR BOCOLES: Prepare a third of the dough recipe as per the method above, adding only 100 ml (3½ fl oz) water, to prepare a very dry dough that can be shaped into a ball. (For cooking instructions, see page 98.)

PAUL'S TIP Tortillas can be prepared in advance and frozen. Simply par-cook and layer the tortillas between pieces of plastic wrap or baking paper. Wrap tightly in plastic wrap and freeze for up to 1 month.

SOPES DOUGH

~~~~~~~~~~~~~~~

+ 150 g (5¹/₂ oz/1¹/₂ cups) masa harina flour
  (see Glossary)
+ ¹/₂ teaspoon sea salt
+ 200 ml (7 fl oz) warm water
+ 30 g (1 oz) lard
+ 250 ml (8¹/₂ fl oz/1 cup) vegetable oil

MAKES 380 G (13¹/₂ OZ) (ENOUGH FOR 12 SOPES)

A basic masa dough similar to tortilla dough with the addition of lard to create a crumblier outcome, which is very appetising as the pastry is short and unctuous. Traditionally the dough is rolled and pressed into small, round thick cakes, partially grilled with the edges raised to create a lip for holding the filling in place. Here I recommend shaping and par-baking them in a muffin tin to form a rustic tart case.

Preheat the oven to 180°C (350°F).

Lightly grease a 12-hole muffin tin with oil.

Combine the flour and salt together in a medium bowl. Gradually add the water, mixing to combine. Add the lard and blend, using your fingertips, into the masa mixture. Knead until it comes together as a dough.

Break off a golf ball-sized piece of dough, shape into a ball and press to flatten – when the dough is the right consistency it should not split at the sides. Add a little more water if necessary.

Shape the dough into 12 equal-sized balls.

Flatten the balls in the palm of your hand and use your thumb and forefinger to mould them into 1 cm (½ in) thick discs approximately 7 cm (2¾ in) in diameter. Press the discs into the prepared muffin holes, raising up the sides to form a rustic tart.

Bake for 10 minutes, or until the sopes hold their shape.

Heat the oil in a medium frying pan and set over medium heat. Shallow-fry the sopes for 5–10 minutes, until they are crisp and golden brown.

TLAYUDAS DOUGH

~~~~~~~~~~~~~~~~

+ 150 g (5½ oz/1½ cups) fine white masa harina flour (see Glossary)
+ 1 teaspoon bicarbonate of soda (baking soda)
+ pinch of salt
+ 180 ml (6 fl oz) soda water (club soda)
+ vegetable oil for shallow-frying
+ sea salt to taste

MAKES 340 G (12 OZ) (ENOUGH FOR 12 TLAYUDAS)

Tlayudas are often referred to as the Mexican pizza. Folded like a quesadilla, filled with grilled slices of steak, rocket (arugula), caramelised onions and chimichurri, it's the perfect comforting street food. The addition of bicarbonate of soda (baking soda) and soda water (club soda) to this masa dough helps the tlayudas to puff up when fried, creating a light and flaky base for a myriad of toppings.

Combine the flour, bicarbonate of soda and salt using an electric mixer fitted with a dough hook.

Mixing at medium speed, gradually pour in the soda water to make a dough. Form the dough into a ball and press to flatten, when the dough is the right consistency it should not split at the sides. Add a little more soda water if necessary. Work the dough on medium speed for 10 minutes, to aerate. Alternatively, knead by hand on a work surface.

Cover with a clean tea towel (dish towel) and rest at room temperature for 30 minutes.

Divide the dough into 12 equal-sized balls.

Using a tortilla press, flatten the balls between 2 pieces of baking paper, creating thin discs. Alternatively roll out between 2 sheets of baking paper using a rolling pin – but your discs will not be so perfectly round.

Heat 50 ml (1¾ fl oz) oil in a medium frying pan over medium–high heat. Once the oil is hot add a disc to the pan, shaking the pan a little to create some airflow and increase the rise of the dough. Cook for 1 minute on each side until puffed, crisp and golden. Transfer onto paper towel to drain. Season lightly with salt.

Repeat with the remaining discs, adding and heating a little oil before cooking each one.

Tlayudas can be prepared in advance, cooled and stored in an airtight container for up to 2 days.

EMPANADA DOUGH

〜〜〜〜〜〜〜〜

+ 350 g (12¹/₂ oz/2¹/₃ cups) plain
  (all-purpose) flour
+ 1 teaspoon smoked paprika
+ 1 teaspoon sea salt
+ 150 g (5¹/₂ oz) butter, chilled
  and cubed
+ 60 ml (2 fl oz/¹/₄ cup) iced water
+ 2 large egg yolks, beaten

MAKES 500 G (1 LB 2 OZ)
(ENOUGH FOR 6 EMPANADAS)

This is a rich, buttery dough, subtly flavoured with
smoked paprika. When baked it produces a short,
crumbly-textured pastry and, when briefly fried before
baking, the pastry becomes more flaky and unctuous.
It can be made in advance and stored in the freezer
to aid speedy empanada preparation.

Combine the flour, paprika and salt in the bowl of an electric
mixer fitted with a dough hook.

Working at medium speed, gradually add the butter, mixing
for 10 minutes or until incorporated to resemble fine crumbs.

Combine the iced water and egg yolks in a small bowl and add to
the flour and butter mixture. Work for a further 10 minutes, or
until it just begins to come together to form a very rough dough.

Transfer to a clean work surface and knead to form a dough.

Divide the dough into 6 equal-sized portions and shape into
balls. Arrange on a plate, cover and rest at room temperature
for 1 hour.

The dough can be stored tightly wrapped in plastic wrap in
the refrigerator for up to 3 days, or in the freezer for up to
3 months.

BASIC MEXICAN GAZPACHO

~~~~~~~~~~~~~~~~

+ 250 ml (8½ fl oz/1 cup) orange juice
+ 5 roma (plum) tomatoes, roughly chopped
+ 1½ red capsicums (bell peppers), roughly chopped
+ ½ Lebanese (short) cucumber, roughly chopped
+ ½ red onion, roughly chopped
+ 1½ slices white bread
+ 1 small handful of oregano leaves
+ 1½ tablespoons reposado tequila (see Glossary)

+ 1 tablespoon cabernet sauvignon vinegar
+ finely grated zest of 1½ oranges
+ ½ jalapeño
+ ½ bird's eye chilli
+ 1 small garlic clove, grated
+ 1 tablespoon extra-virgin olive oil
+ sea salt and freshly ground black pepper to taste

MAKES 1 LITRE (34 FL OZ/4 CUPS)

A fresh soup base infused with the Mexican flavours of oregano, tequila and jalapeño. It makes a perfect summer soup, and is an excellent match with all types of fish and seafood.

Place the orange juice in a small saucepan and simmer over medium–low heat, until reduced to 100 ml (3½ fl oz). Allow to cool.

Process the orange juice reduction with the remaining ingredients in a food processor or blender until smooth. If the mixture appears too thick, moisten with water as required.

Strain through a fine-mesh sieve. Season with salt and pepper. Chill until required.

Store in an airtight container in the refrigerator for up to 3 days.

MEXICAN-STYLE PICKLES

I discovered these pickles while preparing a traditional Yucatán dish called cochinita pibil. The pickles are so versatile for both meat and seafood cooking. They are a great cooling agent and an attractive accompaniment for spicy dishes, barbecues and cured meats. The solution can be used to pickle a variety of vegetables, fruit and chillies as well as for a light dressing for salads.

PICKLING SOLUTION

+ 250 ml (8¹/2 fl oz/1 cup) cider vinegar
+ 220 g (8 oz/1 cup) sugar
+ 1 cinnamon stick
+ ¹/4 teaspoon whole black peppercorns
+ ¹/4 teaspoon cumin seeds
+ zest and juice of 2 oranges
+ 2 garlic cloves, smashed
+ ¹/2 bunch oregano leaves
+ 1 bay leaf

POSSIBLE VEGETABLES & FRUIT FOR PICKLING

+ small red onions, halved, quartered or sliced
+ heirloom radishes, thinly sliced
+ heirloom carrots, thinly sliced
+ jalapeños, thinly sliced
+ nectarines, thinly sliced
+ peeled cherry tomatoes

MAKES 500 ML (17 FL OZ/2 CUPS)
PICKLING SOLUTION

To make the pickling solution, combine the vinegar and sugar in a small saucepan and gently simmer, stirring occasionally, until the sugar dissolves.

Meanwhile dry-fry the cinnamon, peppercorns and cumin seeds in a small frying pan over low heat, until fragrant.

Add the orange zest and juice, garlic, oregano and bay leaf and set aside to cool.

Bring the pickling liquid to the boil and pour over the vegetables or fruit to cover. Allow to cool.

Store in an airtight container in the refrigerator for up to 1 week.

MACADAMIA PASTRY

~~~~~~~~~~

+ 280 g (10 oz/1¾ cups) macadamia nuts
+ 80 g (2¾ oz/⅓ cup) caster (superfine) sugar
+ 450 g (1 lb/3 cups) plain (all-purpose) flour
+ 225 g (8 oz) unsalted butter, at room temperature
+ 1 large egg
+ ½ teaspoon vanilla extract

> MAKES 1 KG (2 LB 3 OZ) (ENOUGH FOR TWO 26–30 CM/10¼–12 IN TART SHELLS)

This recipe makes enough for two large tart cases, one for now and one for later. Simply freeze and then thaw at room temperature when next required. The dough can also be rolled out and cut and baked into cookies. Sprinkle with salt before baking for an added touch. Great filling ideas would be salted caramel, bananas and chocolate, or raspberries with lime curd. This pastry is very short and crisp, so you can't roll it over a tin and trim the edges or it will fall apart. Instead, form it into a thick disc that you place into the bottom of the tart tin and then mould the edges of the pastry up the side of the tin with your fingers.

Place the nuts in a food processor and pulse a few times, until they form a sandy texture. Add the sugar and pulse to make a fine meal. Add the flour and pulse to combine.

Transfer to the bowl of an electric mixer, fitted with a paddle attachment. Add the butter, egg and vanilla and mix to make a smooth dough.

Divide the dough into 2 equal parts and wrap in plastic wrap. Rest in the refrigerator for 30 minutes before use.

Store the pastry in the refrigerator for up to 3 days, or freeze for up to 3 months.

DRIED VANILLA BEANS

~~~~~~~~~~

+ 4 vanilla beans
+ Stock syrup (page 57) for dipping

The scent of vanilla beans is heavenly and will fill your kitchen while you're preparing these dried shards. They're simple to prepare and add a hit of vanilla as well as a lovely textural contrast to desserts, where vanilla is the hero.

Preheat the oven to 80°C (175°F). Set a wire rack over a tray lined with baking paper.

Cut the vanilla beans into fine shards, dip them into the stock syrup and arrange on the prepared rack.

Place in the oven to dry for 4 hours, or until crisp.

Store in an airtight container for up to 6 months.

PAUL'S TIP These vanilla beans can also be dried overnight in a food dehydrator.

CHOCOLATE SAUCE

~~~~~~~~~~~~~~~

+ 225 g (8 oz) best-quality dark
  cooking chocolate, minimum
  60% cocoa solids
+ 150 ml (5 fl oz) full-cream
  (whole) milk
+ 50 ml (1¾ fl oz) dark rum
+ 30 g (1 oz) sugar

+ 2 cinnamon sticks
+ 30 g (1 oz) unsalted butter
+ 1½ tablespoons pouring (single/
  light) cream

MAKES 375 ML (12½ FL OZ/1½ CUPS)

Infused with cinnamon and with the addition of rum,
this is more than an average chocolate sauce. Use it as
an additional element for desserts or serve with ice
cream. Adjust the flavour with your choice of liqueur.

Place the chocolate in a heatproof bowl and set over a saucepan of barely simmering water, ensuring the base is not touching the water. Stir occasionally until melted.

Combine the milk, rum, sugar and cinnamon sticks in a small saucepan and bring to the boil over medium–low heat.

Gradually pour the hot milk mixture into the melted chocolate, whisking continuously, to combine. Add the butter and cream, stirring until the butter has melted, to make a smooth sauce. Strain through a fine-mesh sieve.

Store in an airtight container in the refrigerator for up to 1 week.

SALTED CARAMEL SAUCE

～～～～～～～

+ 145 g (5 oz/²⁄₃ cup) caster (superfine) sugar
+ 180 ml (6 fl oz) pouring (single/light) cream
+ 1¹⁄₂ teaspoons sea salt

MAKES 300 ML (10 FL OZ)

Salt and caramelised sugar are a perfect match and reminiscent of the Latin dulce de leche and Mexican cajeta. It's great on an ice cream sundae or drizzled over chocolate muffins or pancakes.

Sprinkle the sugar over the base of a medium saucepan. Gently heat over low, until the sugar begins to caramelise. Swirl the sugar to help create an even caramel.

Gradually add the cream, stirring continuously, to make a smooth sauce. Add the salt and stir until dissolved. Strain through a fine-mesh sieve.

Store in an airtight container in the refrigerator for up to 1 week.

SORBET SYRUP

～～～～～～～

+ 285 g (10 oz/1¹⁄₄ cups) caster (superfine) sugar
+ 1¹⁄₂ tablespoons liquid glucose

MAKES 500 ML (17 FL OZ/2 CUPS)

A base for most sorbets, this is best stored chilled to aid quick freezing of your sorbet when churned.

Combine the sugar, 250 ml (8¹⁄₂ fl oz/1 cup) water and the glucose in a medium heavy-based saucepan and bring to the boil, stirring occasionally, over medium–low heat. Boil for 3 minutes. Strain through a fine-mesh seive.

Store in an airtight container in the refrigerator for up to 6 months.

STOCK SYRUP

~~~~~~~~~~

+ 660 g (1 lb 7 oz/3 cups) sugar

MAKES 1 LITRE (34 FL OZ/4 CUPS)

Stock syrup can be used to poach a range of fruits, such as pears, quinces, peaches, nectarines and tamarillos. Use the stock as a base and flavour with spices such as cinnamon, star anise, vanilla, cloves or cardamom. The syrup can be used for making cocktails too.

Combine 750 ml (25½ fl oz/3 cups) water and the sugar in a medium saucepan and set over medium–low heat. Bring to a simmer, stirring occasionally, until the sugar dissolves.

Bring to the boil and boil for 2 minutes. Remove from the heat and set aside to cool.

Store in an airtight container in the refrigerator for up to 6 months.

LIME CURD

~~~~~~~~~~

+ 2 large egg yolks
+ 80 g (2¾ oz/⅓ cup) caster (superfine) sugar
+ finely grated zest and juice of 2 limes
+ 100 g (3½ oz) unsalted butter, cubed

MAKES 500 ML (17 FL OZ/2 CUPS)

A deliciously tart, buttery cream, great for scooping onto homemade scones (biscuits), spreading on toast or eating straight from the jar!

Combine the egg yolks and sugar in a medium heatproof bowl. Set over a saucepan of barely simmering water, ensuring the base does not touch the water, and whisk continuously until very thick. When ready you should be able to drizzle the mixture on top to form a figure 8 and it will hold its shape briefly before sinking into the mixture – this is known as the ribbon stage. Add the lime zest and juice and whisk until thick.

Remove from the heat and add the butter, a cube at a time, whisking to incorporate before adding the next cube. Continue until the mixture is thick and all of the butter is incorporated. Strain through a fine-mesh sieve. Cover and refrigerate for at least 4 hours, or preferably overnight, before use.

Store in an airtight container in the refrigerator for 2 months.

02

EGGS & BREAKFAST

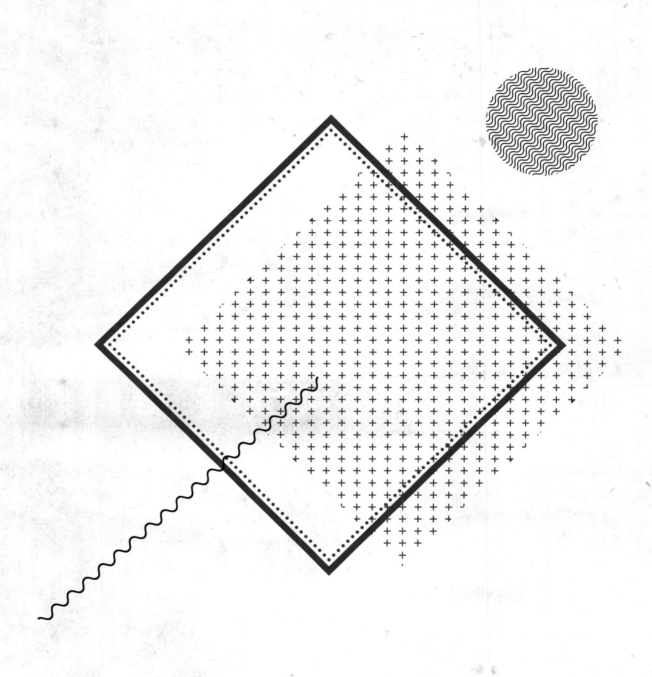

Although every meal is
celebrated in Mexico, breakfast
is particularly special. Mexicans are
hard-working people who need big hearty
dishes to fuel their busy days.

～～～～～

Everyone in Mexico City seems to walk or ride bikes to work, so
street vendors set up roadside grills, serving rib-tickling quesadillas
and tortillas, tamales with chocolate and cauldrons full of beans
and nose-to-tail delights. Most of Mexico's breads and cakes are
gluten-free, as they use masa harina (flour made from corn
instead of wheat), and the ancient grains they use create light
and nutrient-rich textures. In this chapter I've focused
on the more typical cantina-style dishes, with a nod
to our busy lifestyles. Drop these dishes in the
middle of the dining table and you will
never disappoint.

ALL-DAY BREAKFAST MOLLETES

~~~~~~~~~~~~~~~

+ 24 thin slices pancetta, cut into 3 cm (1¼ in) lengths
+ 200 g (7 oz) cherry tomatoes
+ 6 Mexican-style bread rolls, bolillos, small baguettes, kaiser rolls or ciabatta rolls
+ Refried beans (page 42)
+ 2 tablespoons extra-virgin olive oil, plus extra for drizzling
+ 200 g (7 oz) provolone, grated

+ 10 g (¼ oz) butter
+ 6 large organic eggs
+ 2 avocados, cut into thirds
+ 90 g (3 oz) salted ricotta, roughly chopped
+ 1 red onion, thinly sliced
+ 1 large handful of coriander (cilantro) leaves
+ Jalapeño & finger lime crema (page 37)

+ 2 limes, each cut into 3 wedges
+ red leaves, such as bull's blood, to garnish

SERVES 6

Bean-stuffed molletes, or Mexican beans on toast, make a wonderful start to the day. Beans, like corn, underpin Mexican food and refried beans, or frijoles, are a common variation. You will adore these molletes any time of day but they make an especially hearty breakfast. The doughy centres of the bread rolls are removed then crisped under the grill (broiler) or in a sandwich press, leaving you with a crunchy bread shell to pile high with whatever you like - think Mexican bruschetta and a myriad of diverse seasonal toppings. For breakfast I have included the essentials, but let your imagination run wild.

Preheat an overhead grill (broiler) to high.

Place the pancetta on a tray and grill (broil) until crisp. Place the tomatoes on a tray and grill until softened. Keep warm.

Cut the rolls in half lengthways. Remove and discard the soft bread centres to form bread shells. Drizzle with a little olive oil. Grill the bread shells for 1–2 minutes on each side, until crisp and golden.

Reheat the refried beans. Generously spread the beans over the rolls, sprinkle with provolone and grill until melted.

Meanwhile, brush a non-stick pan with the 2 tablespoons of oil, add half the butter and heat over low, until melted. Gently fry the eggs for 2 minutes, or until set. Transfer to a chopping board and trim to make a neat round. Season the egg white with salt.

Place 2 roll halves onto each serving plate. Arrange an egg, the pancetta and tomatoes on top. Garnish with avocado, salted ricotta, red onion and coriander. Drizzle with jalapeño and finger lime crema and serve with a lime wedge. Garnish with the red leaves.

ALL-DAY
BREAKFAST
MOLLETES
(pages 62–3)

CHIA PUDDING WITH STONE FRUIT, AGAVE & VANILLA

Latin food is typically gluten-free, with corn and ancient grains making a nutrient-packed substitute for wheat. Amaranth, an Aztec grain used for centuries, is commonly used in a popped form mixed with caramel or honey and set in candy bars. The indigenous people adore it this way, but it also makes a terrific and healthy alternative to oats in the form of a comforting porridge. High in fibre, vitamins, protein and amino acids, it's even said to reduce the greying of hair! If you can't find amaranth seeds, you can use quinoa flakes. While this recipe does take a little longer than your usual instant porridge, the goodness it provides is worthwhile.

+ 120 g (4½ oz/⅔ cup) amaranth seeds (see Glossary) or quinoa flakes, rinsed
+ 80 g (2¾ oz/½ cup) chia seeds
+ 1 litre (34 fl oz/4 cups) low-fat milk or water
+ 1 teaspoon vanilla extract
+ 1 teaspoon ground cinnamon
+ agave syrup (see Glossary) or raw honey to taste
+ 255 g (9 oz/1⅔ cups) fresh blueberries
+ 2 stone fruit, such as nectarines or peaches, stoned and thickly sliced
+ 250 ml (8½ fl oz/1 cup) light coconut milk
+ 90 g (3 oz) flaked almonds or pistachio nuts, lightly toasted

SERVES 4–6

Combine the amaranth and chia seeds with the milk, vanilla and cinnamon in a medium saucepan. Bring to the boil over medium–low heat, stirring occasionally. Reduce the heat to low and simmer, stirring constantly, for 15–20 minutes, until thick. Sweeten with honey or agave.

Divide the porridge among serving bowls, scatter with the fruit and drizzle with the coconut milk. Scatter over the flaked almonds or pistachio nuts.

SWEETCORN FRENCH TOAST WITH PANCETTA & AVOCADO

~~~~~~~~~~

+ 100 g (3½ oz) thinly sliced pancetta
+ 4 wedges of iceberg lettuce or rocket (arugula) leaves to serve
+ 1 avocado, thickly sliced
+ Salsa mexicana (page 36)
+ Jalapeño & finger lime crema (page 37)
+ micro leaves to serve
+ 1 small red capsicum (bell pepper), thinly sliced in rings, to garnish

SWEETCORN LOAF

+ 125 g (4½ oz) butter
+ 300 g (10½ oz) frozen or fresh corn kernels (about 2 corn cobs), plus extra cooked shards for garnish (optional)
+ 375 g (13 oz) tin condensed milk
+ 60 g (2 oz/¼ cup) sour cream
+ 5 large organic eggs
+ 50 g (1¾ oz/½ cup) masa harina PAN flour (see Glossary)
+ 1½ teaspoons baking powder
+ pinch of sea salt
+ oil for spraying

SERVES 4 (MAKES 1 LOAF)

Preheat the oven to 150°C (300°F) and lightly grease and line a loaf (bar) tin with baking paper.

For the sweetcorn loaf, melt the butter in a large frying pan over low heat. Add the corn, cover and cook for 5 minutes, or until softened.

Add the condensed milk and sour cream and bring to the boil. Reduce the heat and simmer, stirring constantly, for 5 minutes. Transfer to a food processor and blend to make a smooth sauce. Gradually add the eggs, flour and baking powder, processing on low speed to combine. Season with salt.

Pour the batter into the prepared tin and bake for about 30–40 minutes, until golden brown and a skewer comes out clean when tested. Leave in the tin for 10 minutes to cool slightly.

Invert the sweetcorn loaf onto a wire rack to cool completely. Wrap in plastic wrap and refrigerate for at least 4 hours, or preferably overnight.

Preheat an overhead grill (broiler) to high.

Slice the cornbread into 8 slices, 2–3 cm (¾–1¼ in) thick.

Arrange the pancetta slices on a baking tray and grill (broil) until crisp. Drain off any excess fat and keep warm.

Preheat a non-stick frying pan over medium heat. Spray the pan with cooking oil and cook the cornbread slices for 2 minutes on each side or until golden brown.

To serve, arrange 2 pieces of cornbread onto each plate, top with an iceberg wedge and some pancetta and avocado slices. Spoon on some salsa mexicana and a dollop of the crema and garnish with the micro leaves, capsicum and shards of corn, if using.

Mexican food is considered one of the world's first fusion cuisines. This traditional corn cake recipe is normally served cold and here has been adapted so it can be sliced and grilled (broiled) before topping with crispy bacon, avocado and salsa mexicana. It's French toast Mexican style! Maple or agave syrup can be included in this recipe with fresh bananas, if you have a sweet tooth.

BAKED DEVILLED EGGS WITH SOBRASADA

~~~~~~~~~~

+ 2 tablespoons olive oil
+ 2 homemade masa harina flour tortillas (see page 46) or store-bought tortillas
+ 4 slices serrano ham
+ 120 g (4 1/2 oz) Mahón, sliced or grated
+ 250 ml (8 1/2 fl oz/1 cup) Adobo sauce (page 15)

+ 4 large organic eggs
+ 150 g (5 1/2 oz) sobrasada, torn into pieces
+ 185 g (6 1/2 oz/3/4 cup) sour cream to serve
+ 90 g (3 oz) salted ricotta or feta, crumbled
+ 1 large handful of flat-leaf parsley, roughly chopped

SERVES 2

Travelling through Mexico and Spain you get the opportunity to sample many delicious and robust breakfast dishes such as huevos rancheros and chilaquiles. I have a theory that these dishes only exist to provide an antidote to the devilish behaviour of the night before. I created this weekend breakfast dish, which relies on the powerfully flavoured adobo sauce, with layers of tortillas, serrano ham, Mahón, sobrasada (a chorizo-like minced/ground pork pâté) and eggs the way you like best. Like any hearty breakfast, the dish improves with the addition of breakfast accessories. Morcilla, chorizo, avocado, crema or salsa are also great with this dish.

Preheat the oven to 180°C (350°F).

Brush a medium-sized earthenware dish with olive oil. Line the base of the dish with one of the tortillas. Arrange the ham and Mahón on top and cover with the remaining tortilla.

Warm the adobo sauce and pour three-quarters of it over the top. Crack in the eggs. Scatter with pieces of sobrasada and dollops of the remaining sauce.

Bake for 10 minutes, until the eggs begin to set. Cook for a further 5 minutes or until the eggs are set.

To serve, place the dish in the centre of the table, top with sour cream and scatter over the ricotta and chopped parsley.

PAUL'S TIPS Preparing the adobo sauce can be time consuming but it's worth it! If you're time poor, simply blend 50 g (1 3/4 oz) chipotle chillies (see Glossary) with 250 g (9 oz/1 cup) tinned chopped tomatoes to replace the adobo sauce.
  Before baking, you can add pieces of cooked chorizo or morcilla to the dish, if desired.
  Mahón is a cow's milk cheese that can be either soft or hard.

HEALTHY HUEVOS MEXICANA

~~~~~~~~~

+ 6 large egg whites
+ vegetable oil spray
+ 4 large homemade masa harina flour tortillas (see page 46) or store-bought tortillas
+ Tomatillo verde (page 21) or your favourite Latin hot sauce to serve
+ 2 avocados, thickly sliced
+ 4 large handfuls of rocket (arugula) or watercress leaves

SALSA

+ 4 ripe roma (plum) tomatoes, cored, halved and squeezed of excess seeds
+ 200 g (7 oz) goat's feta, crumbled
+ 1 zucchini (courgette), coarsely grated
+ 1 red onion, finely chopped
+ 1 jalapeño, finely chopped
+ 1 garlic clove, finely grated
+ 1 small handful of basil leaves
+ 1 small handful of mint leaves
+ pinch of salt
+ pinch of freshly grated nutmeg

SERVES 4

Huevos mexicana are essentially scrambled eggs laced with salsa and they are indeed a delicious start to the day. It's common to see the addition of savoury morsels, such as broken fried corn (tortilla) chips, bacon or chorizo served in tortillas. For a lighter alternative, here I have used egg whites packed with lean protein. However, the challenge is making egg white texturally pleasing and delicious. I found that baking the egg whites in a shallow dish with flavoursome vegetables, herbs and low-fat cheese is the answer. This recipe will change your opinion of egg white omelettes forever!

Preheat the oven to 180°C (350°F).

To prepare the salsa, finely chop the tomatoes and place in a medium bowl. Add the remaining salsa ingredients and toss to combine.

Lightly beat the egg whites in a medium bowl. Add to the salsa and stir to combine.

Spray a large non-stick frying pan with vegetable oil. Pour in the egg white mixture and bake for 6–8 minutes, until just firm to the touch.

Wrap the tortillas in aluminium foil and place in the oven for 5 minutes to warm.

To serve, cut the egg white pancake into 4 and place a quarter onto each warmed tortilla. Add a little tomatillo verde or hot sauce, avocado, rocket or watercress leaves and roll up.

PISTACHIO & SPICED CHOCOLATE HOTCAKES WITH RASPBERRY CREMA

~~~~~~~~~~

+ 210 g (7¹/₂ oz/1²/₃ cups) fresh raspberries to serve
+ 100 g (3¹/₂ oz/²/₃ cup) pistachio nuts, lightly toasted and coarsely chopped, to serve

RASPBERRY COULIS

+ 115 g (4 oz/³/₄ cup) fresh or frozen raspberries
+ 55 g (2 oz/¹/₄ cup) sugar

PISTACHIO & SPICED CHOCOLATE HOTCAKES

+ 2 large organic eggs
+ 55 g (2 oz/¹/₄ cup) firmly packed brown sugar
+ 2 tablespoons pistachio paste (see Glossary)
+ 75 g (2³/₄ oz) butter, melted
+ 300 g (10¹/₂ oz/3 cups) masa harina PAN flour (see Glossary) or 450 g (1 lb/3 cups) plain (all-purpose) flour
+ 3 teaspoons unsweetened (Dutch) cocoa powder
+ 2 teaspoons ground cinnamon
+ 2 teaspoons baking powder
+ 1 teaspoon ground cloves
+ ¹/₂ teaspoon bicarbonate of soda (baking soda)
+ ¹/₂ teaspoon salt
+ 750 ml (25¹/₂ fl oz/3 cups) buttermilk
+ vegetable oil for cooking
+ 110 g (4 oz) frozen raspberries
+ 100 g (3¹/₂ oz/²/₃ cup) milk chocolate melts (buttons), roughly chopped

RASPBERRY CREMA

+ 1 tablespoon raspberry coulis (see above)
+ 185 g (6¹/₂ oz/³/₄ cup) sour cream

SERVES 6

Spice-infused chocolate is commonplace in Latin cooking. A love for chocolate inspired this spicy breakfast creation. It is made with masa harina, perfect if you're on a gluten-free diet. Plain (all-purpose) flour can be substituted, if preferred. However, you will require less liquid so gradually add it until you get the right consistency. To transform this dish into a dessert, simply serve with salted caramel ice cream (see pages 288-9).

Preheat the oven to 180°C (350°F).

To make the coulis, place the raspberries, 60 ml (2 fl oz/¹/₄ cup) water and sugar in a small saucepan and simmer over low heat for 3–4 minutes until the raspberries have softened. Set aside to cool slightly. Transfer to a small food processor and blend until smooth. Strain through a fine-mesh sieve and set aside.

To prepare the hotcakes, whisk the eggs and brown sugar together using an electric mixer, until pale and creamy. Add the pistachio paste and gradually pour in 50 ml (1³/₄ fl oz) of the melted butter, whisking to combine. Remove to a clean bowl. Sift the masa harina PAN flour, cocoa powder, cinnamon, baking powder, cloves, bicarbonate of soda and salt together into a medium bowl. Add the sifted dry ingredients and buttermilk alternately to the egg mixture, stirring to make a smooth batter. Do not overmix.

Preheat a large ovenproof non-stick frying pan over medium heat. Drizzle with oil and add a little of the remaining butter. Spoon the batter into the pan, approximately 2 tablespoons per hotcake. Scatter with frozen raspberries and the chocolate melts and cook for 1–2 minutes, until the base begins to cook and is light golden.Place the pan in the oven and bake for 8 minutes, or until risen and firm to the touch and a skewer comes out clean when tested. Remove to a plate and keep warm, then repeat until all the batter has been used.

Meanwhile, to make the raspberry crema, combine 1 tablespoon of the raspberry coulis with the sour cream in a small bowl.

To serve, place 2 hotcakes onto each plate, top with a dollop of raspberry crema, drizzle with raspberry coulis and scatter with fresh raspberries and chopped pistachio nuts.

SUMMER BREAKFAST CHILAQUILES

~~~~~~~~~~~~~~~~

+ 350 g (12¹/₂ oz) masa harina flour corn (tortilla) chips
+ 200 ml (7 fl oz) Tomatillo verde (page 21)

VEGETABLE MIXTURE

+ 125 ml (4 fl oz/¹/₂ cup) olive oil
+ 1 chorizo sausage, cut into 1 cm (¹/₂ in) dice
+ 1 red onion, diced
+ 2 garlic cloves, crushed
+ 1 yellow (summer) squash, thinly sliced
+ 200 g (7 oz) fresh or frozen corn kernels (about 1 corn cob)
+ 150 g (5¹/₂ oz) mixed grape and cherry tomatoes, halved
+ 250 g (9 oz) shredded rocket (arugula)
+ 1 large handful of oregano, roughly chopped
+ 1 large handful of coriander (cilantro) leaves, roughly chopped
+ sea salt to taste

EGG MIXTURE

+ 8 large organic eggs
+ 125 ml (4 fl oz/¹/₂ cup) milk
+ 1-2 tablespoons hot sauce
+ ¹/₂ teaspoon ground cumin
+ ¹/₂ teaspoon smoked paprika
+ pinch of sea salt

GARNISH

+ 2 avocados, cubed
+ 3 large handfuls of rocket (arugula), roughly chopped
+ 200 g (7 oz) salted ricotta or feta, crumbled (or your favourite cheese)
+ Jalapeño & finger lime crema (page 37) or sour cream
+ 1 large handful of oregano or coriander (cilantro) leaves to garnish

SERVES 6

Chilaquiles is the name given to tortillas served with chillies and greens. This much-loved comfort food has been adapted so many times, its versatility is its appeal. For me this is why it's a great breakfast dish – you can add so many interesting flavours and ingredients. I like this baked version with colourful summer tomatoes, squash, corn and chorizo. I recommend making the tomatillo sauce the day before and use proper masa harina flour corn (tortilla) chips, as their flavour and texture is much better than mass-produced corn chips.

Preheat the oven to 180°C (350°F).

Lightly grease the base of a large ovenproof ceramic dish with oil.

To prepare the vegetable mixture, heat the oil in a large frying pan over medium heat. Fry the chorizo for 1–2 minutes until golden. Add the onion and garlic and cook until softened. Add the squash and corn and cook for a further minute, or until softened. Remove from the heat, add the tomatoes, rocket, oregano and coriander and stir to combine. Season with salt. Spread the mixture out onto a tray to cool slightly.

To make the egg mixture, whisk the eggs, milk, hot sauce, spices and salt together in a medium bowl. Pour into the prepared dish.

Place the corn chips in a large bowl. Add the tomatillo verde and cooled vegetable mixture and toss to combine. Pile on top of the egg mixture.

Bake for 15–20 minutes, until the eggs are just set.

Remove from the oven and allow the eggs to cool slightly. Scatter with avocado, rocket, cheese, crema or sour cream and coriander to serve.

SAVOURY SUPER-FOOD QUINOA PORRIDGE

~~~~~~~~~~

- + 60 ml (2 fl oz/1/4 cup) rice bran oil
- + 1 small red onion, finely chopped
- + 2 garlic cloves, thinly sliced
- + 2 teaspoons ground cumin
- + 1 teaspoon smoked paprika
- + 1 chipotle in adobo sauce (see Glossary)
- + 1/2 bunch kale, stripped from the stem and roughly chopped
- + 200 g (7 oz/1 cup) red quinoa, soaked in cold water for 30 minutes, drained and rinsed
- + 1 litre (34 fl oz/4 cups) chicken or vegetable stock

- + 200 g (7 oz) fresh or frozen corn kernels (about 1 corn cob)
- + 200 g (7 oz) cherry tomatoes, halved
- + 1 large chorizo sausage, finely chopped
- + sea salt to taste

GARNISH

- + 2 avocados, sliced
- + 6 poached eggs (optional)
- + 200 g (7 oz) sheep or goat's feta, crumbled
- + 1 large handful of coriander (cilantro) leaves, roughly chopped

SERVES 6

This is my super-healthy version of a Latin American-inspired congee. Quinoa is often used to make comforting savoury porridges in the highlands of Peru and Bolivia, from where it originates. It's extremely good for you and high in protein, fibre and magnesium, while being cholesterol- and gluten-free. You can add whatever savoury foods you enjoy and alternate them according to what's in season. Here the broth is flavoured with the smoky chipotle chilli, which is easy to find in most Latin American food stores.

Heat the oil in a medium heavy-based saucepan over low heat. Cook the onion and garlic until softened. Add the spices and chipotle and cook until fragrant. Add the kale and quinoa and stir to combine. Pour in the stock, increase the heat to medium and bring to the boil.

Reduce the heat and gently simmer, stirring occasionally, for 30 minutes. Cover and cook over low heat for another 30 minutes, or until the quinoa has cooked and the liquid has reduced to make a thick porridge. Add the corn, tomato and chorizo and simmer for a further 1–2 minutes to heat through, stirring to combine. Season with salt.

Divide the quinoa porridge among serving bowls and top each with slices of avocado and a poached egg, if desired. Scatter with feta and coriander.

PAUL'S TIP For a seasonal variation, in autumn add dried porcini mushrooms to the broth and replace the corn and tomatoes with chopped sautéed field mushrooms and cooked chickpeas (garbanzo beans).

TIJUANA TRIFLE

~~~~~~~~~~~~

+ 800 g (1 lb 12 oz) seedless
  watermelon, cubed

FLAVOURED YOGHURT

+ 1 kg (2 lb 3 oz/4 cups) extra-
  thick Greek yoghurt
+ 60 g (2 oz) honey
+ 1½ tablespoons pomegranate
  molasses
+ ½ teaspoon chilli powder

TOASTED MUESLI (GRANOLA)

+ 100 g (3½ oz/1 cup) rolled
  (porridge) oats
+ 80 g (2¾ oz/½ cup) macadamia
  nuts, crushed and toasted
+ 50 g (1¾ oz/⅓ cup) pepitas
  (pumpkin seeds)
+ 45 g (1½ oz/½ cup) flaked
  almonds, crushed
+ 2 tablespoons sesame seeds
+ 1½ tablespoons honey, warmed
+ 40 g (1½ oz/⅓ cup) sultanas
  (golden raisins)

SERVES 6

Tijuana has a colourful reputation for partying but you may not know that the food there and along the Baja coast is some of the best you'll find in Mexico. A typical breakfast for me travelling through Baja was fresh fruit from a street vendor - sweet melons and mangoes cut to order and served in clear plastic bags with a squeeze of lime and a pinch of chilli powder. It hit the spot every time. This dish reminds me of being near the water, so I developed this simple, refreshing and healthy breakfast dish for Icebergs restaurant on Bondi Beach in Sydney. Think sun and surf.

Preheat the oven to 180°C (350°F).

To prepare the toasted muesli, combine the oats, macadamia nuts, pepitas, almonds and sesame seeds in a medium bowl. Add the honey and toss to combine. Spread the mixture onto a baking tray. Bake, stirring occasionally, for 10 minutes. Add the sultanas and cook for a further 5 minutes, or until crisp and golden brown. Set aside to cool.

To prepare the flavoured yoghurt, mix the Greek yoghurt, honey, pomegranate molasses and chilli powder together in a medium bowl.

To assemble, spoon a little of the yoghurt into the base of 6 tall serving glasses, add some of the watermelon cubes to make a fruit layer, then additional yoghurt and watermelon to make a further 2 layers. Top with a generous layer of yoghurt to finish. Cover and refrigerate for 1 hour to chill and set.

Sprinkle generously with toasted muesli to serve.

You can store any remaining toasted muesli in an airtight container for up to 3 months.

03

MASA DELICACIES & STREET FOOD

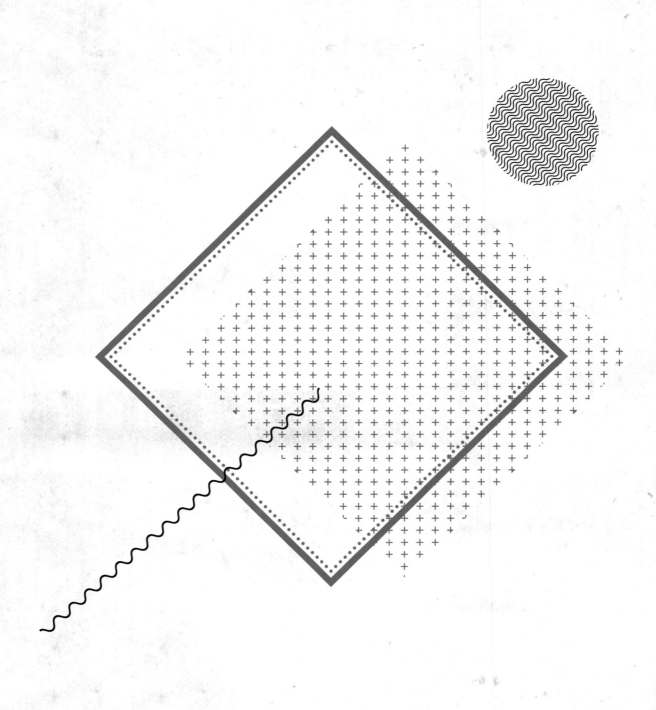

Corn and masa harina
flour underpin the foods of
Mexico. Without them there would be
no antojitos. These are the many small masa
snacks created to satisfy hunger, and the staple
of Mexican street food.

∿∿∿∿∿∿

I find there is something mesmerising and addictive about the flavour
of masa (the dough made from masa harina flour). I always get that
'I just need one more' feeling whenever I eat it, especially when
I am touring the street food highlights of Mexico. In fact, I could
write an entire book about masa delicacies – but that's another
story to be told! Think of this chapter as a beginner's guide
to understanding that there is much more to masa
than the humble taco. Try these recipes and
embrace the endless creations that this
simple dough can offer!

STREETCORN

~~~~~~~~~~~~~

GRILLED CORN

+ 4-6 corn cobs in their husks

```
SERVES 4-6
```

Watching the Pied Piper effect of tourists, families and children appearing and congregating around the aromas of sweetcorn vendors on the streets of Oaxaca was a truly memorable experience. Once one got started, a flurry of vendors would also set up shop nearby as the crowds were guaranteed. It's impossible to resist the smell of streetcorn barbecuing in the husk. The husk is then pulled back to make the ideal handle with the corn smothered in crema, chilli and salty cheese. But why stop there! Try one or all of the Mexi toppings and flavour combinations below and opposite that celebrate the humble corn.

To prepare the corn, preheat a barbecue chargrill (ideally a wood and charcoal combination) to medium.

Moisten the husks with water to help prevent burning.

Place the corn on the barbecue, cover with a lid and grill, turning occasionally, for 15 minutes or until the husks are charred and the corn appears tender.

Allow the corn to cool slightly while you prepare your choice of topping (see below and opposite).

Peel away the charred husks, rinse off any charred splinters of husk, either reheat on the barbecue or warm in the oven.

PAUL'S TIP Substitute baby corn for whole corn cobs. Simply grill or boil for 4 minutes then toss in your favourite sauce.

TOPPINGS

GOAT'S CREMA WITH BLACK OLIVE CRUMBS

+ 200 g (7 oz/1¼ cups) pitted Manzanilla olives
+ 150 g (5½ oz) soft goat's curd
+ 60 g (2 oz/¼ cup) sour cream
+ 1 large handful of basil leaves
+ 1 garlic clove, grated
+ sea salt to taste
+ 150 g (5½ oz) hard goat's cheese, finely chopped or coarsely grated
+ 1-2 teaspoons chilli powder (optional)
+ 1 lime to serve (optional)

PAUL'S TIP Olive crumbs can be made in advance and stored in an airtight container at room temperature for up to 1 week.

Preheat the oven to 100°C (210°F).

To make the olive crumbs, line a tray with baking paper and scatter with the olives. Cook for at least 8 hours, or overnight, until dried to a stale bread-like texture. Finely chop the olives.

To make the goat's crema, combine the goat's curd, sour cream, basil and garlic in a food processor and blend to make a smooth cream. Lightly season with salt, as the dried olives are already salty.

To serve, place the goat's crema in a shallow tray and roll the hot corn around to generously coat.

Spread a large spoonful of goat's crema onto your serving plates and place the corn on top. Sprinkle with goat's cheese and olive crumbs. Dust with chilli powder, if desired, for a fiery and colourful finish! Serve with a squeeze of lime, if desired.

AVOCADO CREMA WITH BACON CRUMBS

+ 1 tablespoon olive oil
+ 200 g (7 oz) streaky bacon or pancetta, diced
+ Avocado crema (page 38)
+ 160 g (5½ oz) salted ricotta, microplaned or grated
+ 1 small handful of chives, finely chopped, to garnish
+ 1 lime to serve (optional)

Heat the oil in a medium frying pan over medium heat. Fry the bacon, stirring occasionally, for 5 minutes or until crispy. Transfer to paper towel to drain.

Adjust the avocado crema, adding a little water to thin down to a coating consistency.

Serve the crispy bacon, avocado crema, salted ricotta and chopped chives alongside the corn and allow your guests to help themselves. Add a squeeze of lime, if desired.

TRUFFLED CREMA & TRUFFLE CHEESE

+ 200 g (7 oz) sour cream
+ 50 g (1¾ oz) salted ricotta, roughly chopped
+ 1 truffle, finely chopped and seasoned with salt
+ 1 garlic clove, finely grated
+ sea salt to taste
+ truffle oil for drizzling
+ 100 g (3½ oz) truffled pecorino
+ 1 lime to serve (optional)

To make the truffled crema, combine the sour cream, salted ricotta, a quarter of the chopped truffle and the garlic in a food processor and blend to make a smooth, thick sauce. Season with salt.

To serve, place the truffled crema in a shallow tray and roll the hot corn around to generously coat.

Spread a large spoonful of truffled crema onto your serving plates and place the corn on top. Drizzle with truffle oil, finely grate over some truffled pecorino and sprinkle with the remaining chopped truffle. Add a squeeze of lime, if desired.

If you prefer a more elegant presentation, you can simply remove the corn kernels from the cob and gently reheat in a pan. Spoon some of the truffle cream into serving glasses, add the warm corn followed by more crema and top with grated truffled pecorino and chopped truffle. Serve with warm tortillas (page 46) or sprinkle with crushed fried corn (tortilla) chips and a squeeze of lime, if desired.

STREETCORN WITH AVOCADO CREMA WITH BACON
CRUMBS (LEFT), AND GOAT'S CREMA WITH BLACK
OLIVE CRUMBS (RIGHT)

(pages 82–3)

LOBSTER TAMALES VERACRUZ-STYLE

~~~~~~~~~~

+ 4 corn husks
+ Zucchini flowers Veracruz-style (page 247)
+ finely chopped salted ricotta to garnish
+ edible flowers to garnish

SWEETCORN PURÉE

+ 1 tablespoon olive oil
+ 175 g (6 oz) fresh corn kernels (about 1 corn cob)
+ 2 garlic cloves, thinly sliced
+ 50 g (1¾ oz) unsalted butter

+ 100 ml (3½ fl oz) chicken stock
+ ½ teaspoon sea salt
+ 300 ml (10 fl oz) pouring (single/light) cream

TAMALE DOUGH

+ 150 g (5½ oz) cold lard
+ 1 teaspoon baking powder
+ ½ teaspoon sea salt
+ 150 g (5½ oz/1½ cups) yellow masa harina flour (see Glossary)
+ 150 g (5½ oz/⅔ cup) reserved sweetcorn purée, chilled (see left)

+ 200 ml (7 fl oz) chicken stock, warmed

FILLING

+ 250 g (9 oz) cooked lobster, langoustine (scampi) or crabmeat
+ 6 spring onions (scallions), thinly sliced
+ 1 small handful of chives, chopped
+ 2 tablespoons finely chopped tarragon leaves

MAKES 12 (SERVES 4)

Tamales are one of my many fantastic culinary discoveries. They are a deserving staple of South American food and every country on that continent has a unique version. In Mexico they are steamed and adored as a corn snack, often filled with vibrant braised meats and sauces, or enjoyed with chocolate. Most recipes use masa harina or masa harina PAN, both flours made from corn and widely available in Latin food stores. Essentially dumplings, tamales can sometimes be heavy but, by adding a fresh corn purée to the batter, you get a super light and creamy, yet still authentic-tasting, tamale.

To prepare the sweetcorn purée, heat the oil in a medium saucepan over low heat. Add the corn and garlic, cover and cook, stirring occasionally, for 4 minutes. Add the butter, chicken stock and salt and cook until the stock has reduced completely. Add the cream and bring to the boil. Simmer, uncovered for 4 minutes, or until reduced to a thick sauce.

Transfer to a food processor or blender and process until smooth. Strain through a fine-mesh sieve. Set aside to cool. Refrigerate until required.

Soak the corn husks in boiling water for 30 minutes, or until they are pliable.

To prepare the tamale dough, combine the lard, baking powder and salt in the bowl of an electric mixer fitted with a whisk. Mix on medium for 2 minutes, or until light and aerated.

Changing to a paddle attachment, gradually add the masa harina flour in fine streams, mixing until a stiff dough has formed. Gradually add the chilled sweetcorn purée, mixing until combined. Add the warm stock and mix on medium speed, until incorporated, to resemble a cake batter. Spoon into a piping (icing) bag.

To prepare the filling, chop the lobster or your seafood of choice into small pieces, approximately 1.5 cm (½ in) dice. Place the seafood, spring onion, chives and tarragon in a small bowl. Add the remaining corn purée and stir to combine.

Drain the corn husks and pat dry with paper towel.

To assemble, trim the corn husks to make 15 cm (6 in) long rectangles, the width of the husk. Lay the corn husks out on a clean work surface. Pipe the tamale dough onto the husks, making a flat zig zag down the length of the husk. Flatten the dough with the back of a wet spoon to cover the husk in an even layer. Pipe around the border creating a well in the centre for the filling.

Spoon the filling inside and pipe over the top with a little more masa dough. Fold the sides of the corn husk over so they meet and overlap in the middle. Fold the ends of the husks over, securing with a toothpick.

Quarter-fill a large saucepan with water and bring to the boil. Cover with a steamer pot or Chinese steamer basket.

Arrange the tamales in the steamer basket and steam gently for 30 minutes.

Gently reheat the zucchini flowers over low heat.

To serve, place the tamales on serving plates and slice through the corn husk skin to open up and expose the dumplings. Spoon over the zucchini flowers and scatter the salad around the outside. Sprinkle with the salted ricotta and edible flowers.

PAUL'S TIP You can omit the zucchini flowers Veracruz-style and make double the sweetcorn purée. It is perfect over the tamales too.

SPICED LAMB TLAYUDAS WITH GOAT'S CHEESE & CRISPY ESCHALOTS

+ 1 quantity Tlayudas (page 49)
+ 460 g (1 lb/2 cups) Refried beans (page 42)
+ 250 g (9 oz) ripe washed-rind goat's cheese, at room temperature

SPICED LAMB

+ 300 g (10½ oz) free-range lamb loin, trimmed of all fat and sinew
+ 50 g (1¾ oz) Latin spice rub (page 30) or cumin salt
+ olive oil for drizzling

SALAD GARNISH

+ 3 large handfuls of wild rocket (arugula) or purslane leaves
+ 250 g (9 oz) jar of peeled piquello peppers, drained and cut into neat strips
+ 1 large handful of oregano leaves
+ 100 ml (3½ fl oz) Latin vinaigrette (page 36)

CRISPY ESCHALOTS

+ 8 eschalots
+ 250 ml (8½ fl oz/1 cup) buttermilk
+ sunflower or rice bran oil for deep-frying
+ 150 g (5½ oz/1 cup) plain (all-purpose) flour
+ sea salt to taste

SERVES 6

Tlayudas are typical street-side snacks where giant paper-thin masa dough discs are cooked over an intense fire on a griddle, causing the dough to puff up and char, resembling an Indian poppadom. Labelled 'the Mexican pizza', these crispy tortillas can be topped with almost anything. The locals are quite partial to tlayudas topped with fried grasshoppers (chapulines), which taste like peanuts. I've also enjoyed a folded-over version. To interpret this classic dish at home, I have adapted the dough recipe so it can be cooked in a hot pan. You can also make tlayudas bite-sized as a great fiesta canapé.

To prepare the spiced lamb, coat the meat with the Latin spice rub, cover and refrigerate for at least 4 hours, or overnight.

To prepare the crispy eschalots, thinly slice the eschalots, using a mandoline and separate into rings. Place the rings in a medium bowl, cover with the buttermilk and soak for 2 minutes, to soften slightly. Drain.

Pour enough oil into a medium heavy-based saucepan to half-fill it and heat the oil to 180°C (350°F).

Dredge the soaked rings in the flour and fry in batches for 2 minutes or until crisp and golden brown. Remove using a slotted spoon and drain on paper towel. Season with salt.

Preheat a barbecue grill plate or large frying pan over high heat. Drizzle with oil and seal the lamb for 1 minute on both sides, or until browned. Reduce the heat to medium and cook, turning occasionally, for a further 5 minutes, or until done to your liking. Remove from the barbecue or pan and set aside on a plate to rest for 5 minutes.

Reheat the precooked tlayudas in the oven for 4 minutes, until they are warm.

Reheat the refried beans over low heat.

To prepare the salad garnish, combine the leaves, pepper and oregano in a medium bowl. Add enough vinaigrette to lightly dress and toss to coat.

To assemble, spread the tlayudas with refried beans. Slice the lamb and arrange on top of the beans. Scatter with knobs of goat's cheese and salad garnish. Sprinkle with crispy eschalots.

PRAWN & QUINOA QUESADILLAS WITH CHIPOTLE REMOULADE SAUCE

+ 12 large raw homemade masa tortillas (page 46) or store-bought tortillas
+ 2 large eggs, lightly beaten
+ 250 ml (8½ fl oz/1 cup) sunflower oil for frying
+ 1 avocado, sliced

FILLING

+ 210 g (7½ oz/1½ cups) peeled and deveined prawn (shrimp) meat (frozen and defrosted is fine)
+ 5 spring onions (scallions), finely chopped
+ 3 large egg whites
+ ½ small red onion, finely chopped
+ 2 jalapeños, finely chopped

+ 25 g (1 oz) achiote paste (see Glossary)
+ 2 garlic cloves, finely chopped
+ 100 g (3½ oz) cooked quinoa
+ 75 g (2¾ oz) salted ricotta, finely chopped
+ 1 large handful of oregano leaves, roughly chopped
+ large pinch of ground cumin
+ large pinch of salt

CHIPOTLE REMOULADE SAUCE

+ 250 ml (8½ fl oz/1 cup) Aïoli (page 28)
+ 150 ml (5 fl oz) Adobo sauce (page 15)
+ grated zest and juice of 2 limes
+ sea salt to taste

SALAD GARNISH

+ 4 breakfast radishes, thinly sliced
+ 1 large handful of flat-leaf parsley or oregano leaves
+ 1 tablespoon sunflower seeds, toasted
+ 2 teaspoons sesame seeds, toasted
+ 50 ml (1¾ fl oz) Latin vinaigrette (page 36)

MAKES 12 (SERVES 6)

Remoulade is classic French sauce, which travels and adapts well. This version celebrates the smoky chocolatey flavours of the chipotle chilli in adobo sauce. These quesadillas are inspired by a street food tour of Mexico City where locals feast on deep-fried quesadillas de Cameron and refreshing seafood coctels. I have adapted the filling and incorporated boiled quinoa, fragrant herbs and salty cheese.

For the filling, place the prawn meat, spring onion, egg whites, red onion, jalapeño, achiote paste and garlic in a food processor and blend to make a coarse paste. Transfer to a bowl and add the quinoa, ricotta and oregano and stir to combine. Season with the cumin and salt. Roll a small ball of the mixture, flatten slightly and shallow-fry. Taste to check the flavours, texture and seasoning and adjust accordingly.

To make the chipotle remoulade sauce, combine the aïoli, adobo sauce and lime zest and juice in a small bowl and mix to combine. Season with salt.

To assemble, place the tortillas on a work surface (floured if using raw homemade tortillas) and brush the edges with the beaten egg. Place a large spoonful of filling in the centre of each, allowing enough room to fold the tortilla in half. Fold the tortillas to enclose the filling and press the edges to seal. Secure with toothpicks if using store-bought or precooked tortillas.

Heat the oil in a large frying pan over medium–high heat. Shallow-fry the quesadillas in batches, for 2 minutes on each side, or until crisp and golden brown. Place on paper towel to drain. Cover and keep warm while you fry the remainder. To prepare the salad garnish, combine the radish, parsley and sunflower and sesame seeds in a small bowl. Lightly dress with vinaigrette and toss to coat.

To serve, arrange the quesadillas on a serving platter. Top each quesadilla with a slice of avocado. Season the salad garnish with a pinch of salt, then arrange over the quesadillas. With gusto, in an artistic Jackson Pollock fashion, dress the quesadillas and serving platter with the chipotle sauce.

PRAWN PLANTAIN & CORN SOPES

+ 1 quantity Sopes (page 48)
+ 250 ml (8½ fl oz/1 cup) Tomatillo verde (page 21)

ACHIOTE PRAWNS

+ 150 g (5½ oz) peeled and deveined prawns (shrimp)
+ 2 tablespoons Achiote relish (page 32)

ASPARAGUS PURÉE

+ 200 g (7 oz) (about 2 bunches) thin asparagus, woody stems removed
+ 1½ tablespoons vegetable oil
+ 20 g (¾ oz) unsalted butter
+ 2 garlic cloves, thinly sliced

+ 2 tablespoons finely chopped tarragon or epazote leaves
+ 90 g (3 oz/⅓ cup) low-fat sour cream
+ pinch of ground cumin
+ sea salt to taste

GARNISHES

+ 50 g (1¾ oz) very thinly sliced streaky bacon, flat pancetta or cheek bacon
+ 1½ tablespoons olive oil
+ 50 g (1¾ oz) ripe plantain, peeled and cut into 1 cm (½ in) slices
+ pinch of sugar
+ pinch of salt

+ 20 g (¾ oz) butter
+ 50 g (1¾ oz) fresh or frozen corn kernels (about 1 corn cob)
+ 50 g (1¾ oz/⅓ cup) fresh and cooked or frozen peas
+ salad burnet, watercress or young snow pea (mangetout) tendrils to garnish
+ salted ricotta, finely crumbled, to garnish

MAKES 12 (SERVES 4)

In Mexico corn masa is used to make all sorts of little delicacies and snacks called antojitos. Here it is used to make sopes (pronounced so-pays). These addictive, crumbly dough cases are tart-like in appearance and traditionally shaped flat with a rim. Sopes can be filled with so many delicious ingredients, such as bean purée, chopped salad, salty cheese, shredded meat or spicy salsa. They can also be made larger for a great breakfast dish filled with braised tomatoes and chorizo topped with poached eggs. Here's a more delicate approach, filling the tart with asparagus purée and achiote prawns (shrimp) along with plantain and corn, both everyday South American staples.

To prepare the achiote prawns, place the prawns and achiote relish in a small bowl and toss to coat. Cover and refrigerate for at least 2 hours or overnight.

Preheat the oven to 180°C (350°F).

For the asparagus purée, cut the tips off the asparagus and set aside. Cut the remaining asparagus into 2 cm (¾ in) lengths.

Heat the oil and butter in a medium frying pan over low heat. Cook the garlic until softened. Add the asparagus and tarragon, cover and cook for 5 minutes, or until tender. Add 60 ml (2 fl oz/¼ cup) water and cook for a further 5 minutes, or until most of the water has been absorbed. Add the sour cream and bring to the boil. Reduce the heat and simmer for 2 minutes, or until reduced to a thick sauce. Transfer to a food processor and blend until smooth. Season with the cumin and salt. Set aside.

To prepare the garnishes, lay the bacon slices on a baking tray, cover with baking paper and place another tray on top to flatten. Cook for 10–15 minutes until crisp and golden brown. Place on paper towel to drain. Tear into small pieces for garnishing.

Heat 1 tablespoon of the oil in a medium frying pan over medium heat. Fry the plantain with the sugar and salt until golden and caramelised all over. Transfer to a bowl.

Increase the heat to medium–high and add the remaining oil and the butter to the pan. Cook the achiote prawns for 30 seconds, add the asparagus tips, corn, peas and caramelised plantain and cook for a further minute or until cooked.

Reheat the precooked sopes in the oven for 4 minutes or until warm.

Reheat the asparagus purée over low heat.

To assemble, fill the sopes with the asparagus purée and top with the achiote prawn and vegetable mixture.

To serve, arrange the sopes on serving plates, placing teaspoons of purée underneath to secure. Drizzle tomatillo verde around and over the tartlets. Garnish with bacon, the salad burnet and salted ricotta.

PAUL'S TIP The dish can be prepared with one garnish, e.g. just asparagus, and the sopes filled with a simple guacamole or Avocado crema (page 38).

SEASIDE SEAFOOD COCKTAIL WITH TARO CHIPS

~~~~~~~~~~~~~

+ 1 litre (34 fl oz/4 cups) Basic Mexican gazpacho (page 51)
+ 2 avocados, sliced, to garnish
+ extra-virgin olive oil for drizzling
+ Taro chips (page 39) to serve

SEAFOOD COCKTAIL SALAD

+ 100 g (3½ oz) cooked prawn (shrimp) meat, diced
+ 100 g (3½ oz) cooked mussels, diced
+ 100 g (3½ oz) cooked crabmeat
+ 100 g (3½ oz) cooked clam (vongole) meat
+ 100 g (3½ oz) cooked octopus, diced
+ 2 white onions, thinly sliced
+ 100 g (3½ oz) breakfast radishes, finely julienned
+ 2 jalapeños, seeded and finely julienned
+ 1 large handful of coriander (cilantro) leaves, coarsely chopped
+ 1 large handful of flat-leaf parsley, coarsely chopped
+ 50 ml (1¾ fl oz) Latin vinaigrette (page 36)

SERVES 4

The prawn (shrimp) cocktail has been reborn in Australia and the United Kingdom and this is its Mexican cousin, inspired by the street food of Mexico – in particular the Baja coast and Campechana. It's a riot of seafood and flavour and you can use whatever seafood you like – the more the merrier! Serve with piles of corn (tortilla) or vegetable chips (crisps). Here I have recommended taro chips.

To prepare the seafood cocktail salad mixture, combine the seafood with the onion, radish, jalapeño, coriander and parsley in a medium bowl. Add the Latin vinaigrette and toss to coat.

To serve, pour approximately 125 ml (4 fl oz/½ cup) of the gazpacho into tall retro sundae or Marie Antoinette glasses. Divide the seafood salad among the glasses and top up with gazpacho until almost overflowing. Garnish with avocado slices and drizzle with olive oil. Serve with the taro chips.

PAUL'S TIP You can replace the gazpacho with 800 ml (27 fl oz) tomato juice blended with the grated zest and juice of 2 oranges and 200 ml (7 fl oz) Adobo sauce (page 15) or 100 g (3½ oz) chipotle in adobo sauce (see Glossary).

STREET-STYLE TOSTADAS WITH SEARED TUNA & WOOD-GRILLED VEGETABLES

TOSTADAS BASE SAUCE – CHOOSE 300 ML (10 FL OZ) FROM ONE OF THE SELECTION BELOW:

+ Veracruz sauce (page 41)
+ Sesame pipian (page 31)
+ Jalapeño & finger lime crema (page 37)

TOSTADAS

+ 6 small homemade masa tortillas (see page 46) or store-bought tortillas
+ 100 ml (3½ fl oz) sunflower oil for frying
+ sea salt to taste

SERVES 6

WOOD-GRILLED VEGETABLES

+ 3 red capsicums (bell peppers)
+ 3 red onions, unpeeled and quartered with roots attached
+ olive oil for drizzling
+ sea salt and freshly ground black pepper to taste
+ 2 green zucchinis (courgettes), cut lengthways into 1 cm (½ in) thick slices
+ 200 ml (7 fl oz) sherry vinegar
+ 200 g (7 oz) sugar
+ 1 large handful of oregano leaves, roughly chopped

TUNA

+ large pinch of ground cumin
+ large pinch of smoked paprika
+ large pinch of salt
+ 3 x 200 g (7 oz) albacore or yellow fin tuna steaks
+ 100 ml (3½ fl oz) extra-virgin olive oil
+ juice of 2 limes
+ 2 garlic cloves, crushed

GARNISH

+ 2 avocados, sliced
+ 1 small handful of oregano leaves
+ 1 small handful of basil or flat-leaf parsley
+ 2 jalapeños, thinly sliced

I found that the detail and care taken in Mexican street food was demonstrated best on the Baja coast, where the seafood tostadas are seriously good! If you find yourself in this part of the world you must seek out the famous seafood street stall, La Guerrerense, in Alvarado. The passionate owner and chef is a local hero and deserves a Michelin star. I was inspired to make these backyard barbecue tostadas, which are great with all types of barbecue toppings - grilled meats, flavoursome cheeses and, of course, great seafood.

Prepare your choice of tostadas base sauce.

Preheat a wood or coal barbecue until the coals have a thin coating of grey ash. Add presoaked aromatic wood, such as mallee oak, hickory or ironbark. Alternatively, if using a gas barbecue, soak smaller wood chips and place them in a smoking box on your barbecue.

To prepare the wood-grilled vegetables, grill the capsicums, turning occasionally, until they are blackened all over and beginning to soften. Transfer to a bowl, cover with plastic wrap and set aside to steam and cool slightly for 10 minutes.

Toss the onion in olive oil and season with salt and pepper and grill, turning occasionally, for 5–10 minutes, until softened and lightly charred all over. Drizzle the zucchini with oil and season with salt and pepper. Grill for 1–2 minutes on each side, until just cooked and lightly charred. Transfer the onion and zucchini to a tray and set aside to cool.

Meanwhile combine the vinegar, sugar and oregano in a small saucepan over low heat, stirring occasionally, until the sugar dissolves. Increase the heat and simmer until reduced to a rich coating consistency. Set aside to cool.

Once cooled, peel the onions and trim off the root. Separate the onion layers and cut each layer in half into neat petal-shaped pieces. Slice the zucchini to make neat ribbons. Peel and seed the capsicums and slice lengthways into neat strips.

Pour the marinade over the vegetables, season with salt and drizzle with olive oil.

To prepare the tostadas, heat the oil in a large frying pan over medium–high heat. Shallow-fry the tortillas in batches for 1 minute on each side, or until crisp and golden. Transfer to paper towel to drain. Lightly season with salt.

To prepare the tuna, combine the spices and salt in a small bowl then season the fish liberally on both sides. Combine the oil, lime and garlic in a medium bowl. Dip the tuna steaks into the oil and lime mixture and grill for 2 minutes on each side, turning every minute, until seared. For a more well-cooked tuna portion, finish in the oven or on a cooler part of the barbecue. Cut into thin slices.

To assemble, spread the tostadas with your chosen sauce, arrange the vegetables, tuna and avocado slices attractively on top and scatter with herbs and jalapeño.

PAUL'S TIP A fast topping for the tostadas would be a homemade guacamole or Avocado crema (page 38).

STREET-STYLE TOSTADAS
WITH SEARED TUNA
& WOOD-GRILLED
VEGETABLES
(pages 94–5)

BLACK BEAN BOCOLES WITH SEARED SCALLOPS & BLACK GARLIC SAUCE

~~~~~~~~~~

+ Black garlic sauce (page 28)
+ Salsa mexicana (page 36)
+ micro herbs to garnish

BOCOLES

+ 250 g (9 oz) Tortilla dough (page 46), very dry
+ 200 g (7 oz) Refried beans (page 42)
+ 100 g (3¹/₂ oz) lard
+ 100 g (3¹/₂ oz) salted ricotta, finely grated
+ ¹/₂ teaspoon baking powder
+ sea salt to taste
+ 250 g (9 oz/2¹/₂ cups) masa harina flour (see Glossary) or 250 g (9 oz/ 1²/₃ cups) plain (all-purpose) flour for dredging
+ 250 ml (8¹/₂ fl oz/1 cup) vegetable oil for frying

SCALLOPS

+ 50 ml (1³/₄ fl oz) olive oil
+ 12-30 large dry diver-caught scallops
+ sea salt to taste
+ 50 g (1³/₄ oz) butter

SERVES 6

These tasty and savoury cakes are very traditional. Originating from Veracruz they are easy to make in a Mexican kitchen because you're likely to already have masa dough and black bean purée in your refrigerator! These cakes can be grilled then baked, but the texture is a bit drier. They are great on their own or slathered in Veracruz sauce (page 41) and finely grated cheese. Here they are topped with sweet scallops and salsa mexicana and striking black garlic sauce.

To prepare the bocoles, place the dry tortilla dough, refried beans, lard, ricotta and baking powder in the bowl of an electric mixer fitted with a paddle attachment. Mix until well combined. Season with salt. Roll a small ball of the dough, flatten slightly and shallow-fry. Taste to check the flavours, texture and seasoning and adjust accordingly.

Divide the remaining dough into 30 equal-sized portions and shape into balls. Flatten slightly to make discs approximately 1 cm (¹/₂ in) thick. Dredge in flour and arrange on a plate.

Preheat the oven to 180°C (350°F).

Heat the oil in a large frying pan over medium-high heat. Fry the discs for 1¹/₂-2 minutes on each side, until crisp, dark golden brown and cooked through. Drain on paper towel. Transfer to a baking tray and place in the oven to keep warm.

Line a tray with a clean tea towel (dish towel).

To cook the scallops, heat a large non-stick frying pan over high heat until it is extremely hot. Add the oil and allow it to reach smoking point.

Season the scallops with salt and briskly fry in batches on one side for 1 minute. Add the butter to the pan, allow this to caramelise, then turn the scallops and remove immediately. Place on the prepared tray to drain.

To serve, spread some black garlic sauce on your serving plates. Place the bocoles on top and then 2-5 scallops on top of the bocoles. Spoon over the salsa and garnish with micro herbs.

MR WILSON'S FISH TACOS WITH SLAW & TWO SAUCES

~~~~~~~~~~

+ 12 small masa tortillas (see page 46) or store-bought tortillas
+ Adobo sauce (page 15)

CHIPOTLE MAYO

+ Aïoli (page 28)
+ 175 g (6 oz) chipotle in adobo sauce, finely chopped (see Glossary)
+ juice of 1 lime
+ sea salt to taste

THE SLAW

+ 150 g (5½ oz/2 cups) very finely shredded savoy or napa cabbage
+ 75 g (2¾ oz/1 cup) finely shredded red cabbage
+ 1 small bulb fennel, thinly shaved
+ 4 breakfast radishes, thinly sliced
+ 1 red onion, finely sliced
+ 1 large handful of flat-leaf parsley, roughly shredded
+ 150 ml (5 fl oz) Zesty lime dressing (page 37)
+ sea salt to taste

FISH

+ sunflower oil or rice bran oil for deep-frying
+ 400 g (14 oz) firm white fish, such as snapper, blue eye trevalla, monkfish, grouper, wahoo, black bass or lemon sole, cut into approximately 40 g (1½ oz) strips
+ plain (all-purpose) flour for coating
+ Mexican beer batter (page 35)

MAKES 12 (SERVES 6)

Visiting Ensenada and the Baja coast was amazing – great fishing, new seafood cultures and fish markets to explore. More importantly, it's where I tried many versions of the area's famous fish tacos. I learnt the fundamentals of this memorable dish and, trust me, there is nothing like it! The secret is choosing the right fish, great crunchy batter, zingy slaw and flavour-packed sauce. But, for the health-conscious, remember they don't have to be fried; grilled fish tacos are great too.

To make the chipotle mayo, whisk the aïoli, chipotle in adobo sauce and lime juice together in a medium bowl. Strain through a fine-mesh sieve. Season with salt. Refrigerate until required.

To prepare the slaw, combine the cabbage, fennel and radish in a medium bowl, cover with damp paper towel and refrigerate until required. Keep the onion and parsley in separate bowls until ready to serve.

To par-cook the fish, half-fill a large heavy-based saucepan with oil, set over medium heat and heat the oil to 180°C (350°F).

Dredge the fish in flour, coat in the batter and fry in batches, for 2–3 minutes, until golden. Remove using a slotted spoon or tongs and place on paper towel to drain.

Heat a medium non-stick frying pan over high heat. Lightly spray with oil and briefly fry the tortillas to warm them. Stack the tortillas, wrap them in a warm damp tea towel (dish towel) and set aside to keep warm.

Combine the slaw ingredients, add the lime dressing and toss to coat. Season with salt.

Re-fry the fish for 1–2 minutes, until crisp, golden and cooked through.

To serve, place the tortillas onto serving plates, drizzle with the chipotle mayo and adobo sauce and top with a little of the slaw and a piece of crispy fish. Drizzle with a little more of the sauces. Serve with napkins, ice cold beer or chilled riesling.

PAUL'S TIP For simpler fish tacos, replace the slaw with chopped iceberg lettuce, sliced radishes and thinly sliced red onion; lightly dress with chipotle mayo and a squeeze of lime.

SEAFOOD TACOS WITH GREEN MANGO & JICAMA SALAD WITH FRAGRANT HERBS

〜〜〜〜〜

+ olive oil for frying
+ 12 small masa tortillas (see page 46) or store-bought tortillas
+ micro coriander to garnish

SEAFOOD

+ 150 g (5½ oz) peeled, deveined prawn (shrimp) cutlets (shelled prawns with tail on, unpeeled), cut into 1 cm (½ in) pieces
+ 150 g (5½ oz) salmon fillet, cut into 1 cm (½ in) cubes
+ 150 g (5½ oz) calamari, cut into 1 cm (½ in) pieces
+ 80 ml (2½ fl oz/⅓ cup) Achiote relish (page 32)

SALAD

+ 1 jicama (see Glossary)
+ 1 green mango
+ 150 g (5½ oz) cherry tomatoes, cut into slices
+ 1 small red onion, thinly sliced
+ 1 jalapeño, thinly sliced
+ 1 small handful of coriander (cilantro) leaves, roughly chopped
+ 1 small handful of Vietnamese mint leaves, roughly chopped
+ 125 ml (4 fl oz/½ cup) Zesty lime dressing (page 37)

> MAKES 12 (SERVES 6)

Jicama is sometimes called Peruvian pear and I was delighted to discover they grow in Australia in Darwin and far north Queensland. In Mexico jicama is often served as an aperitif snack, cut into strips and sprinkled with smoked paprika then served in a tall, narrow glass partially filled with freshly squeezed lime. This is a terrific alternative to any olive in my opinion! This tropical taco is given a Southeast Asian twist with herbs, green mango, chilli and jicama for a lip-smacking and feisty taco treat. The marinade for the seafood is very versatile, the hero being achiote paste with its savoury, citrusy and complex taste.

To prepare the seafood, combine the prawns, salmon and calamari in a medium bowl. Add the achiote relish and toss to coat. Cover and refrigerate for at least 4 hours or up to 48 hours.

To prepare the salad, peel the jicama and mango and, using a mandoline, thinly shave into slices. Place them in separate stacks and cut into thin strips. Combine the jicama and mango with the remaining salad ingredients in a medium bowl, add the dressing and toss to coat.

Heat a medium non-stick frying pan over high heat. Lightly spray with oil and briefly fry the tortillas to warm them. Stack the tortillas, wrap in a warm damp tea towel (dish towel) and set aside to keep warm.

Heat a medium non-stick frying pan over high heat. Add a splash of olive oil and briskly fry the marinated seafood for 1 minute, or until just cooked through.

To serve, place the tortillas onto serving plates, top with the seafood and a neat pile of the salad. Garnish with the micro coriander and eat immediately!

PAUL'S TIPS Choose one seafood or white meat that can be precooked and served as a cold filling.
   If jicama is hard to find, you can substitute breakfast radishes, daikon (white radish) or even nashi pear.

SOFT-SHELL CRAB TACOS WITH GUACAMOLE, SHAVED FENNEL & SWEETCORN SALAD

+ 12 small masa tortillas (see page 46) or store-bought tortillas
+ guacamole or Avocado crema (page 38)
+ Tomatillo verde (page 21)

SOFT-SHELL CRAB

+ sunflower oil for deep-frying
+ 150 g (5½ oz/1 cup) plain (all-purpose) flour
+ 1 tablespoon onion powder
+ 1 tablespoon garlic powder
+ 1 tablespoon chilli powder
+ 1 teaspoon ground cumin
+ sea salt to taste
+ 3 defrosted soft-shell blue crabs, quartered
+ 250 ml (8½ fl oz/1 cup) buttermilk

SHAVED FENNEL & CORN SALAD

+ 2 tablespoons olive oil
+ 2 corn cobs, kernels removed
+ sea salt to taste
+ 1 small bulb fennel, excess stalk removed
+ 100 g (3½ oz) pickled jalapeños, sliced, preferably homemade (see Mexican-style pickles, page 53)
+ 1 red onion
+ 1 small handful of bronzed fennel fronds or dill, picked
+ 125 ml (4 fl oz/½ cup) Latin vinaigrette (page 36)
+ sea salt to taste

MAKES 12 (SERVES 6)

Australia produces some world-class seafood and soft-shell crabs are a great example. Young blue swimmer and mud crabs shed their hard shells at certain times of the year, and these are replaced by paper-thin textured skins. This taco is one of the most popular I've put on any menu. The soft tacos filled with crunchy fried crab, slathered in spicy tomatillo verde and fresh, clean-tasting crisp fennel salad, is an absolute winner.

To prepare the salad, heat the oil in a medium frying pan over medium–low heat. Cook the corn for 1–2 minutes until tender. Season with salt. Transfer to a small bowl and set aside to cool.

Using a mandoline, thinly shave the fennel. Place in a medium bowl and moisten with a little of the pickled jalapeño liquid. Cover and set aside.

Thinly slice the onion with the mandoline and set aside.

To par-cook the crab, half-fill a large heavy-based saucepan with oil, set over medium heat and heat to 180°C (350°F).

Combine the flour, onion, garlic and chilli powders, cumin and salt in a medium bowl. Dip the crab pieces in the buttermilk, coat in the seasoned flour and fry in batches for 2–3 minutes until golden. Remove using a slotted spoon or tongs and place on paper towel to drain.

Heat a medium non-stick frying pan over high heat. Lightly spray with oil and briefly fry the tortillas to warm them. Stack the tortillas, wrap in a warm damp tea towel (dish towel) and set aside to keep warm.

Combine the salad ingredients, add the vinaigrette and toss to coat. Season with salt.

Re-fry the crab for 1–2 minutes until crisp, golden and cooked through.

To serve, place tortillas onto serving plates, add a spoonful of guacamole or avocado crema and a piece of crab. Drizzle with tomatillo verde and top with a small amount of salad. Serve immediately with more tomatillo verde on the side.

PAUL'S TIP Replace the tomatillo verde with chipotle mayo (see page 101) and add coriander (cilantro) to the salad.

BARBECUED LAMB STEAK TACOS WITH POBLANOS RAJAS & CHIMICHURRI

- + oil for brushing
- + 12 small masa tortillas (see page 46) or store-bought tortillas
- + New-style chimichurri (page 22)

MARINATED LAMB

- + 1 kg (2 lb 3 oz) free-range lamb leg steaks
- + 100 g (3¹/₂ oz) Latin spice rub (page 30)
- + 100 ml (3¹/₂ fl oz) extra-virgin olive oil
- + squeeze of lime

POBLANOS RAJAS

- + 100 ml (3¹/₂ fl oz) olive oil
- + 3 poblano or bullhorn chillies (see Glossary), thinly sliced into strips (if using poblano, omit the chipotle in adobo)
- + 4 garlic cloves, thinly sliced
- + 50 ml (1³/₄ fl oz) sherry vinegar
- + 50 ml (1³/₄ fl oz) dark beer
- + 50 g (1³/₄ oz) sugar
- + 50 g (1³/₄ oz) chipotle in adobo, chopped (see Glossary)
- + 500 g (1 lb 2 oz/2 cups) low-fat sour cream
- + salt

CHOPPED SALAD

- + 300 g (10¹/₂ oz) iceberg lettuce hearts, roughly chopped
- + 4 breakfast radishes, thinly sliced
- + 1 red onion, thinly sliced
- + 100 g (3¹/₂ oz) pickled jalapeños, sliced, preferably homemade (see Mexican-style pickles, page 53)
- + 1 large handful of mint leaves
- + 80 ml (2¹/₂ fl oz/¹/₃ cup) Latin vinaigrette (page 36)

MAKES 12 (SERVES 6)

Lamb in a sandwich. The Turks and Greeks have been duelling over who has the best for centuries, but I love both equally! Most Mexican lamb recipes call for slow-cooking barbecoa-style. You could do this with lamb belly for this recipe, but lamb leg steaks during spring are an undervalued cut, in my opinion. You could also use lamb loin and fillets (tenderloin) if you're feeling fancy. Here, the briefly seared spiced lamb is sliced and tossed with a smoky poblano chilli stew and served with fresh chimichurri.

To prepare the lamb, coat the meat with the Latin spice rub, cover and refrigerate for at least 4 hours, or overnight.

To prepare the poblanos rajas, heat the oil in a medium frying pan over medium–low heat. Cook the chilli and garlic for 10 minutes or until softened. Add the vinegar, beer, sugar and chipotle, if using, and simmer, until reduced to a caramel. Add the sour cream and simmer over low, until reduced to a rich stew. Season with salt.

Preheat the barbecue chargrill to medium–high.

Brush the lamb with oil and a squeeze of lime and grill for 4 minutes each side, or until done to your liking. Remove from the barbecue and set aside on a plate to rest for 5 minutes.

Heat a medium non-stick frying pan over high heat. Lightly spray with oil and briefly fry the tortillas to warm them. Stack the tortillas, wrap in a warm damp tea towel (dish towel) and set aside to keep warm.

To prepare the salad, place the lettuce, radish, onion, jalapeño and mint in a medium bowl. Add the dressing and toss to coat. Transfer to a serving bowl.

Thinly slice the lamb, discarding any fat or sinew. Roughly chop and mix with enough rajas to bind. Transfer to a serving bowl.

To serve, place the tortillas, lamb, poblanos rajas, salad and chimichurri in individual serving bowls and plates and arrange on the table. Invite your guests to build their own tacos.

PORK CARNITAS WITH PINEAPPLE ADOBO SAUCE

~~~~~~~~~~

+ 1 kg (2 lb 3 oz) free-range boneless pork belly
+ sea salt
+ 2 litres (68 fl oz/8 cups) Chipotle chicken stock (page 14)
+ 100 ml (3½ fl oz) vegetable oil for frying
+ 8 large homemade masa tortillas (see page 46) or store-bought tortillas
+ guacamole or Avocado crema (page 38)
+ sliced green chilli to garnish
+ lime to garnish (optional)

PICKLED PINEAPPLE

+ 500 g (1 lb 2 oz) ripe pineapple, peeled, cut in half, excess core removed and thinly sliced widthways, then each slice cut in half
+ Mexican-style pickle solution, hot (see page 53)

PINEAPPLE ADOBO SAUCE

+ 500 ml (17 fl oz/2 cups) pineapple juice
+ 250 ml (8½ fl oz/1 cup) sherry vinegar
+ 230 g (8 oz/1 cup) brown sugar
+ 15 g (½ oz) dried chilli flakes
+ 250 ml (8½ fl oz/1 cup) Adobo sauce (page 15)

SALAD

+ 2 gem lettuce hearts, roughly chopped
+ 1 red onion, very thinly sliced
+ 1 small handful of coriander (cilantro) or mint leaves

SERVES 4

Traditional pork carnitas are made from slow-cooked spiced pork shoulder. Once cool, the meat is shredded, refried, then hashed and flavoured with chilli, lime, red onion and coriander (cilantro). It's then smothered over tortillas with guacamole, rolled like a cigar and grilled. This nuevo Latino version has the same flavours, it's just more textural and pleasing to the eye. The spicy and glossy pineapple adobo sauce adds a moist and extra-juicy layer.

To prepare the pork belly, generously season it and place it in a large, wide saucepan. Cover with the stock and bring to the boil over medium-high heat. Reduce the heat until simmering, cover and cook for 1 hour, until fork-tender. Allow to cool in the stock. Once cooled, remove the pork belly from the pan and pat dry with paper towel.

Line a deep tray, large enough to fit the pork, with baking paper. Place the pork belly in the tray, skin side down, cover with another sheet of baking paper and a large tray. Press down with a heavy weight, such as tins of beans, so the pork is pressed flat. Refrigerate overnight.

To prepare the pickled pineapple, place the pineapple in a small, deep tray, and pour over enough hot pickling solution to cover. Set aside for 1 hour or until cooled.

To prepare the pineapple adobo sauce, combine the pineapple juice, vinegar, sugar and chilli flakes in a medium saucepan and simmer over low heat, stirring occasionally, until the sugar dissolves. Increase the heat and simmer until reduced to make a rich caramel. Add the adobo sauce and stir to combine. Set aside.

Cut the pork into 2 cm (¾ in) cubes or rectangles.

Heat the oil in a large non-stick frying pan over high heat. Fry the pork pieces, taking care as they may spit when they cook, until crisp and golden brown. Transfer onto paper towel to drain.

Pour the oil out of the frying pan and wipe clean with paper towel. Add the pineapple adobo sauce to the pan and warm over low heat. Add the crisp pork cubes and baste and coat in the sauce. Keep warm.

Heat a medium non-stick frying pan over high heat. Lightly spray with oil and briefly fry the tortillas to warm them. Stack the tortillas, wrap in a warm damp tea towel (dish towel) and set aside to keep warm.

To prepare the salad, combine the lettuce, onion, coriander or mint in a medium bowl. Add a little of the pickling liquid and toss to coat.

To serve, arrange the tortillas on serving plates, top with guacamole or avocado crema, salad, slices of pickled pineapple and pork. Garnish with chilli and add a squeeze of lime, if desired.

PUFFY TACOS, NAPA CHICKEN SALAD & TOMATILLO VERDE

~~~~~~~~~

+ 1 quantity Tlayudas dough (page 49)
+ plain (all-purpose) flour for dusting
+ sunflower oil for deep-frying
+ 125 ml (4 fl oz/½ cup) Tomatillo verde (page 21)
+ 80 g (2¾ oz) salted ricotta or hard goat's cheese, finely chopped
+ lime to garnish (optional)

NAPA CHICKEN SALAD

+ 1 smoked boneless, skinless chicken breast, finely shredded
+ ⅓ head napa or Chinese cabbage (wombok), very finely shredded
+ 70 g (2½ oz) butternut pumpkin (squash), finely shredded
+ 1 small red onion, thinly sliced
+ 3 breakfast radishes
+ 1 small handful of flat-leaf parsley
+ 1 small handful of tarragon leaves
+ 80 ml (2½ fl oz/⅓ cup) Latin vinaigrette (page 36)

SERVES 4 (MAKES 12)

I've been very fortunate to represent Tourism Victoria at many events in the United States. One such trip to San Francisco was where I first encountered – what the Melbourne food media has dubbed – Cal/Mex food, a kind of fusion of authentic Mexican flavours with American locavore spirit. There were many new, fun, relaxed, produce-focused and really tasty dishes, all of which helped to inspire this napa chicken salad served in crispy and buttery puffy taco shells with lashings of tomatillo verde. These tacos can be cooked well ahead of time and reheated for just a minute in the oven as required.

Roll your dough into 30 g (1 oz) balls. Lightly flour a work surface and roll the dough out into 7 cm (2¾ in) discs, approximately 1 cm (½ in) thick.

If you don't have a special taco frying basket, simply drape the discs over a wooden spoon and pinch the ends together. Place in the freezer for 10–15 minutes to firm up.

Meanwhile, to prepare the salad, combine all of the ingredients, except the dressing, in a medium bowl.

Half-fill a medium heavy-based saucepan with oil and heat the oil to 180°C (350°F).

Arrange the tacos, ends facing upwards, into the oil and place a sheet of folded aluminium foil on top. (This applies just enough pressure to maintain the shape of the tacos.) Cook for about 3–4 minutes, until crisp and golden brown. Remove using a slotted spoon and drain on paper towel. Lightly season with salt. If some tacos are still sealed, simply cut through them with a pair of scissors.

Add the dressing to the salad and toss to coat.

To assemble, spoon a little of the tomatillo verde in the tacos, top with a small pile of chicken salad and sprinkle generously with cheese. Alternatively, place the tacos on a serving plate and the salad, cheese and tomatillo verde in separate serving bowls and invite your guests to build their own tacos. Add other condiments such as jalapeños, avocado, chopped iceberg lettuce, and a squeeze of lime, if desired.

PAUL'S TIP These tacos are great with left-over roast chicken or cooked prawns (shrimp) and Jalapeño & finger lime crema (page 37).

EMPANADAS DE PICADILLO WITH MISSION FIG MOLE

~~~~~~~~~~

+ 1 quantity Empanada dough (page 50)
+ 1 egg, lightly beaten (for egg wash)

LAMB FILLING

+ 750 g (1 lb 11 oz) free-range lamb rib plate (breast), excess fat trimmed
+ 35 g (1¼ oz) Latin spice rub (page 30)
+ 1 tablespoon olive oil
+ 1 large red onion, thinly sliced
+ 3 garlic cloves, thinly sliced

+ 45 g (1½ oz) dried figs, finely chopped
+ 2 tablespoons roughly chopped oregano leaves
+ 100 ml (3½ fl oz) dark Mexican beer or red ale
+ 50 ml (1¾ fl oz) sherry vinegar
+ 50 ml (1¾ fl oz) agave syrup (see Glossary) or honey
+ 375 ml (12½ fl oz/1½ cups) chicken stock
+ 125 ml (4 fl oz/½ cup) Red mole (page 16)
+ sea salt to taste

GARNISH

+ 150 ml (5 fl oz) Dark beer gastrique (page 31)
+ 3 ripe figs, halved lengthways
+ 125 ml (4 fl oz/½ cup) Red mole (page 16)

> MAKES 6

The Australians and English adore their meat pies. However, so do our Latin cousins but they call them empanadas, meaning stuffed bread or pastry. They are also the national dish of Argentina. With Mexican empanadas the term picadillo is often used to describe a flavour-packed meaty hash enriched with fruits, nuts and spices. Here lamb ribs are made into a delicious picadillo after being slow-cooked with dark beer, aromatic red mole, caramelised onions and fig.

To prepare the filling, coat the lamb with the Latin spice rub. Place on a tray, cover and refrigerate for at least 4 hours or, preferably, overnight.

Preheat the oven to 180°C (350°F).

Heat the oil in a large flameproof casserole dish over medium–high heat. Seal the lamb on all sides, until richly coloured and most of the fat has rendered away. Transfer the lamb to a tray for 2 minutes then drain the excess fat from the dish.

Reduce the heat to low and cook the onion and garlic until softened. Add the dried figs and oregano and cook for a further 2 minutes, or until soft. Pour in the beer, vinegar and agave and simmer, until reduced to a rich caramel. Add the stock and mole and stir to combine.

Return the lamb to the dish, cover and bring to the boil. Place in the oven and braise for 1 hour, or until the meat is fork-tender. Remove the lamb from the dish, place on a tray and set aside to cool.

Skim the excess fat off the braising liquid. Set over low heat and simmer, until reduced to a rich, thick coating consistency.

Once the lamb has cooled, remove all the meat from the bone, discarding any unnecessary fat or sinew. Pull and shred the meat using 2 forks and combine with enough of the reduced braising liquid to moisten. Season with salt and set aside.

Roll the rested empanada dough balls out, one at a time, between 2 pieces of baking paper, to make 5 mm (¼ in) thick discs, approximately 10–12 cm (4–4¾ in) in diameter.

Leave each dough disc on the baking paper and place a spoonful of filling in the centre. Brush the edge with egg wash and fold over to enclose, using the paper as a guide. Press around the edge of the filling to remove any air bubbles. Trim to make a curved edge and crimp to seal. Repeat with the remaining dough and filling. Rest in the refrigerator for 30 minutes.

Line 2 baking trays with baking paper.

Arrange the empanadas on one of the prepared trays and brush with egg wash. Bake for 20 minutes, or until golden brown.

To prepare the garnish, heat the dark beer gastrique in a medium frying pan over low heat. Place the figs in the gastrique, cut side up, and spoon over the liquid to coat. Transfer the figs to the remaining tray and bake in the oven for 5 minutes, or until caramelised.

Gently heat the red mole in a small saucepan over low heat.

To serve, spoon a little of the remaining reduced braising liquid onto serving plates, place the empanadas on top and garnish with a caramelised fig half and some red mole.

PAUL'S TIPS Store-bought puff pastry and a heavy seasoning of cumin and allspice can make this recipe simpler.

For fast and perfectly shaped empanadas, special cutters are available online.

For a flakier pastry, empanadas can be deep-fried briefly prior to baking. Simply preheat enough oil for deep-frying to 180°C (350°F). After resting the empanadas, fry them one at a time for 20–30 seconds, until golden brown. Drain on paper towel and bake for 5 minutes until golden brown and heated through. There is no need to brush empanadas with egg wash if pre-frying.

EMPANADAS DE PICADILLO
WITH MISSION FIG MOLE

(pages 110–11)

CHORIZO WITH APRICOT & MESCAL AÏOLI

~~~~~~~~~~

+ 4 authentic chorizo sausages
+ olive oil for drizzling
+ 100 g (3½ oz) padrón peppers (see Glossary)
+ smoked paprika to taste
+ sea salt to taste
+ watercress leaves to garnish
+ flat-leaf parsley to garnish

APRICOT AÏOLI

+ 2 tablespoons olive oil
+ 3 garlic cloves, thinly sliced
+ 1 cinnamon stick
+ ¼ teaspoon dried chilli flakes
+ 1 whole clove
+ 125 ml (4 fl oz/½ cup) chardonnay vinegar
+ 110 g (4 oz/½ cup) sugar
+ 375 ml (12½ fl oz/1½ cups) orange juice
+ 250 g (9 oz) dried apricots
+ 1 large handful of sage or tarragon leaves, roughly chopped
+ 2 teaspoons achiote paste (see Glossary)
+ sea salt and freshly ground black pepper

ARTICHOKE SALAD

+ 6 marinated artichoke hearts, quartered
+ 1 red onion, very thinly sliced
+ 370 g (13 oz/2 cups) shelled broad (fava) beans, blanched (optional)
+ 1 large handful of mint leaves
+ extra-virgin olive oil for dressing

SERVES 4

It's very common to encounter a pop-up roadside barbecue in Mexico selling carne asada - a popular mixed grill-type street food - or various other braised meats. It may look weird, but don't ask questions - just eat! The aromatic fuels from the barbecue and an array of salsas and relishes create a real street-side delicacy. The acid of the fruit helps to digest rich meats and the authentic spirit of Oaxaca - mescal - adds a lingering smoky, warm and complex overtone.

To make the apricot aïoli, heat the oil in a medium saucepan over low heat. Cook the garlic with the cinnamon stick, chilli flakes and clove, until the garlic softens and the spices are fragrant. Add the vinegar and sugar and simmer until reduced to a syrup. Add the orange juice, apricots, sage and achiote paste and stir to combine. Gently simmer for 10–15 minutes to make a semi-dry compote. Remove the cinnamon stick. Transfer the compote to a food processor and blend to a smooth jam consistency. Allow to cool. Adjust the seasoning with salt and pepper and additional vinegar, if necessary. Refrigerate until required.

Preheat a barbecue, preferably one with natural fuels, to medium heat.

Cut each chorizo diagonally into 6 even slices. Drizzle the chorizo with olive oil and cook on the barbecue for 2 minutes on both sides.

Meanwhile, heat a medium frying pan over high heat until very hot. Quickly sauté the padrón peppers for 1 minute until they begin to collapse. Season with smoked paprika and sea salt.

To prepare the artichoke salad, toss the artichoke, onion, broad beans and mint together with a little oil.

To serve, spoon the apricot aïoli onto serving plates, arrange the chorizo on top and garnish with the padrón peppers, artichoke salad, watercress and parsley.

PAUL'S TIPS This apricot aïoli is great with sliced chorizo salami or other cured meats as a simple, cold alternative.
   Fresh apricots can also be used for the recipe. Simply reduce the amount of orange juice to 250 ml (8½ fl oz/1 cup).

04

SOUPS

As with all noteworthy
cuisines of the world, the flavour
of the traditional soups can often set
the stage for understanding the remaining
food of that culture.

~~~~~~~~~~

In my experience, the soups of Mexico and South America are rich,
complex and satisfying. Sweltering over a bowl of steaming pozole at
the Oaxacan markets is a memory that makes me smile to this day.
In this chapter you'll find recipes ranging from aromatic broths and
refreshing gazpachos, to soups featuring smoky chipotle chillies
and unctuous bean purées. Some recipes are a bit 'cheffy' and
might test your patience and skill but, believe me, they are
worth it! I firmly believe you can judge a cook by their
use of stocks and sauces. Unfortunately this skill
is becoming a dying art, but I am happy
to try and keep it alive.

BLACK & BLUE CORN TORTILLA SOUP WITH BACON & PUMPKIN

~~~~~~~~~~

+ 100 ml (3½ fl oz) olive oil
+ 200 g (7 oz) smoked bacon, diced
+ 4 celery stalks, sliced
+ 1 red onion, finely diced
+ 4 garlic cloves, finely chopped
+ 1 red bullhorn chilli, diced (see Glossary)
+ 1½ tablespoons ground cumin
+ 1 tablespoon smoked paprika
+ 1 tablespoon dried chilli flakes
+ 1 kg (2 lb 3 oz) smoked ham hock
+ 3 litres (101 fl oz/12 cups) chicken stock
+ 220 g (8 oz/1 cup) dried black beans, soaked in cold water overnight
+ sea salt and freshly ground black pepper to taste
+ 200 g (7 oz) blue corn (tortilla) chips to serve

PUMPKIN

+ 100 ml (3½ fl oz) olive oil
+ 500 g (1 lb 2 oz) butternut pumpkin (squash), cut into bite-sized pieces
+ 55 g (2 oz/¼ cup) sugar
+ 2 jalapeños, sliced
+ 1 large handful of oregano leaves, roughly chopped

GOAT'S CREMA

+ 400 g (14 oz) soft goat's cheese
+ 250 g (9 oz/1 cup) sour cream
+ 1 tablespoon ground coriander
+ 1 garlic clove
+ juice of 2 limes, or to taste
+ sea salt to taste

SERVES 8

Black bean soup is a classic for a reason. It's comforting, hearty and one of the most versatile soups you will ever come across. You can add your favourite vegetables and herbs and spices to complement and liven up the earthy nature of this soup. This version uses bacon and ham hock to develop a really solid base and is served with pumpkin (winter squash) and goat's cheese crema for sweetness and balance.

Heat the oil in a large heavy-based saucepan over medium heat. Cook the bacon, vegetables, garlic and spices for 5 minutes, or until softened and fragrant. Add the ham hock and chicken stock and bring to the boil. Reduce the heat and gently simmer for 30 minutes. Add the pre-soaked beans, cover and gently simmer for a further 45–60 minutes, until tender.

Meanwhile, to prepare the pumpkin, heat the oil in a large frying pan over medium heat. Fry the pumpkin for 10 minutes, or until it begins to caramelise. Add the sugar and continue to cook, until well coloured. Add the jalapeño and oregano and cook for a further minute. Set aside.

To prepare the goat's crema, combine the goat's cheese, sour cream, coriander and garlic in a food processor and blend to combine. Season with the lime juice and salt.

Once the beans are tender, remove the ham hock and approximately 300 g (10½ oz) of the beans and set aside – you need enough beans to garnish the soup.

Blend the soup using a hand-held blender, until smooth. Strain through a fine-mesh sieve. Return to the pan and season with salt and pepper to taste.

Shred the meat off the ham hock. Add the ham and the reserved beans to the soup and stir to combine.

To serve, place a spoonful of the warm cooked pumpkin, along with the jalapeño and oregano leaves, in a neat pile in the centre of the soup bowls or plates. Pour in the soup and top with a generous spoonful of goat's crema. Serve with the corn chips, crushed if desired.

CHERRY GAZPACHO WITH DUCK CARNITAS

+ 250 ml (8^{1}/2 fl oz/1 cup) Red mole (page 16) or Adobo sauce (page 15)
+ 8 large homemade masa flour tortillas (see page 46) or store-bought tortillas
+ 1 small red onion, finely chopped, to garnish
+ 2 tablespoons sesame seeds, toasted, to garnish

CHERRY SOUP

+ 500 ml (17 fl oz/2 cups) freshly squeezed orange juice
+ 1.5 kg (3 lb 5 oz) cherries, pitted
+ 2 red capsicums (bell peppers), roughly chopped
+ 1 long (telegraph) cucumber, roughly chopped

+ 3 slices white bread, torn
+ 1 red onion, roughly chopped
+ 1 large handful of oregano leaves
+ 60 ml (2 fl oz/^{1}/4 cup) extra-virgin olive oil
+ 50 ml (1^{3}/4 fl oz) reposado tequila (see Glossary)
+ 1^{1}/2 tablespoons cabernet sauvignon vinegar
+ 1 small garlic clove, roughly chopped
+ zest of 3 oranges
+ ^{1}/2 jalapeño
+ ^{1}/2 bird's eye chilli
+ sea salt and freshly ground black pepper to taste
+ sugar to taste

DUCK CARNITAS

+ 4 free-range duck legs, deboned and cut into 4 even-sized pieces
+ 2 tablespoons rock salt flakes
+ 1 tablespoon ground allspice
+ 1 tablespoon ground cumin
+ 500 g (1 lb 2 oz) duck fat
+ 1 large handful of oregano leaves
+ 1 bay leaf

SALAD

+ ^{1}/2 small head savoy cabbage, finely shaved
+ 1 bunch (about 6) breakfast radishes, finely shaved
+ 1 large handful of coriander (cilantro) leaves
+ 1 jalapeño, thinly sliced
+ 125 ml (4 fl oz/^{1}/2 cup) Latin vinaigrette (page 36)

SERVES 8

The combination of cherries and duck is a winner. Cherries, like tomato, make a lovely chilled soup as they are not too sweet. A bowl of soup and a sandwich is a classic lunchtime meal or easy supper in many places and here the duck carnitas, literally 'little meats', take on the sandwich role, making each part more enjoyable. This soup can also be used as a dressing. Try it tossed with peppery greens and thin slices of smoked duck or prosciutto.

To prepare the cherry soup, place the orange juice in a small saucepan and simmer until it's reduced to 170 ml (5½ fl oz/ ⅔ cup), about 5 minutes.

Combine the reduced juice with the remaining soup ingredients in a food processor or blender and process until smooth. Season with salt, pepper and sugar to taste. Refrigerate overnight or for up to 24 hours. The longer the soup has to marinate the better the flavour.

Preheat the oven to 180°C (350°F).

To prepare the duck carnitas, season the duck legs all over with the salt and spices.

Heat 60 g (2 oz) of the duck fat in a wide, shallow ovenproof saucepan over medium-low heat. Cook the duck pieces, skin side down, for 5 minutes, or until the fat renders and the spices caramelise.

Reduce the heat to low, add the oregano, bay leaf and remaining duck fat, cover and cook in the oven for 1 hour, or until fork-tender. Allow the duck to cool in the fat.

To serve, remove the duck from the fat and set on a plate. Heat enough of the fat to shallow-fry in a large frying pan over medium heat. Fry the duck, taking care as it tends to spit, until crispy all over. Transfer onto paper towel to drain.

Warm the red mole or adobo sauce in a small saucepan over low heat, and the tortillas in the oven for 4 minutes. Place the duck in the sauce and heat through.

Make the salad, combining the cabbage, radish, coriander and jalapeño in a medium bowl and lightly dressing with the Latin vinaigrette.

Pour the soup into serving bowls or cups. Arrange the salad on the tortillas then arrange the duck on top. Sprinkle with red onion and sesame seeds. Serve immediately.

CHILLED CHILE DE AGUA SOUP WITH ALMOND SALT COD FRITTERS

~~~~~~~~

CHILE DE AGUA SOUP

+ 500 ml (17 fl oz/2 cups) freshly squeezed orange juice
+ 10 roma (plum) tomatoes, roughly chopped
+ 6 bullhorn chillies, roughly chopped (see Glossary)
+ 1 long (telegraph) cucumber, roughly chopped
+ 3 slices white bread, torn
+ 1 red onion, roughly chopped
+ 1 large handful of oregano leaves
+ 60 ml (2 fl oz/¼ cup) extra-virgin olive oil
+ 50 ml (1¾ fl oz) reposado tequila (see Glossary)
+ 1½ tablespoons cabernet sauvignon vinegar

SERVES 8–12

+ 1 small garlic clove, roughly chopped
+ zest of 3 oranges
+ ½ jalapeño
+ ½ bird's eye chilli
+ sea salt to taste
+ sugar to taste

ALMOND SALT COD FRITTERS

+ 60 g (2 oz/1 cup) panko crumbs (Japanese breadcrumbs)
+ 45 g (1½ oz/½ cup) flaked almonds, toasted and coarsely chopped
+ 2 large eggs, lightly beaten
+ 75 g (2¾ oz/¾ cup) masa harina PAN flour (see Glossary)
+ 1 quantity Salt cod mixture (page 44)
+ sunflower oil for frying
+ sea salt to taste

TO GARNISH

+ 175 ml (6 fl oz) Aïoli (page 28)
+ 1 avocado, sliced
+ 1 tart green apple, such as granny smith, sliced
+ micro coriander (cilantro)

Chile de agua is a chilli that's famous in the Oaxaca region of Mexico. It is known by a few names and you may have seen it called bullhorn chilli, banana chilli, sweet pepper, paprika or heirloom pepper. These chillies have much more flavour than a capsicum (bell pepper) and a gentle heat, hence the name, which means 'water chilli'. Here I make a gazpacho from them, which is a lovely partner for the salt cod fritters.

To make the chile de agua soup, place the orange juice in a small saucepan and simmer to reduce to 170 ml (5½ fl oz/⅔ cup).

Combine the reduced juice with the remaining soup ingredients in a food processor or blender and process, adding a little water to make a smooth, rich soup. Pass through a fine-mesh sieve and adjust the seasoning with salt, sugar and a little more vinegar, if required. Refrigerate overnight or up to 24 hours. The longer the soup has to marinate the better the flavour.

To prepare the almond salt cold fritters, combine the panko crumbs and flaked almonds in a medium bowl, and place the eggs and masa harina flour in separate bowls alongside. Roll the salt cod mixture into golf ball-sized balls, dredge in the flour, dip in the egg mixture and coat in the crumbs.

Pour enough oil for shallow-frying into a large deep frying pan until it is one-third full and heat it over medium heat to 180°C (350°F).

Fry the balls, turning frequently, for 5 minutes, or until golden brown all over and heated through. Season lightly with salt then drain on paper towel.

To serve, place spoonfuls of aïoli into the base of the soup bowls and spread flat with the base of a spoon. Place a fritter on the top and surround with alternating avocado and apple slices. Sprinkle with micro coriander. Transfer the soup to a suitable pitcher and pour into the bowls at the table in front of your guests.

LATIN FISH SOUP WITH PLANTAIN & ORANGE

~~~~~~~~~~~~~~

SOUP

+ 2 dried guajillo chillies, roughly chopped (see Glossary)
+ 1 litre (34 fl oz/4 cups) fish or chicken stock
+ 100 g (3 1/2 oz) achiote paste (see Glossary)
+ 250 g (9 oz/1 1/4 cups) fresh corn kernels (about 1 1/2 corn cobs)
+ 1 large handful of oregano leaves, roughly chopped
+ 80 ml (2 1/2 fl oz/1/3 cup) olive oil
+ 2 bulbs fennel, cut into thin wedges
+ 500 g (1 lb 2 oz) ripe tomatoes, sliced or quartered
+ 200 g (7 oz) kipfler (fingerling) potatoes, peeled and sliced
+ 10 garlic cloves, thinly sliced
+ grated zest of 4 oranges
+ sea salt to taste
+ 400 g (14 oz) kingfish fillet, cut into thick cubes
+ 300 g (10 1/2 oz) large prawns (shrimp), peeled with heads left on
+ 250 g (9 oz) large mussels, cleaned and scrubbed
+ 150 g (5 1/2 oz) clams (vongole), cleaned and scrubbed

GARNISH

+ 60 ml (2 fl oz/1/4 cup) olive oil
+ 300 g (10 1/2 oz) plantain or banana, thickly sliced
+ 300 g (10 1/2 oz) red bullhorn chillies, seeded and thinly sliced (see Glossary)
+ 6 garlic cloves
+ salt and freshly ground black pepper to taste
+ 100 g (3 1/2 oz) unsalted butter
+ 1 red onion, cut into 5 mm (1/4 in) thick rings
+ 4 oranges, segmented
+ 1 small handful of samphire, chopped
+ 1 small handful of flat-leaf parsley, finely chopped

SERVES 4-6

It might seem odd tucking into a bowl of hearty fish soup in the tropical heat of Mexico but sometimes it is just what you want. The rich variety of seafood available along the coast offers many unique Caribbean-influenced recipes. I was served this rustic soup by a fisherman's wife along the coast of Veracruz. It was honest and deeply satisfying. Due to the full-flavoured nature of the dried achiote and guajillo chillies, it's a fairly quick soup to prepare. Any firm white fish is suitable and, if potatoes are not your thing, simply swap them for sweet potatoes or pumpkin (winter squash).

To prepare the soup, dry-fry the chilli in a small frying pan over low heat, until fragrant.

Combine the chilli, stock, achiote paste, corn and oregano in a medium saucepan and heat until simmering.

Heat the oil in a wide paella-type pan over medium heat. Fry the fennel on both sides until golden brown. Add the tomatoes, potato and garlic and cook briefly without colouring.

Add the infused stock and orange zest and gently simmer until the potato is tender. Season with salt.

Add the fish, prawns and shellfish, reduce the heat to low and allow to simmer for 10 minutes until the shellfish open and the fish is cooked through. Remove the mussels and clams from their shells if you prefer.

Meanwhile, to prepare the garnish, heat the oil in a medium frying pan over medium heat. Cook the plantain, chillies and garlic until softened. Season with salt and pepper. Add the butter and onion and cook until the onion begins to soften. Add the orange segments and any residual juice to the pan and heat through.

To serve, spoon the garnish over the soup and sprinkle with samphire and parsley. Present the pan in the centre of the table and allow your guests to help themselves.

HUITLACOCHE & MUSHROOM SOUP WITH TROMPET MUSHROOMS

~~~~~~~~~~~~~

+ 80 ml (2^1/$_2$ fl oz/^{1}/$_3$ cup) olive oil
+ 3 red onions, finely chopped
+ 12 garlic cloves, crushed
+ 300 g (10^1/$_2$ oz/1^1/$_2$ cups) fresh corn kernels (about 2 corn cobs)
+ 300 g (10^1/$_2$ oz) tin huitlacoche corn truffle, drained (see Glossary)
+ 100 g (3^1/$_2$ oz) dried trompet or porcini mushrooms, soaked in warm water for 10 minutes to rehydrate (see Glossary)
+ 100 g (3^1/$_2$ oz) finely diced potato

+ 1 large handful of sage, tarragon or epazote leaves
+ 1 litre (34 fl oz/4 cups) chicken or vegetable stock, heated
+ 100 g (3^1/$_2$ oz) low-fat sour cream

PICKLED RADISH & ONION

+ 6 radishes, thinly sliced
+ 1 small red onion, sliced into rounds
+ 250 ml (8^1/$_2$ fl oz/1 cup) Mexican pickle solution, cooled (see page 53)

GARNISH

+ 50 ml (1^3/$_4$ fl oz) olive oil
+ 250 g (9 oz) cleaned fresh trompet mushrooms (see Glossary)
+ 2 garlic cloves, crushed
+ 1 small handful of flat-leaf parsley
+ 200 g (7 oz) blue corn (tortilla) chips, smashed

SERVES 8

Huitlacoche (pronounced weet-la-KOH-chay) is also known as Mexican corn truffle. It is a fungus that grows in the ear of corn and has a truffle-like taste. It has various nicknames, such as corn smut or raven's poo, but don't let that put you off! It's often hard to find fresh, in which case it's fine to use tinned. Tinned huitlacoche lacks the fungal oomph of the fresh variety, but adding dried porcini or trompet mushrooms to the base of huitlacoche recipes helps create an authentic flavour and colour.

To prepare the pickles, place the radish and onion in a medium bowl and pour over the cooled pickling solution. Cover and set aside to pickle for 1 hour.

Heat the oil in a medium saucepan set over low heat. Cook the onion and garlic until softened.

Add the corn, huitlacoche and rehydrated mushrooms, increase the heat to medium–high and cook until golden. Add the potato and sage and cook for 1 minute. Pour in the stock and bring to the boil. Reduce the heat and gently simmer for 40 minutes.

Transfer the soup to a blender or food processor. Add the sour cream and process until smooth. Strain through a fine-mesh sieve. Return to the pan and gently warm.

For the garnish, heat the oil in a medium frying pan over medium–low heat and cook the mushrooms and garlic for 1 minute, until golden brown. Allow to cool then stir through the parsley.

Drain the pickled radish and onion and arrange into soup bowls along with the mushrooms. Pour in the soup and scatter with smashed corn chips.

PUMPKIN SOUP WITH CHORIZO MIGAS

~~~~~~~~

SOUP

+ 75 ml (2½ fl oz) vegetable oil
+ 2 white onions, finely chopped
+ 10 garlic cloves, thinly sliced
+ 1 kg (2 lb 3 oz) butternut pumpkin (squash), diced
+ 250 g (9 oz) diced potatoes
+ 100 g (3½ oz) achiote paste (see Glossary)
+ grated zest and juice of 4 oranges
+ 1 teaspoon sea salt
+ 1 teaspoon sugar
+ 1 litre (34 fl oz/4 cups) chicken or vegetable stock, heated
+ 1 large handful of oregano or sage leaves

CHORIZO MIGAS

+ 100 ml (3½ fl oz) olive oil
+ 250 g (9 oz) chorizo, coarsely minced (ground)
+ 1 teaspoon smoked paprika
+ 200 g (7 oz) day-old country-style bread, coarsely torn
+ 4 garlic cloves, crushed
+ 1 large handful of oregano or sage leaves, roughly chopped
+ sea salt to taste

TO GARNISH

+ Jalapeño & finger lime crema (page 37)

SERVES 4

A simple, comforting soup with a vivacious topping! There are so many varieties of pumpkin (winter squash) available but you can't go wrong with the good old butternut variety. Here the silky sweetness of the soup interplays nicely with the salty crunchy chorizo migas – a Spanish and Portuguese condiment of torn day-old bread soaked with garlic and paprika, then fried with bacon or chorizo, sometimes even anchovies. It's an exciting addition sprinkled onto many foods and is great for breakfast with eggs.

To prepare the soup, heat the oil in a medium saucepan over low heat. Cook the onion and garlic until softened. Add the pumpkin and potato and cook for 5–10 minutes until soft and caramelised.

Add the achiote paste, orange zest and juice, salt and sugar and cook until the orange juice has reduced to a syrup. Add the stock and oregano or sage and bring to the boil. Reduce the heat and simmer for 40 minutes, or until the pumpkin is soft.

Transfer the soup to a food processor or blender and process until smooth. Strain through a fine-mesh sieve and return to the pan. Adjust the seasoning and keep warm.

To prepare the chorizo migas, heat the oil in a large frying pan over medium heat. Cook the chorizo and paprika until golden brown. Transfer the chorizo to a bowl, retaining the oil in the pan. Add the bread to the pan and cook until crisp and golden. Add the garlic and cook for 1 minute. Return the chorizo to the pan, add the oregano or sage and fry together for 1 minute. Drain the excess oil from the pan. Season with salt and drain on paper towel.

To serve, ladle the soup into bowls, top with some jalapeño and finger lime crema, and scatter over some chorizo migas.

KALE & CACTUS SOUP WITH POBLANO CREMA

~~~~~~~~~~

+ 80 ml (2½ fl oz/⅓ cup) vegetable oil
+ 3 onions, roughly chopped
+ 10 garlic cloves
+ 1 tablespoon ground cumin
+ 1 teaspoon ground cinnamon
+ 1 teaspoon freshly grated nutmeg
+ 400 g (14 oz) kale, stripped off the stems and shredded
+ 250 g (9 oz) tinned or cooked borlotti (pinto) beans
+ 250 g (9 oz) cactus paddle, peeled, grilled and chopped (or pickled cactus from a jar or tin) (see Glossary)

SERVES 6

+ 2 large handfuls of oregano leaves
+ 1 litre (34 fl oz/4 cups) chicken or vegetable stock, heated
+ 200 g (7 oz) English spinach leaves, washed
+ sea salt to taste

POBLANO CREMA

+ 250 g (9 oz/1 cup) sour cream
+ 95 g (3¼ oz) tinned poblanos in adobo sauce (see Glossary)
+ finely grated zest and juice of 1 lime
+ sea salt to taste

GARNISH

+ 2 tablespoons vegetable oil
+ 300 g (10½ oz/1½ cups) fresh corn kernels (about 2 corn cobs)
+ sea salt to taste
+ 250 g (9 oz) corn (tortilla) chips, smashed

This soup could open its very own health food store! Kale, currently so popular as a vitamin-packed super-food, is worth all the fuss afforded it. Likewise, cactus is worth all the fuss the Latin-American countries make about this unusual and versatile vegetable. It's very low in kilojoules, packed full of antioxidants and high in vitamin A. However, the aloe vera-like texture is unfamiliar to most Western palates. If you can't source fresh cactus, tinned or from a jar is fine. The poblano crema adds a lovely smoky note to the soup and the smashed corn (tortilla) chips and corn add texture.

Heat the oil in a medium saucepan over low heat. Cook the onion, garlic and spices until softened and fragrant. Add the kale, cover and cook for 5 minutes, or until wilted. Add the beans, cactus and oregano and cook for 1 minute.

Pour in the stock and bring to the boil. Reduce the heat and simmer for 15 minutes, or until the kale is well cooked. Add the spinach and cook for 2 minutes, or until wilted.

Transfer the soup to a blender or food processor and process until smooth. Season with salt. Strain through a fine-mesh sieve into a bowl – preferably stainless steel if you have one as it will help the soup to cool faster, retaining its green colour. Set the bowl over a larger bowl filled with iced water and stir to chill.

To make the poblano crema, combine the sour cream, poblanos in adobo sauce and lime zest and juice in a food processor or blender and process until smooth. Season with salt. Pass through a fine-mesh sieve and set aside.

For the garnish, heat the oil in a medium frying pan over medium heat. Cook the corn for 2 minutes, or until tender. Season with salt. Transfer to a small bowl and set aside.

Return the soup to the pan and gently heat over medium–low heat, stirring frequently so it does not stick and burn.

To serve, ladle the soup into serving bowls, top with a swirl of poblano crema, then scatter over the corn kernels and smashed corn chips to garnish.

PAUL'S TIP This soup is also great served cold, perfect for a refreshing light lunch. Just thin it down with some vegetable stock and serve topped with thick chunks of avocado.

HEARTY LAMB & TOMATILLO SOUP WITH ALBONDIGAS & ANCIENT GRAINS

~~~~~~~~~~~~~

SOUP

+ 60 ml (2 fl oz/1/4 cup) olive oil
+ 1 free-range lamb shank
+ sea salt and freshly ground black pepper
+ 1 small carrot, sliced
+ 1 small onion, sliced
+ 3 garlic cloves, sliced
+ 50 ml (1³/4 fl oz) sherry
+ 1¹/2 tablespoons sherry vinegar
+ 1¹/2 tablespoons sugar
+ 1 teaspoon ground cumin
+ ¹/2 teaspoon smoked paprika
+ ¹/2 teaspoon ground allspice
+ 1.5 litres (51 fl oz/6 cups) chicken stock
+ 200 g (7 oz) tinned tomatillos, chopped (see Glossary)
+ 60 g (2 oz) chipotle in adobo sauce (see Glossary)
+ 1 small handful of mint leaves, roughly chopped
+ 1 small handful of flat-leaf parsley, roughly chopped
+ sugar to taste
+ sea salt to taste

> SERVES 4-6

ALBONDIGAS

+ 60 ml (2 fl oz/1/4 cup) olive oil
+ ¹/4 onion, finely chopped
+ 5 garlic cloves, crushed
+ 1¹/2 tablespoons cumin
+ 1 teaspoon allspice
+ 1 teaspoon smoked paprika
+ 1 teaspoon chilli powder
+ 750 g (1 lb 11 oz) minced (ground) free-range lamb
+ 150 g (5¹/2 oz) sliced day-old bread, soaked in milk to soften
+ 2 large eggs
+ 50 g (1³/4 oz) salted ricotta, grated
+ 1 large handful of oregano leaves, roughly chopped
+ 1 small handful of mint leaves, roughly chopped
+ sea salt to taste

ANCIENT GRAINS

+ 1¹/2 tablespoons olive oil
+ ¹/2 red onion, diced
+ 3 garlic cloves, crushed
+ 1¹/2 celery stalks, diced
+ ¹/2 carrot, diced
+ 150 g (5¹/2 oz) kale or silverbeet (Swiss chard) leaves, finely chopped
+ 50 g (1³/4 oz) cooked mixed quinoa
+ 40 g (1¹/2 oz) cooked farro (see Glossary)
+ 40 g (1¹/2 oz) cooked or tinned chickpeas (garbanzo beans)
+ 40 g (1¹/2 oz) cooked or tinned Puy lentils
+ 50 g (1³/4 oz/1/3 cup) cooked peas
+ 1 small handful of oregano leaves, roughly chopped

GARNISH

+ Jalapeño & finger lime crema (page 37)
+ mint leaves
+ micro coriander (cilantro)
+ 100 g (3¹/2 oz) salted ricotta, finely chopped

This recipe is commonly eaten for lunch or supper in Mexico. The influence for these albondigas, or 'meatballs' as they translate in Spanish, dates back to the 6th century when a strong Islamic influence dominated the region. In Arabic the word al-bunduq means 'hazelnut', giving you a good idea of the size of these meatballs. Albondigas are also great as party food served on skewers with plenty of salsa verde or romesco sauce. Alternatively, simply serve the soup as a broth rich with grains and pulses.

To prepare the soup, heat the oil in a large heavy-based saucepan over medium–high heat. Season the lamb shank with salt and pepper and seal until it is browned all over. Transfer to a plate.

Add the carrot, onion and garlic to the pan and cook until golden brown. Pour in the sherry and vinegar. Add the sugar and reduce to a syrup. Add the spices and cook until fragrant. Return the lamb shank to the pan, pour in the stock, cover and cook over low heat for 3 hours, or until the lamb is soft and gelatinous.

Remove the lamb, place in a bowl and set aside to cool slightly. Flake the lamb from the bone with a fork, discarding any bone or sinew.

Skim any excess fat off the top of the soup. Add the tomatillos and chipotle in adobo sauce and simmer until the soup has reduced by half. Transfer the soup to a food processor or blender, add the mint and parsley and process until smooth. Season with sugar and salt. Pour the soup into a clean large saucepan, add the shredded lamb and keep warm.

Preheat the oven to 200°C (400°F).

To prepare the albondigas, heat 1 tablespoon of the oil in a medium frying pan over low heat. Cook the onion and garlic until softened. Add the spices and cook until fragrant.

Combine the spiced onion mixture with the lamb, bread, eggs, ricotta, oregano and mint. Mix well using clean hands to knead the mixture together. Season with salt. Roll a small ball and cook in a frying pan to taste and test the seasoning. Adjust if required. Shape the remaining mixture into small hazelnut-sized balls, or larger balls if you prefer.

Heat the remaining oil in a large frying pan over medium–high heat. Seal the meatballs in batches, for 2–3 minutes, until they are browned all over. Transfer the meatballs to a large ovenproof dish and add enough lamb soup to cover. Bake for 8 minutes, turn off the oven and leave the meatballs in the oven to stay warm.

To prepare the ancient grains, heat the oil in a medium saucepan over low heat. Cook the onion and garlic until softened. Add the celery, carrot and kale and cook for 5 minutes, or until the vegetables are tender. Add the precooked grains, pulses, peas and oregano and cook for a further 2 minutes, or until heated through.

To serve, reheat the soup until hot. Divide the vegetable and grain mixture into your serving bowls and arrange the meatballs on top. Spoon on some jalapeño and finger lime crema and scatter over some mint and micro coriander leaves and salted ricotta. Present the soup in the centre of the table for your guests to help themselves.

HEARTY LAMB & TOMATILLO SOUP
WITH ALBONDIGAS & ANCIENT GRAINS
(pages 134–5)

MEXICAN-STYLE SPRING MINESTRONE

~~~~~~~~~~~~~~

SOUP

+ 135 g (5 oz/^{2}/$_3$ cup) dried borlotti (pinto) or black beans, soaked in water overnight
+ 1.5 litres (51 fl oz/6 cups) Chipotle chicken stock (page 14) or vegetable stock
+ 300 g (10^1/$_2$ oz/1^1/$_2$ cups) fresh corn kernels (about 2 corn cobs), husks retained
+ 1 rosemary sprig
+ 50 ml (1^3/$_4$ fl oz) olive oil
+ 1 onion, diced
+ 2 garlic cloves, thinly sliced
+ 1 bunch baby (Dutch) carrots, cut into 1 cm (^{1}/$_2$ in) thick slices
+ 1 small head celeriac, diced
+ 1 small fennel bulb, diced
+ sea salt and freshly ground black pepper

+ 250 g (9 oz/2 cups) sliced green beans
+ 250 g (9 oz) small zucchini (courgettes), sliced
+ 100 g (3^1/$_2$ oz/^{2}/$_3$ cup) peas, cooked
+ 95 g (3^1/$_4$ oz/^{1}/$_2$ cup) podded broad (fava) beans, blanched and peeled
+ 100 g (3^1/$_2$ oz) angel hair pasta, broken into pieces and cooked
+ 100 g (3^1/$_2$ oz) mixed grape tomatoes
+ squeeze of lime juice
+ 125 ml (4 fl oz/^{1}/$_2$ cup) Pasilla chilli relish (page 25)
+ basil leaves to garnish

STUFFED ZUCCHINI FLOWERS

+ 100 g (3^1/$_2$ oz) soft goat's cheese
+ 1 large handful of chives, chopped
+ 1 large handful of tarragon, chopped
+ ^{1}/$_2$ small garlic clove, finely grated
+ sea salt and freshly ground black pepper
+ 4 zucchini (courgette) flowers
+ peanut oil for frying
+ 190 ml (6^1/$_2$ fl oz/^{3}/$_4$ cup) milk
+ 75 g (2^3/$_4$ oz/^{3}/$_4$ cup) masa harina PAN flour (see Glossary)
+ sea salt to taste

SERVES 4

I like giving traditional recipes a cross-cultural twist. Mexican soups are mostly brothy soups rich with beans, braised meats and vegetables. Here I have taken the flavours of Mexico - chilli and lime - to make a lighter minestrone-style soup. The addition of the zucchini (courgette) flowers, which always shout spring to me, stuffed with the soft goat's cheese, works beautifully with the sweet raisin-like flavours of the pasilla chilli.

To prepare the soup, drain and rinse the pre-soaked beans and place them in a medium saucepan. Cover with the stock, add the corn husks and rosemary and bring to the boil over medium heat. Simmer for 1 hour, or until tender.

Heat the oil in a large, wide heavy-based saucepan over low heat. Cook the onion and garlic until softened. Add the carrot, celeriac, fennel and corn kernels and cook until soft. Add the cooked beans and stock and bring to the boil. Remove from the heat, season with salt and pepper and set aside.

To prepare the zucchini flowers, combine the goat's cheese, chives, tarragon and garlic in a small bowl. Season with salt and pepper. Spoon the mixture inside the flowers and twist the ends to secure.

Half-fill a heavy-based frying pan with peanut oil and heat the oil to 180°C (350°F).

To finish the soup, bring it to the boil again then add the beans, zucchini, peas, broad beans, pasta and tomatoes and bring to the boil again. Add the lime juice and adjust the seasoning, if required.

Blend the pasilla chilli relish with enough boiling water to make a smooth liquid for drizzling. Adjust the seasoning. Set aside.

To cook the zucchini flowers, dip them in the milk, then dredge in the masa harina flour and shallow-fry, turning occasionally, for 3–5 minutes, until crisp and golden brown. Remove using a slotted spoon and drain on paper towel. Season with salt.

Ladle the soup into shallow bowls, drizzle with the pasilla chilli relish and garnish with basil leaves. Sit the bowls on slightly larger under-plates. Place the zucchini flowers on the side or on top to serve.

RANCHERO-STYLE BEEF BROTH WITH BONE MARROW & CHIMICHURRI TOAST

BROTH

+ 60 ml (2 fl oz/1/4 cup) olive oil
+ sea salt and freshly ground black pepper
+ 3 kg (6 lb 10 oz) oxtail pieces
+ 2 chorizo sausages
+ 4 carrots, halved lengthways
+ 2 garlic bulbs, halved crossways
+ 2 litres (68 fl oz/8 cups) beef stock
+ 250 g (9 oz) tin poblano chillies in adobo sauce (see Glossary)
+ bouquet garni

SERVES 4

SOUP BASE

+ 5 onions
+ 6 celery stalks
+ 6 bullhorn chillies, seeded (see Glossary)
+ 170 ml (5 1/2 fl oz/2/3 cup) olive oil
+ 10 garlic cloves, thinly sliced
+ sea salt and freshly ground black pepper
+ 8 thyme sprigs, tied in a muslin (cheesecloth) parcel or tied in a bundle with kitchen string
+ 310 ml (10 1/2 fl oz/1 1/4 cups) sherry vinegar
+ 110 g (4 oz/1/2 cup) sugar
+ 250 g (9 oz) cooked or tinned black beans
+ 200 g (7 oz) cooked or tinned chickpeas (garbanzo beans)

BONE MARROW & CHIMICHURRI TOAST

+ 4 thin slices rustic bread
+ extra-virgin olive oil for brushing and drizzling
+ sea salt and coarsely ground black pepper
+ 1 garlic clove, halved, for rubbing
+ 125 g (4 1/2 oz) New-style chimichurri (page 22)
+ 2 cm (3/4 in) thick slices of deboned marrow, rinsed and soaked in iced water for 30 minutes to draw out the blood and discolourations
+ 3 eschalots, thinly sliced into rings
+ 1 large handful of flat-leaf parsley
+ 1–2 pickled jalapeños, sliced
+ baby breakfast radishes to garnish

This is an opulent version of a typical breakfast soup I tried in Oaxaca, Mexico. The key is a rich and full-flavoured stock, which is created after long, slow braising of the oxtail. The marrow toast makes a welcome addition - it is rich but the punchy chimichurri adds a lovely herbaceous acid kick. I am sure you will adore this as much as most chefs and foodies. It's a great beef eater's wintry feast!

Preheat the oven to 200°C (400°F).

To prepare the broth, heat the oil in a deep heavy-based flameproof casserole dish with a lid over medium–high heat. Season the oxtail. Sear the oxtail and whole chorizo on all sides until well browned. Drain off the excess fat and transfer the oxtail and chorizo to a large plate.

Add the carrot and garlic to the dish and cook until lightly coloured. Pour in the stock, add the poblano in adobo and bouquet garni. Return the oxtail and chorizo to the dish. Cover and cook in the oven for 2½–3 hours, until the oxtail meat is soft and gelatinous.

Meanwhile, to prepare the soup base, thinly slice the onion, celery and bullhorn chillies with a mandoline, taking care not to cut too close to your fingers.

Heat the oil in a large saucepan over high heat. Cook the onion, celery, chilli and garlic until softened and all of the liquid has evaporated. Season with salt and pepper. Reduce the heat to low, add the thyme, vinegar and sugar and reduce to a syrup. Remove from the heat.

Once the oxtail is soft and tender, remove the oxtail and chorizo from the broth. Skim off any excess fat and impurities. Strain the broth through a fine-mesh sieve into the soup base.

Remove the oxtail meat from the bone. Trim and discard any fat or gristle.

Cut the chorizo into 2 cm (¾ in) thick slices.

Heat the broth and soup base mixture over medium heat and allow to simmer for 15 minutes. Add the beans, chickpeas, oxtail and chorizo.

Reduce the oven temperature to 190°C (375°F).

Preheat an overhead grill (broiler) to medium–high.

To prepare the chimichurri toasts, brush the bread on both sides with olive oil, season with salt and pepper and rub with garlic. Arrange on a tray and bake in the oven for 10 minutes or until crisp and golden brown. Spread the toast with the chimichurri. Place the marrow slices on top of the toasts and season. Grill (broil) briefly to warm up.

Combine the eschalots, parsley and jalapeño in a small bowl. Drizzle with olive oil, season with salt and pepper and toss to combine.

To serve, pile the soup base, beans, chickpeas, oxtail and chorizo into serving bowls. Ladle enough broth to cover and sprinkle with the eschalot mixture. Top with the marrow toasts and garnish with the baby radishes.

RANCHERO-STYLE BEEF
BROTH WITH BONE MARROW
& CHIMICHURRI TOAST
(pages 140–1)

CHILLED TOMATILLO & AVOCADO SOUP WITH TUNA SASHIMI SALAD

～～～～～～

SOUP

+ 250 ml (8½ fl oz/1 cup) Tomatillo verde (page 21)
+ 4 very ripe hass avocados, peeled and stoned
+ 500 ml (17 fl oz/2 cups) chicken or vegetable stock
+ 90 g (3 oz/⅓ cup) sour cream
+ large pinch of salt

TUNA SASHIMI SALAD

+ 500 g (1 lb 2 oz) sashimi-grade tuna loin, blood-line removed
+ 2 small red onions, thinly sliced

+ 2 small (Lebanese) cucumbers, cut into thin rounds
+ 200 g (7 oz) grape or pear cherry tomatoes, halved
+ 100 g (3½ oz) (about 3) breakfast radishes, sliced into rounds
+ 1 habanero chilli, seeded and thinly sliced (see Glossary)
+ 125 ml (4 fl oz/½ cup) Mexican pickle solution (see page 53)
+ salt and freshly ground black pepper
+ extra-virgin olive oil for brushing and drizzling
+ 1 large handful of green or purple basil leaves

+ 1 large handful of mint leaves
+ 1 avocado, sliced
+ 50 g (1¾ oz) finger lime flesh (see Glossary) or lime segments
+ Taro chips (page 39)
+ 30 g (1 oz/¼ cup) pepitas (pumpkin seeds), toasted, to garnish
+ assorted micro herbs to garnish

SERVES 8

This soup takes its inspiration from ajo blanco, which is a delicious garlic and almond soup from Andalusia, Spain. Seafood loves the acid kick of lemon and lime, and tuna sashimi is no exception. The king of chillies, the habanero, spices up the accompanying salad and provides a contrast to the cooling soup – just be careful as habaneros are VERY hot! This soup is incredibly versatile – in addition to seared tuna it can also be served with sweetcorn, salsa and smashed corn (tortilla) chips or even torn poached chicken and peppery greens.

To make the soup, combine the tomatillo verde and avocados in a food processor or blender and process, gradually adding the chicken stock, until smooth. Add the sour cream and process to combine. Season with salt. Strain through a fine-mesh sieve and chill until required.

To prepare the tuna sashimi salad, wrap the tuna loin tightly in several layers of plastic wrap, twisting the ends to seal, creating a round log of tuna. Chill in the freezer for 30 minutes, or until firm.

Meanwhile, combine the onion, cucumber, tomato, radish and habanero in a medium bowl. Pour in the Mexican pickle solution and set aside for 30 minutes to pickle.

Once firm, cut the tuna into four 125 g (4½ oz) steaks. Season with salt and pepper.

Heat a barbecue chargrill to high heat.

Generously brush the tuna steaks with oil and grill briefly for 30 seconds on each side. Remove from the pan and set aside to cool slightly.

To serve, drain the pickled vegetables and combine with the basil and mint leaves in a medium bowl. Drizzle with a little olive oil and toss to coat. Season with salt.

Using a very sharp knife, slice the tuna steaks diagonally, making 5 slices from each steak.

Arrange the tossed salad ingredients across 8 chilled soup bowls. Neatly arrange the tuna, avocado, lime flesh or segments and taro chips among the salad and sprinkle with pepitas.

Transfer the soup into a pitcher and pour around the salad. Garnish with micro herbs and a drizzle of olive oil.

RED TURKEY POZOLE

~~~~~~~~~~

BROTH

+ 1 kg (2 lb 3 oz) turkey breast (skinless, boneless with wing attached), or turkey bones from a left-over roast
+ good pinch of salt
+ 2 litres (68 fl oz/8 cups) chicken stock
+ 250 g (9 oz/1 cup) Pasilla chilli relish (page 25)
+ 2 corn cobs, cut into 4
+ 2 red onions, quartered
+ 2 large handfuls of tarragon leaves
+ 1 large handful of sage leaves
+ 4 bay leaves
+ 300 g (10½ oz) cooked or tinned hominy (see Glossary)

GARNISH

+ 1 small white cabbage, very finely shredded
+ 6 breakfast radishes, thinly sliced
+ 2 white onions, thinly sliced
+ 1 large handful of coriander (cilantro) leaves, roughly chopped
+ 3 pickled jalapeños, sliced
+ 200 g (7 oz) sour cream
+ 200 g (7 oz) homemade masa flour tortillas (see page 46) or store-bought tortillas, fried and smashed

SERVES 6

Pozole is an incredibly full-flavoured and hearty soup. Dating back to pre-Colombian times, this ceremonial soup is primarily made from nixtamalised (a process of soaking and boiling) white corn, also known as hominy. It is available rehydrated and tinned. History tells us it was originally made with human meat by cannibals and used at special rituals. This is now replaced with pork – or pig's head, to increase the flavour and theatre of the dish. Here I've created a more celebratory version using turkey, perfect for Christmas or Thanksgiving left-overs. The spice element, fresh salad component and array of condiments make for a perfect pick-me-up after too much fun at a festive event.

To prepare the broth, place the turkey breast or bones in a large saucepan with the salt. Pour in the stock and bring to the boil over medium–high heat. Skim off the impurities that have come to the surface.

Add the pasilla chilli relish, corn, onion and herbs. Reduce the heat and simmer for 30 minutes. Remove the turkey breast and set aside to cool slightly. Simmer for a further hour. Remove the corn cobs, set aside to cool slightly. Cut off the kernels and set aside.

Once cooled, shred the turkey, pulling the meat into fine strips lengthways. Cover until required.

Strain the stock through a fine-mesh sieve, return to a clean pan and gently simmer until it is reduced to a well-balanced and flavoured broth of approximately 1.5 litres (51 fl oz/6 cups).

Add the hominy, corn, shredded meat and half of the cabbage, radish and onion prepared for the garnish to the broth.

To serve, ladle the soup into serving bowls. Place the remaining garnish ingredients into individual serving bowls and encourage guests to add as desired.

CORAL TROUT POZOLE

~~~~~~~~~~

BROTH

+ 500 g (1 lb 2 oz) coral trout, scaled and filleted (ask your fishmonger to retain the head and bones)
+ 1 litre (34 fl oz/4 cups) chicken stock
+ 1 kg (2 lb 3 oz) ripe tomatoes, chopped
+ 2 bunches bulb spring onions (scallions), cut into quarters
+ 2 small bulbs fennel, 1 quartered and 1 thickly sliced
+ 2 corn cobs, husks retained and kernels removed

+ 1 large handful of oregano leaves
+ 2 bay leaves
+ 2 tablespoons olive oil plus extra for drizzling (optional)
+ 1 kg (2 lb 3 oz) prawns (shrimp), bodies peeled and deveined, shells retained
+ 250 ml (8$\frac{1}{2}$ fl oz/1 cup) Pasilla chilli relish (page 25) plus extra to garnish (optional)
+ 250 g (9 oz) cooked or tinned hominy (see Glossary)
+ sea salt and freshly ground black pepper to taste

+ 300 g (10$\frac{1}{2}$ oz) mussels, cleaned and scrubbed

GARNISH

+ 200 g (7 oz) cherry tomatoes, halved
+ 6 radishes, sliced
+ 2 limes, thinly sliced
+ 60 g (2 oz/$\frac{1}{2}$ cup) pitted black olives, roughly chopped
+ 1 large handful of coriander (cilantro) leaves
+ 2 avocados, peeled and quartered

SERVES 4

To prepare the broth, place the fish bones and heads in a large saucepan, cover with stock and bring to the boil over medium–low heat.

Add the tomato, half the spring onions, the fennel quarters, the corn husks, oregano and bay leaves. Simmer for 30 minutes, skimming off the impurities as they rise to the surface.

Heat the oil in a large frying pan over medium–high heat. Fry the prawn shells for 3–4 minutes until caramelised. Add the shells to the stock and simmer for 3 minutes. Remove from the heat and set aside to cool.

Strain the fish stock, taking care not to disturb the bones and other ingredients too much or the stock will become cloudy. Discard the solids.

Reheat the clear broth in a clean large saucepan. Add the pasilla chilli relish, remaining onions and fennel slices and gently simmer for 5 minutes, or until tender. Add the hominy, corn kernels and prawns and cook until the prawns change colour. Remove the prawns, place in a bowl and set aside. Season with salt and pepper.

Add the mussels to the stock and cook for 5 minutes, or until just opened. Remove, place in a bowl and set aside.

Set a large bamboo steamer lined with baking paper over a saucepan of simmering water.

Cut the fish into 4 equal-sized portions. Arrange the fish in the steamer and steam for 5 minutes or until just cooked through.

Place the fish portions into deep serving bowls suitable for noodles. Add the cherry tomatoes and ladle in a little of the broth. Surround with the vegetables and cooked shellfish. Garnish with slices of radish and lime, olives and coriander. Add the remaining broth, top with avocado and drizzle with oil or pasilla chilli relish.

There are many types of pozole, both red or green are great with seafood. Chilli is my muse for this dish in the form of pasilla chilli relish, so it's red pozole here. For green, tomatillo verde is added to the broth. The key to a good pozole is the stock. For meaty pozole I like ham stock because it's always clear, smoky and fragrant. You can add chorizo or chicken wings but, for this recipe, it's all about the seafood. I use roasted prawn (shrimp) shells and coral trout bones to make a great seafood broth. Don't forget to enjoy the cheeks from the fish head – they're a deserving cook's prize!

05

FISH & SEAFOOD

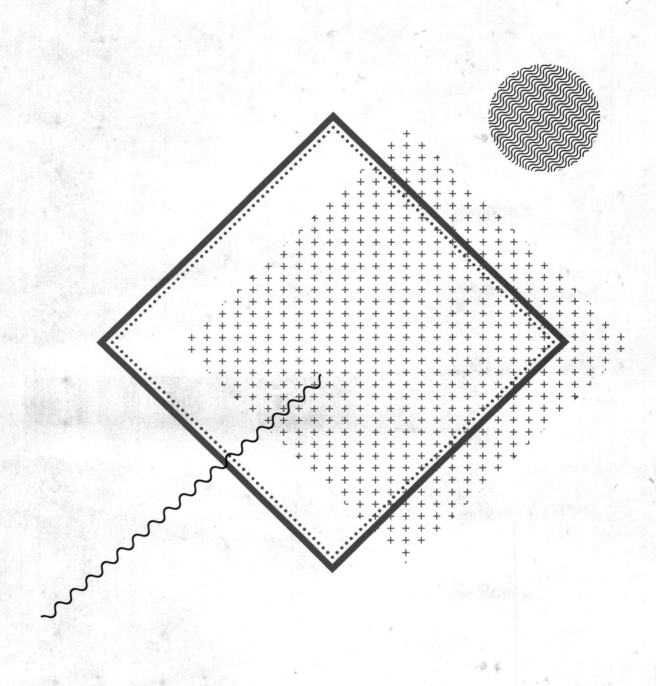

Seafood is popular and
plentiful in Mexican cuisine,
which is evident when you visit the
central markets of Mexico City and the Baja
coast. I came across so many new species of
fish while I was there.

~~~~~~~

As eating fish is so healthy, I have included recipes promoting lesser
known fish, prepared in new and exciting ways with Latin flavours
to create exotic and nutritious dishes. You will discover how the
flavours of the sea can be transformed into delicate appetisers.
My new-style of cebiche provides a safe, fresh and vibrant
way to eat raw seafood. The simply grilled or fried seafood
with refreshing mojo sauces and the whole baked fish,
slathered in sesame pipian, will transport you
straight to the beach-side restaurants of
the Yucatán Peninsula.

ALBACORE TUNA CEBICHE WITH JICAMA, PEAR & GREEN SALMOREJO

~~~~~~~~~~

+ 500 g (1 lb 2 oz) sashimi-grade albacore tuna or salmon
+ 250 ml (8½ fl oz/1 cup) Green salmorejo (page 39)

SALAD

+ 2 jicamas, julienned (see Glossary)
+ 3 nashi pears, quartered, cored and shaved
+ 1 handful of perfect watercress tops or micro daikon (white radish)
+ 1 red onion, thinly sliced
+ 100 g (3½ oz) pepitas (pumpkin seeds), toasted
+ 1 jalapeño, thinly sliced
+ 4 avocados, halved and stoned
+ juice of 2 limes
+ 100 ml (3½ fl oz) olive oil
+ pinch of sea salt

SERVES 4

Albacore tuna was a seafood discovery for me this year. Albacore, or bincho, tuna is white tuna and the type normally used for tinned tuna because of its pale appearance. I find this tuna to be the perfect texture for cebiche as it really takes to the lime, chilli and fragrant herbs, almost melting in your mouth. At the restaurant we get a bit fancy and cut small barrels from the loin that we marinate in the salmorejo dressing for 5 hours so the tuna starts to cook on the outside, giving the impression it's been seared and adding a wonderful flavour.

Slice the tuna into two 6 x 3 cm (2½ x 1¼ in) pieces.

Place the tuna in a 3 cm (1¼ in) deep container and coat with 150 g (5½ oz) of the green salmorejo. Cover and marinate in the refrigerator for 4 hours.

To prepare the salad, just before serving, combine the jicama, nashi pear, watercress, onion, pepitas and jalapeño in a medium bowl.

Cut the avocados very thinly into a straight fan shape. Add a little of the lime juice and drizzle with a bit of the oil. Arrange the avocado fans neatly on serving plates.

Toss the salad ingredients together, dressing with the remaining olive oil and lime juice. Season with salt.

Cut the tuna pieces, using a very sharp knife, into thin 15 cm (6 in) long slices.

Arrange four or five slices of tuna on each avocado fan. Surround with the remaining salmorejo sauce and arrange the salad decoratively on top. Serve immediately.

PAUL'S TIP For a more traditional approach you can simply cut the tuna into cubes and toss in the dressing just before serving. If you wish, marinate for 2 minutes. Toss with cubes of avocado and arrange over the tossed salad.

OCEAN TROUT & WATERMELON CEBICHE WITH PRICKLY PEAR DRESSING

+ 500 g (1 lb 2 oz) lime-cured ocean trout fillet, belly flap removed (see Lime cure for fish, page 45)
+ 400 g (14 oz) seedless watermelon

PRICKLY PEAR DRESSING

+ 350 ml (12 fl oz) freshly squeezed prickly pear juice (see Glossary) or blood orange juice
+ 350 ml (12 fl oz) freshly squeezed lime juice
+ 4 serrano chillies (see Glossary) or red jalapeños, seeded
+ sea salt and sugar to taste and balance

SALAD

+ 1 red onion, thinly sliced
+ 4 breakfast radishes, thinly sliced plus extra to garnish
+ 1 large handful of coriander (cilantro) leaves, finely shredded
+ olive oil for drizzling
+ pinch of sea salt

GARNISH

+ 1 jalapeño, thinly sliced into rounds
+ 75 g (2¾ oz) finger lime flesh (about 8-12 limes) (see Glossary)
+ edible flowers

SERVES 4-6

Slice the cured trout thinly into neat 3 cm (1¼ in) round slices. Layer on baking paper. Cover and refrigerate until ready to serve.

Cut the watermelon into rounds using a 5 cm (2 in) diameter cookie cutter. Slice into 1 cm (½ in) thick discs. Ensure you have 20-30 discs, depending on how many you are serving – you will need 4-5 per serve.

To prepare the prickly pear dressing, blend the prickly pear juice, lime juice, chilli and any watermelon offcuts (without rind) in a food processor until smooth. Season lightly with salt and sugar, remembering the dressing still needs to be sharp with acid but balanced.

Combine the salad ingredients, except the oil and salt, in a small bowl.

To serve, arrange 5 watermelon discs with alternate slices of cured ocean trout on serving plates. Drizzle the salad with olive oil, toss to dress and season with salt. Garnish each slice of trout with a slice of jalapeño and a neat pile of finger lime flesh. Generously spoon over the dressing and lightly drizzle with olive oil. Garnish with edible flowers and thin slices of radish. Serve immediately along with the salad.

I am continuing the theme of seafood cebiche with exotic fruits, as it is such a revelation to me. I feel the need to share this as prickly pear season was upon us when I opened the new cantina. Prickly pears are menacing to prepare for a novice due to their transparent, razor-like spikes and I suggest you wear heavy-duty gloves when you handle them. Allow them to ripen in the sun where they start to split as they become ripe. Cut down the centre of the fruit and the skin should peel away in one piece. The bright colours and flavours here are sensational.

PACIFIC OYSTER CEBICHE WITH MELON SALSA

~~~~~~~~~~~

+ 24 freshly shucked Pacific oysters
+ iced water
+ crushed ice for serving
+ micro coriander (cilantro) to garnish

MELON SALSA

+ 100 g (3½ oz) finely diced seedless watermelon
+ 100 g (3½ oz) finely diced rockmelon (cantaloupe/netted melon)
+ 2 red onions, finely chopped
+ 1 short (Lebanese) cucumber, halved lengthways, seeded and finely diced
+ flesh from 6 finger limes (see Glossary)
+ ½ habanero chilli, finely chopped (see Glossary)
+ 1 large handful of coriander (cilantro) leaves, finely chopped
+ finely grated zest and juice of 6 limes
+ 100 ml (3½ fl oz) extra-virgin olive oil

SERVES 4

We've actually been eating cebiche for years – think freshly shucked oysters with a squeeze of lemon, a spoonful of eschalot vinegar and some Tabasco sauce! Purists would scorn at the thought of melon and oysters together, but it works. The salty, briny oysters interplay well with this fragrant, zesty melon salsa and, dotted with finger lime, it makes the sometimes daunting oyster bright and friendly. Try this versatile salsa with briefly cooked scallops or grilled fish steaks.

To prepare the melon salsa, combine the watermelon, rockmelon, onion, cucumber, finger lime flesh, chilli and coriander in a medium bowl. Add the lime zest and juice and olive oil and toss to coat. Cover and refrigerate for 1 hour, for the flavours to develop.

To shuck the oysters, wrap the rounded end of the oyster within a folded tea towel (dish towel) and hold it down securely on a bench. With the other hand insert the end of an oyster knife into the point of the oyster, wedging it just underneath the shell. Leverage up carefully, angling your knife up and away from the meat, to open. Carefully remove the muscle, known as the foot, which attaches the oyster to shell.

Fill a medium bowl with salted iced water. Using a pastry brush, brush away any oyster shell fragments with the iced water.

Cover the serving plates with crushed ice and arrange the oysters on top. Spoon generous amounts of melon salsa over the oysters and top with micro coriander. Serve immediately.

WARM BONITO & FENNEL CEBICHE SALAD WITH FIGS & POMEGRANATE

~~~~~~~~~~

+ olive oil
+ 800 g (1 lb 12 oz) lime-cured, boneless sashimi-grade bonito fillet, blood-line removed, or you can use cobia fish or any firm oily fish (see Lime cure for fish, page 45)
+ 9 ripe figs, roughly torn into quarters
+ 250 ml (8½ fl oz/1 cup) Pomegranate mojo (page 22)
+ pomegranate seeds for garnish (optional)

SALAD

+ 200 g (7 oz) black radishes, thinly sliced
+ 2 small bulb spring onions (scallions), thinly sliced
+ 1 bulb fennel, thinly sliced
+ 2 serrano chillies, seeded and finely cut into matchsticks (see Glossary)
+ 50 g (1¾ oz) bronzed fennel or dill tops, roughly chopped
+ 1 large handful of purple basil leaves or mint
+ 100 ml (3½ fl oz) Zesty lime dressing (page 37)

SERVES 4-6

Bonito is a strangely undervalued fish in some places. We are so conditioned to eating Japanese-flavoured sashimi salads with traditional sashimi fish, but I urge you to source more interesting fish with Latin flavours to excite the palate. After all, Latin cuisine is all about balance of flavours, heat and acidity. I recommend you cure the fish first as perfect sashimi-grade fish is becoming harder to source and, while adding more flavour to the fish, this also allows you the comfort of working ahead when entertaining. This dish would be perfect as a shared table starter.

To prepare the salad, combine the radish, onion, sliced fennel, chilli, fennel tops and basil in a medium bowl.

Preheat a medium non-stick pan over high heat and drizzle with a little olive oil.

Sear the bonito for 30 seconds on each side to seal. Sear slightly longer on the skin side, so it is crisp and golden. Place on paper towel to drain and cool.

Add the dressing to the salad and toss to coat. Arrange the salad and torn figs neatly to one side of each plate.

Cut the fish, skin facing up, diagonally into 1 cm (½ in) thick slices. Arrange the fish next to the salad. Dress the fish with pomegranate mojo and garnish with extra pomegranate seeds, if desired. Serve immediately.

BARBECUED MAHI MAHI WITH PASILLA CHILLI & SWEETCORN CREMA

~~~~~~~~~~

+ 4 x 200 g (7 oz) mahi mahi fish fillets, or any other meaty fish
+ 250 ml (8½ fl oz/1 cup) Pasilla chilli relish (page 25)
+ 4 corn husks
+ 2 limes, thinly sliced
+ butcher's twine to secure
+ Sweetcorn crema (page 38)

SERVES 4

This is a classic 'marinate, wrap and grill' fish dish. The sweet and savoury herbaceous pasilla chilli is made into a pesto-like relish and chunks of firm meaty fish are then marinated, placed into a corn husk and grilled over an aromatic fire. The sweetcorn crema adds more pleasure to the dish. Other choices of side dish that would work well are Ancient grain seven vegetable super-food salad (pages 226-7), Hominy rice (page 43) or Cool cucumber salad (page 231). Boneless skinless chicken breasts or pork fillets (tenderloins) would make a nice substitute for the fish too.

Place the fish on a plate and rub with pasilla chilli relish to coat. Cover and refrigerate for at least 4 hours, or overnight.

Ideally a wood-fired or charcoal barbecue will impart greater flavour when cooking your fish. If you have one, preheat a barbecue with a hood until the coals have a thin coating of grey ash. Add presoaked aromatic wood, such as oak, mallee oak, ironbark or hickory. If using a gas barbecue soak smaller wood chips and place them in a smoking box on your barbecue.

To prepare the parcels, drain the husks and pat dry with paper towel. Lay the husks out on a clean work surface. Place the marinated fish pieces onto the husks and cover with the lime slices. Twist the husks at either end and tie with twine. Stand at room temperature for 5 minutes prior to cooking. Place the corn parcels on the barbecue, cover with the lid and bake for 10 minutes, until just cooked through.

To serve, simply unwrap the fish and coat with sweetcorn crema or serve on the side along with your choice of accompaniments.

CHIA-CRUSTED MACKEREL WITH POMEGRANATE MOJO

+ Refried beans (page 42)
+ 250 ml (8$^1/_2$ fl oz/1 cup) Pomegranate mojo (page 22)

CRUSTED FISH

+ 40 g (1$^1/_2$ oz/$^1/_3$ cup) chia seeds
+ 50 g (1$^3/_4$ oz/$^1/_3$ cup) sesame seeds
+ sea salt flakes
+ 4-8 mackerel fillets (180 g/6$^1/_2$ oz per person)
+ olive oil for brushing and shallow-frying

GARNISH

+ 200 g (7 oz) yellow frisée lettuce hearts
+ 3 eschalots, thinly sliced
+ 2 breakfast radishes, thinly sliced
+ 1 large handful of flat-leaf parsley
+ 1 large handful of tarragon leaves
+ 150 ml (5 fl oz) Latin vinaigrette (page 36)

SERVES 4

Chia seeds and oily fish are packed with Omega-3 fatty acids, which help your heart, brain and eyes, so it's the perfect food for a chef! As a chef I've eaten so poorly all my career that I feel compelled to promote some good eating habits among my colleagues. Of course, food should be pleasurable and indulgent but I am learning that balance keeps you in the game longer and allows you to enjoy your life. We haven't embraced mackerel in Australia yet, but it's having somewhat of a resurgence in Europe. Refried beans essentially mellow the oily flavours of the fish, as does the pomegranate mojo. Salmon would be a terrific replacement for the mackerel.

Preheat the oven to 180°C (350°F).

For the crusted fish, spread the chia and sesame seeds onto a baking tray. Cook in the oven for 4 minutes until toasted and golden. Season lightly with salt and set aside to cool.

To prepare the garnish, combine the frisée, eschalot, radish, parsley and tarragon in a medium bowl.

Lightly brush the mackerel fillets with oil. Lay the fillets, skin side down, in the toasted seeds to coat on one side.

Preheat a large non-stick frying pan with a splash of oil over high heat. Cook the fish fillets, skin side down, for 2 minutes or until crisp. Turn over and cook for a further 2 minutes until still slightly pink.

Dress the garnish with the Latin vinaigrette.

To serve, place a neat spoonful of refried beans in the centre of the serving plates and spread out into a thin circle. Top with the fish fillets. Arrange a small pile of garnish on the plates and top and surround with pomegranate mojo.

PLANK-GRILLED SPICED SALMON SALAD WITH PUMPKIN SLAW & POMEGRANATE MOJO

~~~~~~~~

+ Pomegranate mojo (page 22)

SALMON

+ 1 kg (2 lb 3 oz) side salmon fillet, preferably centre cut, pin-boned
+ extra-virgin olive oil for drizzling
+ 50 g (1¾ oz) Latin spice rub (page 30)
+ large pinch of sea salt
+ freshly ground black pepper

SERVES 6

PUMPKIN SLAW

+ 500 g (1 lb 2 oz) sweet variety of pumpkin (winter squash), finely julienned
+ 2 fennel bulbs, thinly sliced
+ 2 red onions, thinly sliced
+ 200 g (7 oz) snow peas (mangetout), stringed and finely julienned
+ 4 jalapeños, seeded and finely julienned
+ 90 g (3 oz) chia seeds, toasted and seasoned with sea salt
+ 90 g (3 oz/⅔ cup) pepitas (pumpkin seeds), toasted and seasoned with sea salt

+ 1 large handful of coriander (cilantro) or basil leaves, roughly chopped
+ 1 large handful of oregano leaves, roughly chopped
+ Zesty lime dressing (page 37)

GARNISH

+ seeds of ½ pomegranate
+ 200 g (7 oz) salted ricotta, finely chopped
+ 1 large handful of snow pea (mangetout) or daikon (white radish) shoots

Specialty barbecue planks can be purchased from hardware or barbecue stores. The plank protects the fish from the intense heat of the barbecue, allowing it to gently steam and remain incredibly moist and tender. Although soaked beforehand to help prevent burning, a little charring of the wood imparts a lovely smoky flavour to the fish. To me, eating raw pumpkin (winter squash) is as appealing as eating a roasted pumpkin. There are now so many pumpkin varieties available, but for this salad choose a soft sweet variety like butternut. The contrast of the tart pomegranate with the sweet pumpkin is a lovely match for the smoky barbecued salmon.

Soak your planks in water for 3–4 hours, to help prevent them from burning. For more flavour you can add citrus juice and herbs to the soak.

Preheat a natural fuel or gas barbecue with a lid to medium.

Place the wet plank on the barbecue rack and grill for 10 minutes, or until it begins to char slightly.

Drizzle the salmon with oil, coat in the Latin spice rub and season with salt and pepper. Lay the salmon fillet, flesh side down, on the plank. Close the lid and cook for 10 minutes. Carefully remove the entire plank from the barbecue and cover with foil. Set aside to cool.

To prepare the pumpkin slaw, combine the pumpkin, fennel, onion, snow peas, jalapeño, chia seeds, pepitas and coriander and oregano leaves in a large bowl. Add the dressing and toss to coat.

Once the salmon has cooled enough to handle, peel back and remove the skin completely. Scrape off and discard the blood-line.

To assemble, tear the salmon into nice chunks and arrange on a serving platter. Top with some slaw, then build another layer of fish and slaw. Spoon the pomegranate mojo over and around and scatter with pomegranate seeds, salted ricotta and shoots.

DORY PESCADO ASADA

~~~~~~~~~~~~~

+ 12 small homemade masa flour tortillas
  (see page 46) or store-bought tortillas

FISH

+ 4 x 200 g (7 oz) fillets of king, smooth,
  mirror or silver dory
+ 1 quantity Smoky rojo sauce (page 23) plus extra
  to serve
+ olive oil for drizzling

CONDIMENTS & GARNISHES

+ 1 bunch bulb spring onions (scallions), halved
+ 1 large handful of bronzed fennel, roughly chopped
+ 1 handful of basil or oregano leaves
+ 1/2 iceberg lettuce, torn
+ 1 Lebanese (short) cucumber, peeled and sliced
+ 2 ripe tomatoes, sliced
+ 2 radishes, thinly sliced
+ Tomatillo verde (page 21) to serve
+ Peruvian salsa criolla (page 26) or guacamole
  to serve
+ 4 limes, cut into cheeks

SERVES 4

As part of my crusade for us all to eat less meat and more fish, I've created a piscatorial version of the Mexican classic, carne asada, which is a mixed grill of meat and chorizo cooked street-side on wood barbecues. When grilling fish it's all about choosing the right cut for the job. Fish on the bone, such as a whole fish or cutlet, is best as it keeps moist and doesn't fall apart. If using fillets ensure they are the same thickness, wrap them in foil and bake on the highest setting with the barbecue lid closed. I prefer to use the dory species on the grill. Give John a break and try another variety, such as king, smooth, mirror or silver, they are all delicious!

For the fish, place the fillets on a plate and rub with the smoky rojo sauce to coat. Cover and allow to marinate in the refrigerator for 2–3 hours before cooking.

Ideally a wood-fired or charcoal barbecue will impart greater flavour when cooking your fish. If you have one, preheat a barbecue with a hood until the coals have a thin coating of grey ash. Add presoaked aromatic wood such as oak, mallee oak, ironbark or hickory. Alternatively, if using a gas barbecue soak smaller wood chips and place them in a smoking box on your barbecue.

Drizzle the fish fillets with oil and cook on one side for 3 minutes. Do not attempt to move the fillets. Slide a roasting fork underneath the fish fillets and carefully lift them to gently loosen from the grill. Turn onto a new clean area of the grill and cook for a further 1–2 minutes. Char the onions until blackened and softened. Transfer the fish and onions to a serving platter and garnish with the herbs, lettuce, cucumber, tomato and radish.

Warm your tortillas on the grill also, briefly grilling them to heat them through.

Arrange the fish, tortillas, condiments and limes on the table and encourage your guests to help themselves.

PAUL'S TIP If you don't have time to prepare all three relishes, simply make the smoky rojo sauce and use it both as a marinade and a condiment.

CLOUDY BAY CLAMS WITH SESAME PIPIAN

~~~~~~~~~~

+ 1 kg (2 lb 3 oz) Cloudy Bay, cherry stone or turtle neck clams (vongole)
+ 200 ml (7 fl oz) dry cider
+ Sesame pipian (page 31)
+ 310 g (11 oz/2 cups) peas, blanched
+ toasted sesame seeds to garnish

SERVES 4

New Zealand has some wonderful seafood, in particular the clams and abalone. This version of a traditional pipian sauce is elegant and piquant. It is lovely with the briny clams and makes a great simmer sauce for vegetables too.

Rinse and scrub the clams to ensure there is no sand.

Preheat a large wide saucepan with a lid over high heat until intensely hot.

Add the clams and cider, cover and cook for 2–3 minutes, until the clams just begin to open. Add the sesame pipian and bring to the boil – by then the clams should be fully open. Remove the clams from the sauce and place in a bowl.

Gently simmer the sauce until it reduces to a nice coating consistency, about 5 minutes. Add the peas to the sauce and heat through, stirring to combine.

While the sauce is reducing, separate the clams into half shells and arrange on serving plates, facing upwards. Pour the reduced sauce over the clams and sprinkle with sesame seeds. Serve immediately with spoons and finger bowls.

HAPUKA, CLAM & SEA VEGETABLE CAZUELA

~~~~~~~~~~

+ olive oil
+ 1 kg (2 lb 3 oz) skinless, boneless hapuka, cod or grouper, cut into 75 g (2¾ oz) chunks
+ sea salt
+ 300 g (10½ oz) small vongole-type clams
+ 200 ml (7 fl oz) fruity white wine
+ 300 g (10½ oz) mixed sea vegetables, such as sea blight, karkalla, samphire, warrigal greens or other edible sea succulent

+ 250 g (9 oz/1 cup) Mexican salsa verde (page 20)
+ 155 g (5½ oz/1 cup) fresh peas, blanched
+ 150 g (5½ oz) broad (fava) beans, blanched and skinned
+ juice of 1 lemon
+ 50 g (1¾ oz) unsalted butter

SERVES 6

Preheat the oven to 200°C (400°F).

Preheat a cazuela/ovenproof dish with a lid in the oven.

Once the cazuela is hot, add a dash of oil. Season the fish with salt and add it to the cazuela.

Bake the fish for 4 minutes. Turn the fish over, add the clams and pour in the wine. Cover and return to the oven for 2 minutes, until the clams open.

Remove the fish and clams, place on a plate and set aside.

Add the sea vegetables, salsa verde, peas, broad beans, lemon juice and butter and return to the oven to cook for a further 1–2 minutes, to make a light herbaceous sauce from the clam juices. Remove from the oven and whisk briefly to combine.

Arrange the vegetables and sauce onto serving plates and spoon the fish and clams on top.

Sea vegetables are more readily available than you think! Most coastlines have wild edible sea succulents like karkalla, also known as beach bananas or pig face. Sea blight and samphire have a delicate marine flavour and are now available in specialty greengrocers or fish merchants. This hotpot is inspired by some rustic food I had in Mexico City. Here I've used clams for their juices and sea vegetables for their fresh taste.

YUCATÁN-STYLE BAKED FISH WITH HOMINY RICE

~~~~~~~~~~~~

+ 8 large homemade masa flour tortillas (see page 46) or store-bought tortillas
+ Smoky rojo sauce (page 23)
+ Hominy rice (page 43)

FISH PARCEL

+ 500 g (1 lb 2 oz) kingfish fillet
+ 100 g (3½ oz) Achiote relish (page 32)
+ 1 x 40 cm (16 in) length of banana leaf
+ 1 x 20 cm (8 in) length of baking paper
+ 1 ripe ox-heart tomato, sliced
+ Mexican-style pickles (page 53)
+ 1 handful of coriander (cilantro) with root attached
+ wooden skewer to secure

GARNISH

+ 1 large handful of coriander (cilantro) leaves
+ 1 large handful of mint leaves
+ olive oil for drizzling
+ cheeks of 3 limes

SERVES 4

When I think of the Yucatán Peninsula I smile - great fishing, white beaches and interesting food. I believe it will become a serious holiday destination in the near future. This dish was a highlight of my trip and, once you master all the Mexican techniques and select your favourite accompaniments, this will be a regular crowd-pleaser at your dinner table. For the dish to stay moist, select fish with a high oil content like salmon, ocean trout, kingfish or river trout. Farmed fish are also good choices for this dish as the marinade boosts the flavour profile - Murray cod, barramundi, yellow tail, halibut or sea bass would be my picks.

For the fish parcel, place the fillet on a plate and rub with achiote relish to coat. Cover and refrigerate for 2–3 hours.

Soak the banana leaf in boiling water for about 10 minutes, or until pliable.

Place the banana leaf out on a clean work surface and put the piece of baking paper in the centre. Place the marinated fish in the middle of the paper. Top with the tomato slices, some of the pickles and the coriander. Fold the left-hand side of the banana leaf over, then fold up the ends, securing in place with the skewer. If the parcel looks unstable you can also wrap it in foil for added protection when cooking.

Preheat a barbecue with a lid to 160°C (320°F). Alternatively the fish can be cooked in the oven.

To cook the fish, place the parcel on the grill, close the lid and bake for 20 minutes. To test if the fish is cooked, insert a metal skewer or roasting fork into the centre of the parcel and into the fish. If it is warm when removed, the heat has transferred through the fish and it will be cooked. Remove from the grill and set aside for 5 minutes.

Heat a medium non-stick frying pan over high heat. Lightly spray with oil and briefly fry the tortillas to warm. Stack the tortillas, wrap in a warm, damp tea towel (dish towel) and set aside to keep warm.

To serve, organise the smoky rojo sauce, the remaining pickles, rice and tortillas in colourful serving dishes and arrange on the table. Transfer the fish onto a platter and unwrap at the table – the smells will waft out and impress your guests. Sprinkle with the herbs, drizzle with oil and serve with lime cheeks to garnish.

PRAWN CAZUELA VERACRUZ

~~~~~~~~~~~~~~~

+ 1.5 kg (3 lb 5 oz) extra-large prawns (shrimp), peeled with heads left on
+ oil for brushing
+ 125 ml (4 fl oz/1/2 cup) medium-dry sherry or tequila (see Glossary)
+ Veracruz sauce (page 41)

MARINADE

+ 150 ml (5 fl oz) extra-virgin olive oil
+ 4 serrano chillies, seeded and finely chopped (see Glossary)
+ 4 garlic cloves, crushed
+ 1 large handful of oregano leaves, finely chopped
+ squeeze of lime juice
+ sea salt to taste
+ pinch of ground cumin to taste

GARNISH

+ 65 g (21/4 oz/3/4 cup) flaked almonds
+ olive oil
+ sea salt to taste
+ smoked paprika to taste
+ 2 tablespoons capers
+ 160 g (51/2 oz) padrón peppers, briefly fried in olive oil to soften (see Glossary)
+ 1 handful of caperberries
+ 1 small handful of flat-leaf parsley

SHERRY CARAMEL

+ 200 ml (7 fl oz) Pedro Ximénez sherry
+ 200 ml (7 fl oz) sherry vinegar

SERVES 4

Food from Veracruz is heavily influenced by colonial Spain and a cazuela is a rustic Spanish cooking method. A nice piece of marinated fish, a splash of wine, some aromatic broth and some salsa in a hot oven and you have a quick and utterly delicious meal. When preparing a seafood stew add the quicker-cooking seafood towards the end of the cooking so everything cooks evenly. I love the smell of the caramelising prawn (shrimp) shells roasting in an intense wood oven, and the speed with which they cook leaves them moist and juicy. You can add vegetables such as cooked sweet potatoes or split raw okra too if you like.

Preheat the oven to 200°C (400°F). Preheat a cazuela/ovenproof dish with a lid in the oven.

To prepare the marinade, combine the olive oil, chilli, garlic, oregano and lime juice in a medium bowl. Season with salt and cumin. Add the prawns to the marinade and toss to coat. Cover and refrigerate until required.

To prepare the garnishes, place the almonds in a small bowl, drizzle with oil, season with salt and smoked paprika and toss to coat. Bake in the oven, stirring once or twice, for 3–5 minutes, until golden. Set aside.

Meanwhile, pour enough olive oil into a small frying pan for shallow-frying. Fry the capers for 1–2 minutes, until crispy. Remove using a slotted spoon and drain on paper towel. Season with salt.

To prepare the sherry caramel, combine the Pedro Ximénez sherry and sherry vinegar in a small saucepan and simmer over low heat, until reduced to a syrup. Set aside.

Remove the preheated cazuela dish from the oven and brush with oil. Place the prawns in the dish and bake in the oven for 2 minutes. Turn the prawns over and cook for a further 2 minutes. Pour in the dry sherry and Veracruz sauce, shaking the pan a little to combine the flavours. Return to the oven and cook for 4 minutes, until the prawns are just cooked through.

To serve, arrange the prawns in sauce on serving plates. Sprinkle with the toasted almonds, fried capers, peppers and caperberries. Lightly dress the parsley with a little oil and scatter on top and drizzle artfully with the sherry caramel.

PAUL'S TIP A fast tomato sauce flavoured with chilli, capers and orange would also be a nice alternative to the complex restaurant-style sauce used here.

SOFT-SHELL CRABS AL PASTOR

~~~~~~~~

- + 8 soft-shell mud crabs, feathery glands removed
- + 125 g (4½ oz/½ cup) Al pastor marinade (page 34)
- + rice bran oil for deep-frying
- + sea salt to taste
- + Smoky rojo sauce (page 23)

COATING

- + 200 g (7 oz/2 cups) coarse masa harina flour (see Glossary)
- + 1 tablespoon smoked paprika
- + 1 tablespoon ground cumin
- + 2 teaspoons garlic powder
- + ½ teaspoon chilli powder

CARAMELISED PINEAPPLE

- + 200 g (7 oz) fresh pineapple, cut into 5 mm (¼ in) slices
- + small pinch of cumin seeds
- + 50 ml (1¾ fl oz) olive oil
- + 55 g (2 oz/¼ cup) brown sugar
- + 50 g (1¾ oz) unsalted butter
- + 1½ tablespoons sherry vinegar

SERVES 4

Coat the crabs in the al pastor marinade. Place on a tray, cover and refrigerate for at least 4 hours or overnight.

To prepare the caramelised pineapple, preheat a medium non-stick frying pan over high heat until extremely hot. Add the pineapple slices facing down flat so they char and begin to caramelise. Add the cumin seeds then the olive oil and sugar and cook until the sugar begins to caramelise. Stir in the butter. Continue to cook the pineapple, turning to coat. Add the vinegar and simmer until reduced to a thin caramel. Remove from the heat and set aside to cool, turning the pineapple occasionally, to coat.

Half-fill a large heavy-based saucepan with rice bran oil and heat the oil to 180°C (350°F).

To prepare the coating, combine the flour and spices in a large bowl. Dredge the crabs in the coating and shake off any excess.

Cook the crabs in the oil in batches, for 2–3 minutes, until golden. Remove from the oil and drain on paper towel. (The crabs are being fried twice, so they do not need to be cooked all the way through the first time.)

Refry the crabs for 2 minutes, or until crisp, golden brown and cooked through. Drain on paper towel and season with salt. Arrange the crab either on one communal plate or on individual serving plates with the caramelised pineapple and rojo sauce and serve immediately.

Tacos al pastor, meaning shepherd's style, involves titanic spits of marinated pork shoulder - a truly deserving cult street food from Mexico. The cumin flavours of the marinade against the tangy sweet and sour pineapple add a lovely tropical note. As a seafood lover I wanted to try a seafood version of this dish, which led me to the soft-shell crab. My travels have taught me crab likes spices and spices like crab! Serve with tortillas (see page 46) or a fresh cooling salad if desired.

SPRING BAY MUSSELS IN CERVEZA NEGRA & ADOBO SAUCE

〜〜〜〜〜〜〜〜〜

+ 1.5 kg (3 lb 5 oz) mussels, washed and cleaned of any excessive sea debris
+ 500 ml (17 fl oz/2 cups) dark Mexican beer or red ale
+ 500 ml (17 fl oz/2 cups) Adobo sauce (page 15)
+ 200 g (7 oz) jicama, finely shaved (see Glossary)
+ 100 g (3½ oz) cooked black or red quinoa
+ 1 large handful of oregano leaves, roughly chopped
+ sea salt to taste

GARNISH

+ sea parsley or other sea succulent
+ olive oil

SERVES 4

Australia is blessed with cool-climate regions with terrific shellfish. Tasmania produces really diverse and world-class food products because of its unique fertile climate. On a recent trip I visited Spring Bay and the mussels, which are large and healthy due to the nutrient-rich water, were absolutely amazing! This sauce is underpinned by the smoky chipotle chillies in the adobo sauce. Allow your imagination to run wild and try adding chorizo, strips of piquillo peppers, corn (tortilla) chips, cherry tomatoes and coriander (cilantro), then you'll have chilaquiles!

Preheat a large saucepan with a lid over high heat until intensely hot. Add the mussels and beer, cover and cook for 3–5 minutes, until the mussels just begin to open. Add the adobo sauce and bring to the boil – by then the mussels should be fully open.

Working quickly, to not overcook the mussels, add the jicama, quinoa and oregano and cook for 4 minutes.

To serve, remove the mussels from the sauce and place in a serving dish. Check the flavour of the sauce and season and reduce as required to make a rich broth. Ladle the broth over the mussels.

Combine the parsley and a little olive oil in a small bowl and toss to coat. Scatter the mussels with the sea parsley to garnish.

PAUL'S TIP For a fast adobo sauce, blend 50 g (1¾ oz) chipotle in adobo sauce with 500 ml (17 fl oz/2 cups) tomato passata (puréed tomatoes) in a food processor. Add a good pinch of sugar and a splash of sherry vinegar to the mussels with 100 ml (3½ fl oz) beer. This will result in a lovely sauce.

BARBECUED TUNA SALAD WITH PERUVIAN SALSA CRIOLLA

~~~~~~~~~~

+ 50 g (1¾ oz) sea salt flakes
+ pinch of ground cumin
+ pinch of smoked paprika
+ pinch of ground allspice
+ 4 x 200 g (7 oz) sashimi-grade tuna steaks
+ olive oil for drizzling
+ Peruvian salsa criolla (page 26)

GARNISH

+ cheeks of 3 limes
+ 1 small handful of micro herbs, such as coriander (cilantro), purple basil, mint or oregano (optional)
+ best-quality extra-virgin olive oil to drizzle

SERVES 4

Peruvians are very fussy about the treatment of onions. They love raw onions but not as much as their Mexican cousins, as they find them a little harsh. So to make them less aggressive and the onion flavour less dominating, they purge them briefly in boiling, salted water. Equally important is to cut the onions 'a la pluma', or 'like feathers'. To do this, slice them into very thin half moons, retaining the curve of the onion, so that they look like little curls on the plate. The mellowed onion and piquant lime of the salsa in this dish make a wonderful accompaniment to the seared rich and oily tuna. Source sashimi-grade tuna for the best result.

Heat a barbecue chargrill plate to high.

Combine the salt and spices in a small bowl.

Drizzle the tuna with oil and sprinkle liberally with the spiced salt mix.

Sear the tuna briefly on the barbecue, on both sides, for 1 minute. Transfer the tuna to a chopping board and cut into thick slices.

Serve with the salsa criolla and garnish with lime cheeks, a sprinkling of herbs and a drizzle of extra-virgin oil.

CHILLI & SALT COD RELLENOS WITH ORANGE AÏOLI

~~~~~~~~~~~~~~~~~~~

+ vegetable oil for deep-frying
+ 3 large handfuls of perfect wild rocket (arugula) to garnish
+ 50 ml (1¾ fl oz) Zesty lime dressing (page 37)

ORANGE AÏOLI

+ grated zest and juice of 6 oranges
+ 250 ml (8½ fl oz/1 cup) Aïoli (page 28)

CHILLI & SALT COD RELLENOS

+ 400 g (14 oz) (about 12) poblano (see Glossary) or jalapeño chillies
+ 50 ml (1¾ fl oz) olive oil
+ sea salt flakes
+ 1 small handful of sage or oregano leaves
+ Salt cod mixture (page 44)
+ 150 g (5½ oz/1½ cups) masa harina flour (see Glossary) or 225 g (8 oz/1½ cups) plain (all-purpose) flour
+ Mexican beer batter (page 35)

SERVES 4

Chillies rellenos, 'stuffed chillies', is Mexican comfort food at its best. Generally the poblano chilli is filled with spiced minced (ground) meat or rich cheese, then shallow-fried in an airy batter. Here I have used savoury salt cod to make a croquette stuffing. This is great with a glass of sherry or chilled añejo tequila.

To make the orange aïoli, combine the orange zest and juice in a small saucepan and simmer over medium-low heat, until reduced to 100 ml (3½ fl oz). Allow to cool. Mix the cooled orange reduction through the aïoli. (This can be stored in an airtight container in the refrigerator for up to a week.)

Preheat the oven to 180°C (350°F).

Cut the chillies lengthways down the centre, without cutting all the way through, just to make an opening for the stuffing. Arrange on a baking tray and lightly drizzle with the olive oil. Season with a pinch of salt and insert a sage leaf into each chilli. Bake for 10 minutes, or until softened.

Spoon the salt cod mixture into a piping (icing) bag fitted with a large plain nozzle. Pipe the filling into the chillies. Using a palette knife smooth over the chilli opening. Refrigerate until required.

Half-fill a large heavy-based saucepan with vegetable oil and heat it to 180°C (350°F).

To cook the stuffed chillies, dredge them in the flour and drop them into the batter. Fry them in batches for 3 minutes, or until they are crisp and golden brown. Remove using a slotted spoon and drain on paper towel. Season with salt.

Dress the rocket with the zesty lime dressing.

To serve, arrange the stuffed chillies on serving plates and garnish with rocket and a dollop of orange aïoli.

PAUL'S TIP If you don't feel like making the salt cod mixture, fill your chillies with firm goat's cheese instead and serve with a salad of thinly sliced pickled baby beetroot (beets). See Mexican-style pickles (page 53).

GRILLED OCTOPUS BAJA–MED STYLE

~~~~~~~~~~

OCTOPUS

+ 125 ml (4 fl oz/$1/2$ cup) chardonnay vinegar
+ 110 g (4 oz/$1/2$ cup) sugar
+ finely grated zest and juice of 2 oranges
+ 2 bay leaves
+ sea salt
+ 1.2 kg (2 lb 10 oz) best-quality large octopus tentacles
+ extra-virgin olive oil
+ pinch of smoked paprika

SALSA PICADA

+ 1 litre (34 fl oz/4 cups) orange juice
+ 50 ml ($1^3/4$ fl oz) chardonnay vinegar
+ 2 jalapeños, roughly chopped
+ 2 garlic cloves, finely grated
+ 1 small handful of mint leaves
+ 45 g ($1^1/2$ oz) day-old coarse breadcrumbs fried in 75 ml ($2^1/2$ fl oz) olive oil
+ 50 g ($1^3/4$ oz/$1/3$ cup) hazelnuts, roasted, peeled and roughly chopped
+ 1 large handful of oregano leaves, finely chopped
+ habanero hot sauce to taste

SALAD

+ 100 g ($3^1/2$ oz) padrón peppers (see Glossary)
+ oil for frying
+ pinch of smoked paprika
+ 300 g ($10^1/2$ oz) green beans, blanched, split lengthways and cut into 3 cm ($1^1/4$ in) lengths
+ 4 oranges, segmented
+ 2 red onions, thinly sliced
+ 160 g ($5^1/2$ oz) black olive cheeks
+ 1 large handful of basil leaves
+ 100 ml ($3^1/2$ fl oz) Latin vinaigrette (page 36)

SERVES 8

On a recent trip to Los Angeles I read about a new trend in Mexican food in Tijuana and Ensenada. Local celebrated chefs were creating a fusion of classic Mexican food with a modern Mediterranean influence. I crossed the border to see for myself and was amazed by the originality. Together with the quality of the local wine industry, with white wine styles similar to Galicia in Spain, this area is truly similar to the Mediterranean. This salsa takes its inspiration from the Mediterranean, in particular the Catalonian salsa picada.

To prepare the octopus, combine 500 ml (17 fl oz/2 cups) water with the vinegar, sugar, orange zest and juice and bay leaves in a large saucepan and heat until simmering. Season with salt. Add the octopus and cook over low heat for 2 hours, or until very tender. Leave the octopus in the cooking liquid and set aside to cool.

Meanwhile to prepare the salsa picada, boil the orange juice in a medium saucepan until reduced to 100 ml (3½ fl oz). Combine the orange juice reduction with the vinegar, jalapeño, garlic and mint in a food processor and blend to combine. Strain through a fine-mesh sieve.

Once the octopus has cooled, remove any excess skin or suckers that have been disturbed by the cooking process. Cut the tentacles into lengths, roughly 75 g (2¾ oz) each.

Preheat a wood-fired or coal barbecue until the coals have a thin coating of grey ash. Add presoaked aromatic wood such as oak, mallee oak, ironbark or hickory. Alternatively, if using a gas barbecue soak smaller wood chips and place them in a smoking box on your barbecue. If you don't have a barbecue you can seal the octopus in a large pan. Simply stir-fry in olive oil with a pinch of smoked paprika and sea salt for 2 minutes. Then reduce the heat and keep warm until serving.

To prepare the salad, briefly fry the peppers in the oil and paprika, till softened.

Combine the peppers, beans, orange segments, onion, olives and basil in a large bowl.

Lightly drizzle the octopus with olive oil and season with salt and paprika. Grill for 4 minutes, turning occasionally, until cooked through.

While the octopus is cooking, combine the breadcrumbs, hazelnuts, oregano and orange reduction and season with salt, hot sauce and a little olive oil to moisten to a spoonable consistency. (It's important this is done just before serving otherwise you lose the crunchy texture.)

Dress and toss the salad with the vinaigrette.

To serve, arrange the octopus on a serving platter. Spoon over the salsa picada and arrange the salad alongside. Serve immediately.

PAUL'S TIPS Serve simply with the salsa picada and use frozen octopus, as it tends to cook quicker.
   The salsa picada can be made in advance and stored in an airtight container in the refrigerator for up to a week.

GRILLED OCTOPUS
BAJA-MED STYLE
(pages 182–3)

SLOW-COOKED CALAMARI ESCABECHE SALAD

~~~~~~~~~~

+ Tomatillo verde (page 21)

SLOW-COOKED CALAMARI

+ 500 ml (17 fl oz/2 cups) extra-virgin olive oil
+ 6 garlic cloves, split
+ 3-4 tarragon sprigs
+ 1 tablespoon cumin seeds, toasted and smashed
+ good pinch of sea salt
+ 500 g (1 lb 2 oz) best-quality fresh, cleaned calamari tubes and tentacles, cut into quarters

DRESSING

+ 250 ml (8½ fl oz/1 cup) fruity white wine
+ 125 ml (4 fl oz/½ cup) freshly squeezed orange juice
+ finely grated zest of ½ an orange
+ 2 garlic cloves, shaved or very thinly sliced
+ 2 anchovy fillets
+ pinch of saffron threads
+ 100 ml (3½ fl oz) extra-virgin olive oil (retained from cooking the calamari, above)
+ squeeze of lime
+ sea salt to taste

SALAD

+ 2 bulb spring onions (scallions), thinly sliced
+ 1 large handful of flat-leaf parsley
+ 90 g (3 oz/¾ cup) pitted black olives
+ 2 bulbs fennel, thinly shaved using a mandoline
+ 200 g (7 oz) mixed variety of heirloom tomatoes
+ 200 g (7 oz) cooked heirloom beetroot (beets)

SERVES 4

Slow-cooked calamari will raise an eyebrow as chefs and home cooks are always taught to cook calamari, squid and cuttlefish briskly with gusto or it becomes rubbery. This still remains best practice, but a thinking person's chef will advise it's the temperature that supports a pleasing texture, not just the time. Here the calamari is cooked in flavoured olive oil at 70°C (160°F) for 3 minutes only, which is considered slow-cooked for calamari! Like all good salads it's the dressing that underpins this dish and the bright flavoursome tomatillo verde does the trick.

To prepare the calamari, heat the oil, garlic, tarragon, cumin seeds and salt together in a medium saucepan set over low heat until it reaches 70°C (160°F). Use a thermometer to monitor the temperature.

Once it reaches the correct temperature, add the calamari to the oil and gently 'slow cook' for 3 minutes. The calamari will change colour from transparent to white. Remove using a slotted spoon and place on paper towel to drain. Cover and set aside to cool. Measure out 100 ml (3½ fl oz) of the cooking oil into a heatproof pitcher and set aside for the dressing.

To prepare the dressing, combine the wine, orange juice and zest, garlic, anchovy and saffron in a small saucepan and boil until reduced by half. Add the reserved cooking oil and process with a hand-held blender to combine. Season with lime juice and salt and set aside to cool.

To prepare the salad, combine the onion, parsley and olives in a medium bowl. Add some dressing and toss to combine. Separately combine the calamari with the fennel and toss in the remaining dressing.

Slice the tomatoes and beetroot into rounds and arrange on serving plates in a circular fashion allowing room for the salad in the centre. Pile the vegetable salad neatly in the centre, top with the combined fennel and calamari and surround with the tomatillo verde.

PAUL'S TIPS If you are time-poor, this salad still tastes great without the tomatillo verde.
   This salad can also be enjoyed in a tortilla (see page 46) with some guacamole.

06

MEAT, MOLES & BARBECUES

It would have been easy
to simply list the great steak
dishes of South America. However,
I wanted to introduce you to the magical
Mexican sauce, mole - as well as the techniques
of barbecoa, brining and twice-cooking meat.

~~~~~~~~~

This chapter will also show you the way experts prepare many
nuevo Latino dishes. There are also interesting rubs, marinades
and condiments that will transform the simple barbecue or
weekend roast and transport you to the aromatic markets of
Oaxaca and the sun-kissed beaches of the Yucatán Peninsula.
These poultry, meat and game recipes are designed for
feasting, which is increasingly dominating the modern
restaurant landscape, so fire up the barbecue,
shake up the cocktails, chill the cerveza
and enjoy my meat fiesta!

PORK FILLET LOMO-STYLE WITH MORCILLA

~~~~~~~~~~~~

- + 1.2 kg (2 lb 10 oz) free-range pork fillet (tenderloin), trimmed of fat and sinew
- + olive oil for drizzling
- + smoked paprika to taste
- + 1 large handful of sage leaves
- + 2 packham pears, peeled, cored and cut lengthways into 5 mm (1/4 in) thick slices
- + 600 g (1 lb 5 oz) morcilla sausage, cut into 1.5 cm (1/2 in) thick slices (see Glossary)
- + 4 large handfuls of watercress, picked
- + sea salt to taste
- + huitlacoche mustard to serve (see page 195)

PORK BRINE

- + 500 ml (17 fl oz/2 cups) water
- + 250 ml (8 1/2 fl oz/1 cup) apple juice
- + 125 ml (4 fl oz/1/2 cup) cider vinegar or white wine vinegar
- + finely grated zest and juice of 2 oranges
- + 1 large handful of sage leaves
- + 100 g (3 1/2 oz) smoked paprika
- + 100 g (3 1/2 oz) ground cumin
- + 30 g (1 oz) sea salt
- + 25 g (1 oz) ground allspice
- + 1 1/2 tablespoons honey
- + 3 garlic cloves, smashed
- + 2 teaspoons black peppercorns, smashed
- + 3 bay leaves

SHERRY CARAMEL

- + 200 ml (7 fl oz) sherry vinegar
- + 200 g (7 oz) sugar
- + 100 ml (3 1/2 fl oz) sherry
- + 1 tablespoon reposado tequila (see Glossary)

SERVES 6

Lomo is a Spanish cured and air-dried pork loin served as tapas like jamón. Here is my barbecued version in which the pork is initially brined overnight to prevent it from drying out, and flavoured with cumin and smoked paprika. It is then simply barbecued or sealed in a pan and gently roasted. As the pork fillet (tenderloin) can be dull on its own, it's served with rich morcilla sausage and huitlacoche mustard.

Combine all of the pork brine ingredients in a large bowl. Add the pork fillet, cover and refrigerate overnight.

Preheat a barbecue, ideally a wood-fired or charcoal barbecue as it will impart greater flavour. If using a wood or charcoal barbecue, heat until the coals have a thin coating of grey ash. Alternatively, if using a gas barbecue, preheat to medium–high.

Preheat the oven to 140°C (275°F).

Drain the pork and pat dry.

Heat a large frying pan over medium heat.

Drizzle the pork with oil and season with paprika. Seal on the grill, turning frequently, until browned all over.

Transfer the pork to a roasting tray, scatter with the sage and bake for 40 minutes, or until almost firm to the touch and a meat thermometer reads between 60 and 65°C (140 and 150°F) for medium, or until cooked to your liking. Remove from the oven. Place the pork on a rack or overturned plate set inside the cooking tray and set aside to rest for 10 minutes.

To prepare the sherry caramel, combine the sherry vinegar, sugar and sherry in a small saucepan and simmer, stirring occasionally, until the sugar dissolves. Boil until reduced to a syrup. Add a splash of tequila and set aside to cool to room temperature.

Add the pear slices to the cooled caramel.

If the barbecue is still hot, very briefly sear the morcilla slices on both sides. Alternatively cook in a large frying pan over medium–high heat. Transfer to a plate.

Slice the pork into 2 cm (3/4 in) thick slices.

To serve, arrange the pork and morcilla slices alternating on a serving plate and season with a sprinkling of sea salt. Toss the pear with the watercress and a tablespoon of the caramel and arrange next to the pork. Serve with the huitlacoche mustard.

HANGER STEAK WITH HUITLACOCHE MUSTARD & SALSA NEGRA

~~~~~~~~

+ 4 x 300 g (10½ oz) grain-fed hanger steaks
+ olive oil for drizzling
+ 100 g (3½ oz) Latin spice rub (page 30)
+ cheeks from 2 limes to serve

HUITLACOCHE MUSTARD

+ 50 g (1¾ oz) dried porcini mushrooms
+ 60 ml (2 fl oz/¼ cup) olive oil
+ 1 small brown onion, finely chopped
+ 3 garlic cloves, finely chopped
+ 50 g (1¾ oz) butter
+ 400 g (14 oz) field mushrooms, washed
+ 400 g (14 oz) tin huitlacoche, drained (see Glossary)
+ 1 large handful of oregano leaves, roughly chopped
+ sea salt to taste
+ truffle oil for drizzling (optional)

SALSA NEGRA

+ Salsa mexicana (page 36)
+ 100 g (3½ oz) cooked black beans

PARSLEY SALAD GARNISH

+ 100 g (3½ oz) eschalots, thinly sliced
+ 50 g (1¾ oz) Lilliput capers
+ 1 large handful of flat-leaf parsley
+ 100 ml (3½ fl oz) Latin vinaigrette (page 36)

SERVES 4

I've always presented a hero steak dish in my restaurants. The hanger steak is one of these killer steaks and is an usual piece of meat that hangs between the liver and kidney. It's full of lovely fatty fibres that run through the meat. Its structure makes it like a flavour mop for marinades. The huitlacoche mustard works so well with the flavours of the meat and salsa.

Ideally preheat a wood-fired or charcoal barbecue to cook your steak as it will impart greater flavour. Alternatively use a hot frying pan on the stove top. If using a wood or charcoal barbecue, heat until the coals have a thin coating of grey ash.

To make the huitlacoche mustard, place the porcini mushrooms in a small bowl, cover with boiling water and set aside for 10 minutes to rehydrate. Drain, reserving the liquid.

Heat the oil in a medium saucepan over medium–low heat. Cook the onion and garlic until softened and they just begin to colour. Increase the heat to high, add the butter, field and porcini mushrooms and sauté for 2–3 minutes until softened.

Reduce the heat to low, add the huitlacoche and porcini liquid and cook for a further 10 minutes, until the liquid has reduced to a glossy sauce. Add the oregano, season with salt and drizzle with truffle oil, if desired. Set aside but keep warm.

Drizzle the steaks with a little olive oil and coat in the Latin spice rub. Grill the steaks on the barbecue or fry in a hot frying pan, for 3 minutes on each side, for medium–rare, or until done to your liking. Transfer to a tray, loosely cover with foil and set aside to rest for 10 minutes.

Meanwhile for the salsa negra, toss the salsa mexicana and black beans together in a medium bowl.

To prepare the parsley salad garnish, combine the eschalot, capers and parsley in a small bowl. Add the dressing and toss to coat.

To serve, cut the steaks diagonally into 2 cm (¾ in) thick slices and spread out neatly on individual platters or serving boards. Spoon the salsa negra over the steaks, garnish with parsley salad, a neat spoonful of huitlacoche mustard and a cheek of lime.

KANGAROO WITH YAM MASH & BLACK MOLE

+ 800 g (1 lb 12 oz) (about 4) yams
+ olive oil for drizzling
+ Wild mushrooms in Mexican salsa verde (page 250) to serve

KANGAROO

+ 1.2 kg (2 lb 10 oz) kangaroo fillet (tenderloin), trimmed of fat and sinew
+ 50 g (1¾ oz) ground cumin
+ 50 g (1¾ oz) sea salt
+ 100 ml (3½ fl oz) vegetable oil

+ 550 ml (18 ½ fl oz) Black mole (page 19), prepared the day before

CORN & OLIVE SALSA

+ 200 ml (7 fl oz) olive oil
+ 600 g (1 lb 5 oz/4 cups) fresh corn kernels (about 4 corn cobs)
+ 95 g (3¼ oz) chopped black olives
+ ½ small red onion, finely diced
+ 2 jalapeños, seeded and finely chopped

+ 1 large handful of coriander (cilantro) leaves, roughly chopped
+ juice of 4 limes
+ sea salt to taste

SERVES 6

Kangaroo is an under-utilised meat. It's a delicious lean protein that must be cooked rare or it's very tough. It's similar to venison so black mole, with its complex fruit notes and spices, is a natural partner in my mind. Yams are white sweet potatoes and here they are baked and crushed with corn salsa and olives. You will need to prepare the mole the day before. Serve with Wild mushrooms in Mexican salsa verde (page 250).

To prepare the kangaroo, rub the fillet with the cumin and salt to cover. Place on a tray, cover and refrigerate overnight.

Preheat the oven to 180°C (350°F).

Place the yams on a baking tray, drizzle with olive oil and bake for 40 minutes, or until tender.

Remove the kangaroo from the refrigerator 20 minutes before cooking.

When the yams are tender, cut them in half and scoop out the flesh. Place in a medium bowl and roughly mash with a fork. Cover and keep warm.

To prepare the salsa, heat 2 tablespoons of the oil in a medium saucepan over medium-low heat. Add the corn, cover and cook, stirring occasionally, for 2 minutes, or until tender.

Add the cooked corn, olives, onion, jalapeño and coriander to the mashed yam. Pour in the lime juice and the remaining oil to moisten and stir to combine. Season with salt. Cover and keep warm.

To cook the kangaroo, heat a large frying pan over medium-high heat. Add the vegetable oil and heat until shimmering. Sear the kangaroo, turning frequently, for 2 minutes, until browned all over. Cook, turning frequently, for a further 3 minutes, for rare. Remove from the pan, place on an upside-down dinner plate, roughly cover with aluminium foil and rest somewhere warm for 5 minutes.

Place the black mole in a medium saucepan and reheat, stirring occasionally, over medium-low heat.

To serve, slice the kangaroo into 2 cm (¾ in) thick slices. Place approximately 100 ml (3½ fl oz) of the mole onto each serving plate, top with kangaroo slices and arrange a spoonful of the yam and salsa mixture and a little extra sauce alongside. Serve the mushrooms separately.

RED MOLE & CERVEZA NEGRA-BRAISED BEEF CHEEKS

~~~~~~~~~~

+ Refried beans (page 42) to serve
+ large homemade masa flour tortillas (see page 46) or store-bought tortillas, warmed, to serve

BRAISED BEEF CHEEKS

+ 4 beef cheeks (about 1.35 kg/ 3 lb in total), trimmed of excess sinew
+ sea salt flakes to taste
+ Spanish smoked paprika to taste
+ 60 ml (2 fl oz/1/4 cup) olive oil
+ 2 onions, roughly chopped
+ 2 garlic cloves, roughly chopped

+ 750 ml (25 1/2 fl oz/3 cups) cerveza negra beer (dark Mexican beer)
+ 100 ml (3 1/2 fl oz) agave syrup (see Glossary)
+ 50 ml (1 3/4 fl oz) sherry vinegar
+ 500 ml (17 fl oz/2 cups) Red mole (page 16)

PICKLED JALAPEÑO SALAD

+ 3 large handfuls of upland cress or watercress
+ Mexican-style pickled jalapeños (see page 53)

SERVES 4

Chefs will tell you that the muscles close to the mouth of an animal taste the best – the tongue, cheek and neck are naturally nutrient-rich and hard-working. They are as good as a fillet, rib or sirloin and, when cooked appropriately, they become equally luxurious and gastronomic. Here beef cheeks are slowly braised with dark beer and red mole until fork-tender.

Preheat the oven to 180°C (350°F).

To prepare the beef cheeks, season the beef with salt and paprika. Heat 2 tablespoons of the oil in a large frying pan set over high heat, until smoking. Seal the beef cheeks all over, until nicely coloured, then remove from the pan and set aside. Reduce the heat to low, add the remaining oil and cook the onion and garlic until softened. Pour in the beer and bring to the boil. Add the agave and vinegar and simmer until reduced to a syrup.

Pour the syrup and red mole into an ovenproof dish and stir to combine. Add the beef cheeks, cover with a lid and braise in the oven for 3 hours, or until tender. Remove the beef cheeks from the braising liquid, place on a tray and set aside.

Pour the braising liquid into a medium saucepan and simmer over low heat until reduced to a rich sauce. Strain through a fine-mesh sieve, return to a clean pan and keep warm.

Slice the beef cheeks into 2 cm (3/4 in) thick slices and return to the sauce to warm through.

For the pickled jalapeño salad, combine the cress, jalapeños and a little of the pickling liquid in a medium bowl and toss to combine.

To serve, arrange the beef slices and sauce on serving plates, garnish with the pickled jalapeño salad, refried beans and warm tortillas.

ROAST CHICKEN MEXICO CITY-STYLE WITH BLOOD ORANGE & AVOCADO SALSA

+ Sweetcorn crema (page 38) to serve
+ Cool cucumber salad (page 231) to serve
+ Ancient grain seven vegetable super-food salad (page 226) to serve

CHICKEN

+ 1.5 kg (3 lb 5 oz) free-range or organic chicken, butterflied
+ 100 g (3½ oz) Achiote relish (page 32)

+ sea salt to taste
+ 3 corn cobs, each cut into 4
+ 2 red onions, each cut into 4-6 wedges
+ 1 bulb fennel, cut into 4-6 wedges
+ 2 limes, sliced
+ oil for drizzling
+ 125 ml (4 fl oz/½ cup) chicken stock
+ 100 g (3½ oz) unsalted butter

SALSA

+ 4 blood oranges, segmented
+ 2 avocados, cubed
+ 1 red onion, diced
+ 1 jalapeño, thinly sliced
+ 1 large handful of tarragon or oregano leaves
+ 1 large handful of coriander (cilantro) leaves
+ 150 ml (5 fl oz) Zesty lime dressing (page 37)
+ sea salt to taste

SERVES 4-6

Place the chicken on a tray and rub it with the achiote relish on both sides to coat. Season with salt. Cover and refrigerate for at least 4 hours, or overnight.

Preheat the oven to 180°C (350°F).

Lay the chicken flat, skin side up, in a large roasting tray.

Place the vegetables and lime slices in a large bowl. Drizzle with oil, season with salt and toss to combine. Arrange the vegetables tightly around the chicken.

Roast in the oven for 1 hour, or until the chicken is golden and cooked through. Approximately 10 minutes before the cooking time is up, pour the stock into the dish and dot the chicken with the butter.

Meanwhile to prepare the salsa, combine the orange, avocado, onion, jalapeño and herbs in a medium bowl. Add the zesty lime dressing and toss to combine. Season with salt.

Either serve the chicken whole or cut it into pieces and arrange on a serving platter then drizzle with any pan juices. Surround with the vegetables and scatter the salsa over the top. Accompany with the sweetcorn crema, cool cucumber salad and the ancient grain salad.

PAUL'S TIP Instead of making zesty lime dressing, simply drizzle 80 ml (2½ fl oz/⅓ cup) of both lime juice and olive oil over the salad.

On a recent trip to Mexico City I observed chicken
rotisserie shops dotted throughout the crazy metropolis
with snaking lines of people down the streets, just like
you see in Paris outside the pâtisseries. The chickens
are butterflied, stained with annatto seeds and spun over
charcoal and wood fires. They are simply cut with scissors
and bagged up with some salsa, then away you go to find
some tortillas! Here's my version. Serve hot or cold.

LAMB BELLY RIBS WITH POMEGRANATE & FLOR DE JAMAICA

〰〰〰〰〰〰

+ Mexican-style pickles (page 53) to serve (optional)
+ Refried beans (page 42) to serve (optional)
+ Cool cucumber salad (page 231) to serve (optional)

LAMB

+ 2 litres (68 fl oz/8 cups) Chipotle chicken stock (page 14)
+ 200 g (7 oz) rosella (wild hibiscus flower) (see Glossary)
+ 2 kg (4 lb 6 oz) free-range lamb belly ribs, chine bone removed
+ olive oil for drizzling
+ 200 g (7 oz) Latin spice rub (page 30)
+ 400 ml (13½ fl oz) Pomegranate mojo (page 22)

CARAMELISED FIGS

+ 6 ripe figs, halved
+ icing (confectioners') sugar for dusting
+ sea salt to taste

SERVES 6

Flor de Jamaica, also known as rosella or wild hibiscus in the Western world, has a lovely acidity that cuts through rich meats. It is available in most Latin food stores and is also great for cocktails. Pork ribs are universally popular, so much so that they are quite expensive these days. Therefore, try these lamb ribs for a delicious change, cooked barbecoa-style with a sweet-and-sour glaze. You can cook them ahead of time, and cool. Remove any excess fat with a sharp knife before reheating on the barbecue or re-roasting in a pan. You can tear chunks of the glazed rib meat into warm tortillas with a fragrant herb salad. I love serving these with Pasilla chilli relish (page 25).

Ideally preheat a wood-fired or charcoal barbecue to char your ribs as it will impart greater flavour. Alternatively, you can use a hot frying pan on the stove top. If using a wood or charcoal barbecue, heat until the coals have a thin coating of grey ash.

Preheat the oven to 180°C (350°F).

To prepare the lamb, combine the stock and rosella in a large saucepan and bring to the boil. Set aside to infuse for 15 minutes.

Drizzle the lamb ribs with olive oil and season with the spice rub, coating all over. Grill the ribs until charred all over. Transfer to a pan and set over low heat. Cook the ribs gently to render the excess fat.

Place the ribs in a large roasting dish. Pour over the infused stock. Cover and cook in the oven for 2 hours, or until the meat is falling off the bone. Remove the lamb from the braise and place on a rack set over a tray, to drain. Cover and allow to cool. Refrigerate if time permits. Once cold, shave the excess fat off the lamb.

To prepare the caramelised figs, arrange the fig halves on a baking tray, dust with icing sugar and sprinkle with salt. Bake for 5 minutes, or until caramelised.

Meanwhile, heat a large frying pan over medium heat. Drizzle with oil. Cook the lamb, fat side down, for 5 minutes, or until crisp and golden. Drain off the excess fat. Pour in 200 ml (7 fl oz) of the pomegranate mojo and simmer until reduced to a syrupy glaze. Brush the glaze over the lamb.

To serve, place the lamb ribs on a platter and drizzle with the remaining pomegranate mojo. Arrange the figs and pickles, if using, decoratively to garnish. Serve with the refried beans and cool cucumber salad, if desired.

LAMB SHOULDER BARBECOA-STYLE WITH MESCAL & CHESTNUTS

~~~~~~~~

+ 1.5 kg (3 lb 5 oz) free-range lamb shoulder, bone in
+ extra-virgin olive oil for drizzling
+ Large homemade masa flour tortillas (see page 46) or store-bought tortillas to serve
+ Green rice with black cabbage (page 246) to serve

MARINADE

+ 750 ml (25½ fl oz/3 cups) Tempranillo wine
+ 1 carrot, roughly chopped
+ 1 red onion, roughly chopped
+ 10 garlic cloves, smashed
+ 4 cinnamon sticks
+ 1 tablespoon juniper berries, crushed

SERVES 6

+ 1 teaspoon coarsely ground black pepper
+ 2 bay leaves
+ 50 ml (1¾ fl oz) extra-virgin olive oil

SAUCE

+ 300 ml (10 fl oz) agave syrup (see Glossary)
+ 300 ml (10 fl oz) balsamic vinegar
+ 1.5 litres (51 fl oz/6 cups) chicken stock or 1 litre (34 fl oz/4 cups) stock combined with 500 ml (17 fl oz/2 cups) Red mole (page 16)
+ 50 g (1¾ oz) cornflour (cornstarch)
+ 100 g (3½ oz) bitter dark chocolate, minimum 50% cocoa solids, roughly chopped
+ sea salt to taste

GARNISH

+ 25 ml (¾ fl oz) olive oil
+ 4 garlic cloves, sliced
+ 175 g (6 oz) smoked bacon or kaiserfleisch, cut into lardons
+ 1 large handful of sage leaves
+ 200 g (7 oz) peeled chestnuts, fresh or frozen
+ 75 ml (2½ fl oz) mescal reposado (see Glossary)
+ 500 ml (17 fl oz/2 cups) chicken stock
+ 100 g (3½ oz) unsalted butter
+ 200 g (7 oz) cooked or tinned flageolet beans, drained and rinsed if using tinned
+ 200 g (7 oz) cooked or tinned lentils, drained and rinsed if using tinned
+ 200 g (7 oz) cooked peas

To prepare the marinade, combine all of the ingredients in a medium bowl.

Place the lamb in a deep casserole dish, pour the marinade over the top and drizzle with oil. Cover and refrigerate, turning occasionally to marinate evenly, for 3–4 hours but not longer as the wine will overpower the meat.

Meanwhile, to prepare the sauce, combine the agave and vinegar in a medium saucepan and boil over medium heat until reduced by half. Add the stock, or stock and mole combination, boil and reduce by half once more. If using just stock, dilute the cornflour with a little water in a small bowl. Whisk the cornflour mixture into the sauce, boiling until it just thickens to a coating consistency. Set aside until required. If the stock and mole combination is already thick enough, skip the cornflour step. Add the chocolate and stir to combine.

Ideally a wood-fired or charcoal barbecue will impart greater flavour when cooking this dish. If you have one, preheat it until the coals have a thin coating of grey ash. However if you don't, below are instructions for how to prepare barbecoa using a conventional stove top and oven.

Preheat the oven to 140°C (275°F).

Remove the lamb from the marinade. Strain the marinade through a fine-mesh sieve into a small saucepan, reserving the vegetables. Bring the marinade to the boil, skimming off the impurities that rise to the surface until clear.

Grill and char the lamb on the barbecue, or alternatively in a hot pan, until well coloured all over. Transfer the lamb to an ovenproof casserole dish. Grill the reserved vegetables until coloured and add to the dish with the lamb. Pour the sauce and boiled marinade into the dish. Cover with a piece of baking paper with a hole in the middle. This allows air to circulate into the braise, causing the liquid to reduce more, resulting in a richer sauce.

Cook for 3–4 hours until the lamb is soft and gelatinous. Remove the lamb from the dish and place on a serving tray, cover and keep warm.

Strain the braising liquid through a fine-mesh sieve into a saucepan. Simmer over low heat until reduced to a rich sauce. Season with salt. Keep warm.

To prepare the garnish, heat the oil in a medium frying pan over low heat. Cook the garlic until softened. Increase the heat to medium, fry the bacon lardons and sage until crisp. Drain the excess oil from the pan. Add the chestnuts and mescal and tilt the pan towards the flame to flambé. Allow the flame to burn out. Add the chicken stock and butter and simmer for 5 minutes, until the chestnuts are tender. Add the beans, lentils and peas and heat through, stirring to combine.

To serve, spoon the bacon and chestnut mixture over and around the lamb. Add plenty of sauce. Serve with the warmed tortillas and green rice with black cabbage.

PAUL'S TIP Substitute borlotti (pinto) beans for the flageolet beans, if unavailable.

PORK HOCK PIBIL WITH LETTUCE CUPS & FRAGRANT JICAMA SALAD

~~~~~~~~~~~~~~~~~~~~~

+ 1 iceberg lettuce, large outer leaves discarded, remaining separated into small cups
+ 250 ml (8½ fl oz/1 cup) green mole (see pages 218-19) or Mexican salsa verde (page 20)

PORK HOCK PIBIL

+ 1 litre (34 fl oz/4 cups) pork brine (see page 192)
+ 250 ml (8½ fl oz/1 cup) Achiote relish (page 32)
+ 1 x 3 kg (6 lb 10 oz) free-range pork hock or shoulder, skin scored
+ oil for brushing
+ salt to taste

CARAMEL

+ 250 ml (8½ fl oz/1 cup) agave syrup (see Glossary) or honey
+ 250 ml (8½ fl oz/1 cup) cider vinegar
+ 1 litre (34 fl oz/4 cups) seville or bitter orange juice
+ 2 cinnamon sticks
+ 2 tablespoons fennel seeds
+ 4 whole cloves

SALAD

+ 2 jicamas, cut into matchsticks (see Glossary)
+ 6 large handfuls of watercress
+ 3 oranges, segmented
+ ½ red onion, thinly sliced
+ 1 large handful of oregano leaves, shredded
+ 1½ tablespoons sesame seeds, toasted
+ 200 ml (7 fl oz) Zesty lime dressing (page 37)

SERVES 6

Pibil pork is an ancient dish from the Yucatán Peninsula, another barbecoa classic that is worth the lengthy preparation. Once you discover the flavour of achiote, you will find yourself looking forward to the next experience. This particular pork cut is all about the dramatic presentation and everyone feasting together. If you can't find jicama, substitute pears, celeriac or radishes. The marinade will make a roast pork cut taste delicious too.

To prepare the pork hock, combine the pork brine with 125 ml (4 fl oz/½ cup) of the achiote relish in a container large enough to hold the hock. Place the pork in the brine, cover and refrigerate, turning occasionally for even brining, for 48 hours.

Remove the pork from the brine. Rub the remaining achiote relish over the hock, cover and refrigerate for at least 4 hours, or overnight.

Preheat the oven to 240°C (465°F).

Brush the pork with oil, sprinkle with salt and place in a roasting tray. Cook for 20 minutes until the skin begins to crisp.

Reduce the heat to 160°C (320°F) and cook for 2 hours, until fork-tender.

To prepare the caramel, combine the agave and vinegar in a medium saucepan and simmer over medium heat until reduced to a glaze. Add the orange juice and spices and simmer until reduced to a rich syrup. Strain through a fine-mesh sieve and keep warm.

Ensure the pork is crispy all over – in a restaurant they would fry it until the skin blisters, after long, slow cooking. You could also do this at home using a deep-fryer without the basket.

Once crisp, brush the pork with some of the caramel and place the remaining caramel in a small serving bowl.

To serve, combine the salad ingredients, except the dressing, in a bowl. Dress and toss to coat. Arrange the salad in a large serving bowl and surround with lettuce cups. Gently warm the green mole and place it in a small serving bowl and serve alongside the caramel. Place the pork hock on a large serving plate and present it in the centre of the table. Pull the meat apart in front of your guests and allow them to serve themselves, filling the lettuce cups with salad and shredded pork and topping with green mole and caramel.

LOW & SLOW BEEF SHORT RIBS WITH CERVEZA-CARAMELISED ONIONS & ANCIENT GRAIN SALAD

~~~~~~~~~~

+ 2 tablespoons olive oil
+ 2 teaspoons sugar
+ 50 ml (1³/4 fl oz) sherry vinegar
+ 50 ml (1³/4 fl oz) agave syrup (see Glossary)
+ Ancient grain seven vegetable super-food salad (page 226)

BEER MARINADE

+ 2 kg (4 lb 6 oz) free-range rack beef short ribs
+ 2 unpeeled red onions, halved
+ 1 purple and 1 yellow carrot, peeled
+ 1 litre (34 fl oz/4 cups) dark Mexican beer, plus an extra splash for glazing

+ 100 ml (3¹/2 fl oz) honey or agave syrup
+ 1 small handful of sage leaves
+ 2 cinnamon sticks
+ 2 garlic cloves, thinly sliced
+ 1 tablespoon black peppercorns, crushed
+ 1 star anise
+ 1 bay leaf

BRAISE

+ 1 l (34 fl oz/4 cups) Red mole (page 16) or 2 litres (68 fl oz/ 8 cups) beef stock

SERVES 6

Short ribs are gaining popularity mainly, I think, due to farmers' markets where foodies get the chance to buy like a chef! Chefs love short ribs because they generate so much flavour. A rack of beef short ribs should take up to 14 hours to cook in a pit barbecue. You can get favourable results in a kettle-type barbecue but someone's got to tend the fire. You could also cook them in the oven in a fragrant beer sauce for 6-8 hours. I suggest you serve this dish with a dark beer, like an ale or malty red ale, but dark Mexican beers are excellent for this dish too.

To prepare the marinade, place the beef ribs, onion and carrots in a large roasting tray. Cut the ribs into 6 individual portions, if necessary, to fit in the tray. Add the remaining ingredients and mix to combine and coat. Cover and refrigerate for at least 4 hours, or ideally overnight.

Preheat a wood-fired or coal barbecue until the coals have a thin coating of grey ash. Add presoaked aromatic wood such as ironbark, mesquite or apple. Alternatively, if using a gas barbecue, soak smaller wood chips and place them in a smoking box on your barbecue. If you don't have a barbecue you can seal the meat in a large pan.

Preheat the oven to 120°C (250°F).

Remove the meat from the marinade and pat dry using paper towel. Remove the onion and carrots from the marinade and dry in the same way. Pour the marinade into a medium saucepan and simmer over low heat until reduced to make a syrupy glaze.

Seal the ribs on the barbecue or in a large frying pan over medium heat, turning frequently, until coloured all over. Take care as the ribs will colour very quickly due to the honey.

Place the ribs in a large casserole dish. Add the glaze and carrots. Pour in the beef stock or the mole. If using mole, it will be concentrated, so add 300 ml (10 fl oz) water. Cover the beef and braise in the oven for 5–6 hours until extremely soft. Remove from the oven and set aside for 10 minutes.

Heat the oil and sugar in a medium ovenproof frying pan over medium heat. Arrange the onions, cut side down, in the pan and cook until richly caramelised. Add a splash of beer and simmer until evaporated. Add 125 ml (4 fl oz/½ cup) of the beef braising juices and cook in the oven for 5 minutes. Remove from the oven and allow to cool in the pan.

Pour the braising liquid into a medium saucepan and simmer over medium heat until reduced to a rich sauce.

Combine the vinegar and agave in a small saucepan and simmer over low heat until reduced to a syrup. Add to the sauce and taste for balance – not too bitter, not too sweet and smooth-tasting to the palate. Strain through a fine-mesh sieve into a pan large enough to fit the beef.

Cut the beef into single-bone portions, return to the sauce and gently reheat.

Cut the carrots into decorative pieces, peel the caramelised onions and allow them to fall apart naturally. Add to the sauce and gently reheat.

To serve, arrange the ribs, carrot and onion decoratively on serving plates with the ancient grain salad to accompany.

PAUL'S TIP The beef can be added to the finished sauce and stored (marinating further) in an airtight container in the refrigerator for up to 3 days, or in the freezer for up to 3 months.

LOW & SLOW BEEF SHORT RIBS
WITH CERVEZA-CARAMELISED
ONIONS & ANCIENT GRAIN SALAD

(pages 206–7)

SKIRT STEAK VERACRUZ WITH BUTTERMILK ONIONS & SALSA VERDE

~~~~~~~~~~

+ 1.5 kg (3 lb 5 oz) grain-fed skirt (flank) steak
+ olive oil
+ 250 ml (8½ fl oz/1 cup) Mexican salsa verde (page 20) to serve
+ Veracruz sauce (page 41) to serve

MARINADE

+ 1 small handful of oregano leaves, finely chopped
+ 25 g (1 oz) best-quality anchovy fillets
+ 25 g (1 oz) capers
+ 1 garlic clove, sliced

ONION RINGS

+ rice bran oil for deep-frying
+ 200 g (7 oz/2 cups) masa harina flour (see Glossary) or 250 g (9 oz/2 cups) semolina
+ 1 teaspoon onion powder
+ 1 teaspoon chilli powder
+ 200 ml (7 fl oz) buttermilk
+ 1 white onion, sliced into 1 cm (½ in) rounds, separated into rings
+ sea salt to taste

HERB SALAD

+ 1 small handful of flat-leaf parsley
+ 1 small handful of tarragon leaves
+ 1 small handful of oregano leaves
+ olive oil for drizzling
+ ½ lime

SERVES 6

Skirt (flank) steak is another thinking person's steak as it requires some skill and is the only steak you will see in rural Mexico. This recipe is a summery type of beef dish. Veracruz sauce is a delicious all-rounder in the way that napoletana sauce is in Italy. The salty capers and anchovies are a great match for the beef. Fried onion rings were first served to me at the restaurant Pujol in Mexico City with veal tongue, and they work well with this steak too. This is a domestic version of the recipe, inspired by my travels.

To prepare the marinade, blend the ingredients together using a food processor or mortar and pestle, until they resemble a pesto-like relish.

Cut the beef into 6 even-sized portions and coat in the marinade. Cover and refrigerate for at least 1 hour, or up to 4 hours.

Preheat the oven to 180°C (350°F).

To make the onion rings half-fill a large heavy-based saucepan with rice bran oil and heat to 140°C (275°F).

Combine the masa harina flour and onion and chilli powders in a medium bowl. Pour the buttermilk into a separate medium bowl and soak the onion rings for 2 minutes.

Drain then dredge the onion rings in the flour. Fry in batches until just coloured. Remove using a slotted spoon and drain on paper towel.

Increase the oil temperature to 180°C (350°F).

Heat a good splash of olive oil in a large frying pan over high heat, until almost smoking. Sear the steak for 1 minute on each side. Transfer to a tray and place in the oven to keep warm.

Refry the onions for 1–2 minutes, until a rich golden brown. Drain on paper towel and season with salt.

For the herb salad, place the herbs in a small bowl, drizzle with oil and a squeeze of lime juice and toss to coat.

To serve, thinly slice the steak, garnish with the herb salad and a tower of onion rings and serve with the salsa verde and Veracruz sauce.

WOOD-BARBECUED CHILLI CHICKEN WITH CUMIN & PINEAPPLE CARAMEL

〰〰〰

+ 1.5 kg (3 lb 5 oz) free-range boneless chicken thighs
+ Latin spice rub (page 30)
+ olive oil

PICKLED PINEAPPLE

+ 1 small ripe pineapple
+ 1 jalapeño, thinly sliced
+ Mexican pickle solution (see Mexican-style pickles, page 53), hot

CUMIN & PINEAPPLE CARAMEL

+ 170 ml (5 1/2 fl oz/2/3 cup) sherry vinegar
+ 125 g (4 1/2 oz/2/3 cup) brown sugar
+ 350 ml (12 fl oz) pineapple juice
+ 150 ml (5 fl oz) Adobo sauce (page 15)
+ 75 g (2 3/4 oz) ripe pineapple flesh, diced
+ 60 g (2 oz/1/4 cup) tamarind pulp
+ 1 tablespoon ground cumin
+ 1 serrano chilli, seeded and finely chopped to taste

GARNISH

+ Tomatillo verde (page 21)
+ toasted sesame seeds to sprinkle
+ 3 large handfuls of watercress or upland cress, perfect leaves picked

SERVES 6

Grilling chicken can be tricky, as the delicate breast meat can overcook and easily become dry. Choose boneless chicken thighs as they marinate well and can be precooked in fragrant stock, or baked, before finishing on the grill. I like to dress them with a sweet-and-sour tamarind and pineapple glaze. You could also serve this chicken with green mole sauce (see pages 218-19).

Rub the chicken with the spice rub to coat. Cover and refrigerate for at least 4 hours or overnight.

To prepare the pickled pineapple, peel, quarter and core the pineapple. Very thinly slice and place in a medium bowl with the jalapeño. Cover with hot pickling liquid and set aside to cool.

Preheat the oven to 120°C (250°F).

Preheat a wood-fired or coal barbecue until the coals have a thin coating of grey ash. Add presoaked aromatic wood such as hickory, ironbark, oak or mallee oak. Alternatively, if using a gas barbecue soak smaller wood chips and place them in a smoking box on your barbecue.

Brush the chicken with olive oil and grill lightly for 4 minutes on each side. Transfer to a tray and bake for 20 minutes, or until just cooked through.

Meanwhile to prepare the pineapple caramel, combine the vinegar and sugar in a small saucepan over low heat and simmer until reduced to a syrup. Add the remaining ingredients, except the chilli, and simmer over low heat for 15 minutes, until the pineapple has softened. Transfer to a food processor or blender and process until smooth. Strain through a fine-mesh sieve and return to the pan. Add as much of the chilli as you like and simmer over low heat, until reduced to a glaze.

To serve, return the chicken to the grill and cook until crisp and evenly charred. Transfer to a tray and generously brush with the pineapple caramel.

Drain the pickled pineapple and place in a serving bowl.

Arrange the chicken on a serving platter, dress with some of the remaining pineapple caramel and tomatillo verde, sprinkle with sesame seeds and garnish with cress. Serve with the remaining sauce and the pickled pineapple on the side.

BLACK MOLE WITH DUCK, CARAMELISED FIGS & FARRO & PISTACHIO PILAF

+ sesame seeds for sprinkling

DUCK IN BLACK MOLE

+ rice bran oil for shallow-frying
+ 6 duck legs
+ large pinch of ground allspice
+ large pinch of sea salt
+ Black mole (page 19)
+ 250 ml (8^1/$_2$ fl oz/1 cup) chicken stock

FARRO & PISTACHIO PILAF

+ 400 g (14 oz/2 cups) farro, soaked in cold water for 1 hour, drained and rinsed (see Glossary)

+ 1 litre (34 fl oz/4 cups) chicken stock, plus additional stock to moisten
+ 60 ml (2 fl oz/^{1}/$_4$ cup) olive oil
+ 25 g (1 oz) butter
+ 2 red onions, finely sliced
+ 6 garlic cloves, finely sliced
+ 2 large handfuls of oregano leaves, roughly chopped
+ 175 g (6 oz) Manzanilla olives, pitted and roughly chopped
+ 110 g (4 oz/^{3}/$_4$ cup) pistachio nuts, toasted and roughly chopped
+ sea salt to taste

GLAZED FIGS

+ 6 ripe figs, halved lengthways
+ 100 ml (3^1/$_2$ fl oz) sherry vinegar
+ 50 ml (1^3/$_4$ fl oz) honey
+ 1 cinnamon stick
+ icing (confectioners') sugar for dusting

SERVES 6

Preheat the oven to 160°C (320°F).

To cook the duck, pour enough rice bran oil into a large frying pan to shallow-fry and heat over medium heat. Season the legs with allspice and salt and shallow-fry, skin side down, until crisp and golden brown. Transfer to a casserole dish and pour over the mole and chicken stock.

Place a piece of baking paper over the duck and cover with a lid. Cook in the oven for 1 hour or until tender and the meat pulls away from the bone easily. Remove from the oven and allow the duck to cool in the sauce.

To prepare the farro and pistachio pilaf, place the soaked farro grains in a large saucepan, cover with the chicken stock and bring to the boil. Boil for 15–20 minutes until tender.

Heat the olive oil and butter in a large saucepan over low heat. Cook the onion, garlic and oregano until softened. Add the olives, pistachio nuts and cooked farro, moisten with additional stock if required, and stir to combine. Season well with salt. Remove from the heat, cover and keep warm.

Either leave the duck legs whole and reheat in the sauce or shred the meat.

For the glazed figs, heat a medium frying pan over low heat. Arrange the fig halves in the pan, cut side down. Add the vinegar, honey and cinnamon stick and gently simmer until the liquid has reduced to a syrup. Dust with icing sugar and transfer to the oven to cook, basting occasionally, for 5 minutes, or until the figs are caramelised.

To serve, place the black mole duck on serving plates and sprinkle with sesame seeds. Serve with the caramelised figs and farro and pistachio pilaf.

A simplified version of the famed mole of Oaxaca, Mexico, this sauce is typically served with turkey as a celebration dish or on a fiesta like Day of the Dead. Mexicans believe in life after death and celebrate this holy day with wonderful dishes. I enjoy eating this dish with nutty grains like farro. The figs work well with the spices, but blood plums or cherries can be substituted also. The bright green pistachio nuts look amazing with the dark sauce and taste great too!

GLAZED MEXICAN SPICED LAMB CHOPS WITH ANCIENT GRAINS & PICKLES

~~~~~~~~~

+ 1 perfect square sheet of banana leaf
+ Ancient grain seven vegetable super-food salad (page 226) to serve

LAMB CHOPS

+ 2 tablespoons olive oil
+ 1.25 kg (2 lb 12 oz) trimmed lamb cutlets (3 per serve)
+ Large pinch of sea salt
+ Large pinch of dried chilli flakes
+ Large pinch of Mexican spice blend (page 30) or ground cumin
+ 60 ml (2 fl oz/1/4 cup) agave syrup (see Glossary)
+ 60 ml (2 fl oz/1/4 cup) sherry vinegar
+ 400 ml (13 1/2 fl oz) Red mole (page 16)
+ hot sauce to taste (optional)
+ sesame seeds to sprinkle

GARNISHES

+ Mexican-style pickles (page 53) to serve
+ 3 oranges, segmented
+ 4 breakfast radishes, sliced into 1 cm (1/2 in) rounds
+ 2 large handfuls of upland cress or watercress
+ 1 sliced jalapeño

SERVES 6

This recipe truly transforms the humble lamb chop into a Mexican delight! With its lacquering of agave syrup and sherry vinegar it takes on a brilliant sheen. It's lovely served with the ancient grains and pickles.

For the lamb, heat the oil in a large frying pan over medium heat. Season the cutlets with the salt and spices. Cook the cutlets, fat side down, for 2 minutes. Seal the meat on both sides, for approximately 4 minutes, until nicely coloured but still pink inside. Transfer to a tray, loosely cover and set aside to rest.

Add the agave syrup to the pan and caramelise. Add the vinegar and caramelise once more. Add the mole and simmer until reduced to a rich sauce. Add a little hot sauce if you prefer a bit more heat.

Coat the cutlets in the sauce and sprinkle with sesame seeds.

To serve, lightly brush the banana leaf with oil and place on a platter. Arrange the lamb cutlets on top and garnish with the pickles, orange, radish, watercress and jalapeño. Serve in a communal fashion with the ancient grain salad on the side.

PAUL'S TIP The red mole glaze is a versatile and delicious sauce to use to glaze pork or beef ribs or lacquer a slow-roasted crisp pork belly. It is heaven with Mexican-style pickles (page 53).

GOAT BARBECOA, GREEN MOLE & GREEN RICE

~~~~~~~~~~

+ Green rice with black cabbage (page 246) to serve
+ Goat's crema (see page 120) to serve

GOAT

+ 100 ml (3½ fl oz) olive oil
+ 1 x 2 kg (4 lb 6 oz) goat shoulder, cut through the bone into 5-8 cm (2-3¼ in) thick pieces osso buco-style (ask your butcher to do this for you)

SERVES 6

+ 200 g (7 oz) Mexican spice blend (page 30) or a mixture of 100 g (3½ oz) ground cumin, 50 g (1¾ oz) ground cinnamon, 50 g (1¾ oz) smoked paprika
+ large pinch of salt flakes
+ 750 ml (25½ fl oz/3 cups) Red mole (page 16)
+ 500 ml (17 fl oz/2 cups) chicken stock

GREEN MOLE

+ zest and juice of 6 limes
+ 2 large handfuls of mint leaves
+ 1 large handful of coriander (cilantro) leaves

+ 1 large handful of flat-leaf parsley
+ 2 jalapeños
+ 100 ml (3½ fl oz) sherry vinegar
+ 100 ml (3½ fl oz) agave syrup (see Glossary)
+ 100 g (3½ oz) bitter chocolate, minimum 45-60% cocoa solids

GARNISH

+ 70 g (2½ oz/½ cup) pepitas (pumpkin seeds), toasted
+ 60 g (2 oz/½ cup) sunflower seeds, toasted

Barbecoa is said to have been invented in the Caribbean. In Mexico the term is used to describe the cooking process where whole animals or joints of meat are spiced then charred and cooked over an open fire, then wrapped in plant leaves and slow-cooked with hot coals under the earth for several hours. It's like a giant slow cooker, really. This recipe highlights another staple ingredient from the Caribbean - goat. Though not used much in Western cooking, goat is a really delicious meat. It is a lean protein so the long, gentle barbecoa cooking style is perfect for a tender outcome.

Ideally a wood-fired or charcoal barbecue will impart greater flavour when cooking this dish. If you have one, preheat a barbecue with a hood until the coals have a thin coating of grey ash. However if you don't, below are instructions for how to prepare barbecoa using either a conventional oven or a stove top.

If using an oven preheat to 100°C (210°F).

If using the stove-top, heat the oil in a large frying pan over high heat.

Season the goat pieces with the spices and salt. Fry a few pieces at a time, until nicely coloured all over. Transfer to a tray and set aside.

Gently heat the red mole and chicken stock together in a large heavy-based saucepan over medium–low heat until simmering. Add the goat to the pan and coat in the sauce. Reduce the heat to the lowest possible setting, cover and cook on the stove-top for 3 hours. Alternatively, if using the oven, cook in the pan or transfer to an ovenproof dish and bake for 4–5 hours until fork-tender.

If wood barbecoa is your mantra, place the meat onto a large, double-layered square of foil lined with baking paper. Spoon over 350 ml (12 fl oz) of the red mole and carefully wrap up the edges to seal. (Traditionally, banana leaves are used as they impart extra flavour to the sauce.) Check the internal temperature of the barbecue – it should be around 60–100°C (140–210°F). Place the parcel on a rack set over the hot coals. Cover with the hood and barbecoa, moving the parcel around the cool spots of the fire from time to time, for 2 hours, or until fork-tender.

Remove the tender meat from the sauce and set aside on a tray to cool slightly.

Meanwhile to prepare the green mole, combine the remaining red mole braising liquid from the goat and the lime zest and juice, herbs and jalapeño in a food processor or blender and process until smooth.

To finish the mole, simmer the vinegar and agave together in a small saucepan, until reduced to a caramel. Adjust the flavour of the mole, adding the caramel and chocolate, a little at a time, until refined to suit your personal taste. Return the mole to the pan and gently reheat.

Once the meat is cool enough to handle, either leave whole or flake into equal bite-sized pieces. Add the meat to the mole and heat through.

Serve the mole, green rice with black cabbage and goat's crema alongside each other in colourful ceramic dishes. Sprinkle the mole with toasted pepitas and sunflower seeds to garnish.

GOAT BARBECOA, GREEN
MOLE & GREEN RICE
(pages 218–19)

07

ANCIENT GRAINS & VEGETABLES

Ancient Mayan and nuevo
Latino flavours work well with
so many diverse seasonal vegetables and
ancient grains. These side dishes and salads
are never dull accompaniments to the main event!

~~~~~~~~

The bright, smoky and mysterious notes of charred tomatillo
salsa verde freshen up market staples as do goat's and brined
cheeses, and guajillo and poblano chillies ensure that your
vegetables are always fiercely seasoned. Roast pumpkin seasoned
with pomegranate mojo takes the Sunday roast to the streets
of Cuba, and the aromatic barbecue continues to make
its mark, with waxy potatoes and spring onions (scallions)
dressed with sesame pipian. Ancient grains, seeds
and nuts ensure nutrition-enriched foods,
vibrant antojitos and interesting additions
to the festive table.

ANCIENT GRAIN SEVEN VEGETABLE SUPER-FOOD SALAD

~~~~~~~~~~~

+ 65 g (2¼ oz/⅓ cup) farro, rinsed (see Glossary)
+ 100 g (3½ oz/½ cup) mixed quinoa (red, black and white), soaked in cold water for 30 minutes, drained and rinsed
+ 100 g (3½ oz) (about ½ bunch) broccolini
+ 100 g (3½ oz) (about ½ bunch) kale, stripped from the stem
+ 2 tablespoons olive oil
+ 100 g (3½ oz) butternut pumpkin (squash), finely diced
+ 100 g (3½ oz) fresh or frozen corn kernels

+ 80 g (2¾ oz/½ cup) fresh or frozen peas
+ 30 g (1 oz/¼ cup) pepitas (pumpkin seeds)
+ 30 g (1 oz/¼ cup) sunflower seeds
+ 30 g (1 oz/¼ cup) chia seeds
+ 150 g (5½ oz) salted ricotta, finely chopped
+ seeds of ½ pomegranate
+ 90 g (3 oz) tinned chickpeas (garbanzo beans), drained and rinsed
+ ½ red onion, finely chopped

+ 1 large handful of oregano leaves, roughly chopped
+ 1 small handful of flat-leaf parsley, roughly chopped
+ 1 jalapeño, seeds removed and finely chopped
+ 150 ml (5 fl oz) Latin vinaigrette (page 36)
+ sea salt and freshly ground black pepper to taste
+ edible flowers to garnish

SERVES 4–6

Cook the farro in a saucepan of boiling water for 15–20 minutes, or until tender. Drain and rinse.

Rinse the quinoa thoroughly and place in a small saucepan. Add 310 ml (10½ fl oz/1¼ cups) water and bring to the boil over medium heat. Reduce the heat to low and simmer for 10 minutes. Cover and cook over low heat for a further 5 minutes. Remove from the heat and set aside, with the lid on, for 5 minutes to finish cooking. Fluff the grains with a fork and spread out on a tray to cool.

Bring a medium saucepan of water to the boil. Cook the broccolini and kale for 1–2 minutes, until tender. Drain and refresh in a bowl of iced water to retain their colour. Chop to roughly the same size as the other vegetables.

Heat the oil in a large frying pan over medium heat. Add the pumpkin and cook for 5–7 minutes, until just tender and beginning to colour. Add the corn and peas and cook for a further 2 minutes, or until tender. Set aside to cool.

Combine the pepitas and sunflower and chia seeds in a dry medium frying pan and cook over medium–low heat, tossing frequently, for 3–4 minutes, until lightly toasted.

Combine the farro, quinoa, broccolini, kale, pumpkin, corn, peas and toasted seeds in a large bowl. Add the salted ricotta, pomegranate seeds, chickpeas, onion, chopped herbs and jalapeño and stir to combine. Pour in the dressing and toss to combine. Season with salt and pepper. Transfer to a decorative bowl and serve garnished with the edible flowers.

Think of this as a type of tabouleh and a healthy salad as a base for anything you like! The farro and quinoa are rich in nutrients and add a lovely nuttiness to the final salad. You can add seasonal vegetables and herbs throughout the year. For summer think cherry tomatoes, grilled eggplant (aubergine), summer squash, zucchini (courgettes), corn, pumpkin (winter squash), sweet potatoes or basil.

BEER-BRAISED BEANS

~~~~~~~~~~

+ 500 g (1 lb 2 oz/2 1/2 cups)
  borlotti (pinto) beans, soaked in
  cold water for at least 4 hours,
  or overnight
+ 1/2 teaspoon bicarbonate of soda
  (baking soda)

BARBECUE SAUCE

+ 250 ml (8 1/2 fl oz/1 cup) beer,
  preferably dark Mexican beer
  or red ale
+ 1 onion, finely chopped
+ 60 ml (2 fl oz/1/4 cup) honey
+ 250 g (9 oz/1 cup) tinned chopped
  tomatoes
+ 250 ml (8 1/2 fl oz/1 cup) tomato
  sauce (ketchup)
+ 125 ml (4 fl oz/1/2 cup) freshly
  squeezed orange juice
+ 2 tablespoons freshly squeezed
  lime juice
+ 2 tablespoons cider vinegar
+ 1 tablespoon brown sugar
+ 2 teaspoons English mustard
+ 2 teaspoons Spanish smoked
  paprika
+ 2 teaspoons tamarind paste
+ 1/2 teaspoon chilli powder
+ 1/4 teaspoon garlic powder
+ sea salt and freshly ground
  black pepper to taste

SERVES 6

These beer-braised beans are a fun Tex-Mex dish and they have a nice kick. The beer is a good bitter-sweet addition. Select red ale or dark beer for a richer taste. These beans are great for breakfast with barbecued meats and ribs - think boozy baked beans to start the day!

Drain and rinse the beans and place them in a large saucepan. Cover with 4 times their quantity of water, add the bicarbonate of soda and bring to the boil. Reduce the heat and simmer for 1 hour, or until tender.

Meanwhile, to make the barbecue sauce, combine the beer, onion and honey in a medium heavy-based saucepan and simmer over medium–low heat for 10 minutes, or until reduced by half to make a rich glaze. Add the remaining ingredients and gently simmer, stirring occasionally, for a further 15 minutes, or until reduced to a thick rich sauce. Transfer to a food processor or blender and purée. Strain through a fine-mesh sieve.

Drain the beans and return to the pan. Pour in the sauce and stir to coat. Serve warm or at room temperature.

DRUNKEN BEAN SALAD

~~~~~~~~~~

+ 1 kg (2 lb 3 oz) ham hock
+ 1 carrot, peeled
+ 1 large handful of oregano leaves
+ 2 litres (68 fl oz/8 cups) chicken stock
+ 220 g (8 oz/1 cup) dried black beans, soaked overnight in cold water
+ 200 g (7 oz/1 cup) dried borlotti (pinto) beans, soaked overnight in cold water
+ 185 g (6½ oz/1 cup) dried brown lentils, rinsed
+ 235 g (8½ oz/1½ cups) fresh or frozen peas, cooked

+ 250 g (9 oz) fresh or frozen corn kernels, cooked
+ 2 celery stalks, cut into 1 cm (½ in) dice
+ ½ red onion, cut into 1 cm (½ in) dice
+ 200 ml (7 fl oz) Latin vinaigrette, using tequila (page 36)
+ 1 large handful of flat-leaf parsley, roughly chopped
+ 1 large handful of tarragon or oregano leaves, roughly chopped
+ sea salt and freshly ground black pepper to taste

SERVES 8

It's not uncommon to find a good whack of tequila in a recipe in Mexico! Good tequila always imparts a refined mysterious flavour to food. In this recipe – based on a French peasant salad from the Lyonnais in France – I like to use ham hock as it generates a lovely stock, but fried bacon pieces are good too. Serve it with meat or fish.

Place the ham hock, carrot and oregano in a medium heavy-based saucepan with the chicken stock and bring to the boil over high heat. Reduce the heat, cover and gently simmer for 2–2½ hours, until the meat is tender and is beginning to fall off the bone.

Remove the ham hock and carrot from the stock and set aside to cool.

Drain and rinse the beans and place them in the pan with the hot stock. Simmer for 50 minutes, or until becoming tender. Add the lentils and simmer for a further 15–20 minutes, until both beans and lentils are tender. Cover towards the end if the stock is getting low. Leave the beans and lentils in the pan to cool.

Dice the carrot to a similar size as the beans.

Combine the beans, carrot, peas, corn, celery and onion in a large bowl. Pour over the dressing and toss to coat. Set aside for 10 minutes to allow the beans to soak up the dressing.

Flake the ham hock, discarding the skin, sinew and bone. Add the ham and herbs to the bean mixture and toss to combine. Season with salt and pepper and serve.

COOL CUCUMBER SALAD

~~~~~~~~~~~~~~~~

+ 50 g (1³/4 oz/¹/3 cup) sesame seeds
+ 30 g (1 oz/¹/4 cup) chia seeds
+ 600 g (1 lb 5 oz) baby short (Lebanese) cucumbers (qukes), peeled and sliced into 1.5 cm (¹/2 in) rounds
+ 2 bulbs fennel, finely shaved and tops roughly chopped
+ 250 g (9 oz) seedless white grapes, cut in half
+ 30 g (1 oz) Lilliput capers
+ 1 large handful of mint leaves, finely chopped
+ 1 large handful of bronzed fennel tops or dill, roughly chopped (optional)
+ 150 ml (5 fl oz) Zesty lime dressing (page 37)
+ 150 g (5¹/2 oz) salted ricotta, finely chopped

SERVES 4

Mexican cucumbers look really cool - they look like tiny striped watermelons and taste like a more juicy cucumber. They are not easily available but you can substitute baby Lebanese (short) cucumbers, often sold as qukes. This salad typically includes beans and corn but here I have created a refreshing light alternative. I feel the role of the cucumber is to cool and make spicy foods more enjoyable. This salad is the perfect coolant for some Mexican heat.

Combine the sesame and chia seeds in a dry frying pan and cook over medium-low heat, stirring occasionally, until lightly toasted. Set aside to cool.

Combine the cucumber, fennel, grapes, capers, mint and bronzed fennel tops in a medium bowl. Add the toasted seeds and pour in the dressing. Toss to combine.

Arrange flat on a serving plate and sprinkle with salted ricotta.

PAUL'S TIP You can substitute baby capers if Lilliput are unavailable.

SNOW PEA, AVOCADO & BACON SALAD

〰〰〰〰〰〰〰

+ 1 tablespoon olive oil
+ 300 g (10½ oz/1½ cups) fresh corn kernels (about 2 corn cobs)
+ 500 g (1 lb 2 oz) snow peas (mangetout), trimmed and blanched
+ 250 g (9 oz) cherry tomatoes, quartered
+ 1 red onion, thinly sliced
+ 4 breakfast radishes, thinly sliced
+ 2 large handfuls of coriander (cilantro) leaves, roughly chopped
+ 1–2 jalapeños, thinly sliced
+ 200 ml (7 fl oz) Zesty lime dressing (page 37)

+ pinch of ground cumin
+ pinch of ground allspice
+ pinch of sea salt
+ 3 large hass avocados, stoned

BACON

+ 80 ml (2½ fl oz/⅓ cup) vegetable oil
+ 500 g (1 lb 2 oz) smoked bacon, cut into lardons
+ 150 g (5½ oz/1 cup) pepitas (pumpkin seeds)
+ 1 large handful of oregano leaves, roughly chopped

SALAD LEAVES

+ a combination of the following leaves (about 3 large handfuls in total):
+ yellow frisée lettuce hearts
+ baby radicchio leaves
+ rocket (arugula)
+ flat-leaf parsley sprigs
+ picked watercress leaves

SERVES 6

I like adding bacon to my guacamole, which gave me the idea for this salad. It's an absolute crowd-pleaser at outdoor barbecues. Choose hardy leaves to support the warm bacon and sharp dressing – you don't want to end up with a pile of wilted leaves! You can also add your favourite touches, like smoked chicken or hot smoked fish, for a more substantial meal.

Heat the olive oil in a medium frying pan over medium heat. Cook the corn for 3 minutes, or until tender. Set aside to cool.

To prepare the bacon element, heat the vegetable oil in a large frying pan over medium heat. Cook the bacon for 4–5 minutes until golden. Drain off the oil, add the pepitas and oregano and cook for a further 2 minutes, or until the seeds are lightly toasted and the bacon and oregano are crisp. Transfer to paper towel to drain.

Combine the corn, snow peas, tomatoes, onion, radish, coriander and jalapeño in a medium bowl. Lightly dress, tossing to coat. Season with cumin, allspice and salt.

Place the salad leaves in a separate bowl and lightly dress, tossing to coat.

Quarter the avocados and lightly dress.

To assemble, spread the vegetable mixture flat onto a large serving plate, arrange the avocado on top and scatter with salad leaves and the bacon and pepita mixture.

KALE CAESAR!

~~~~~~~~~~

DRESSING

+ 125 g (4 1/2 oz/1/2 cup) low-fat sour cream
+ 100 g (3 1/2 oz) low-fat feta, crumbled
+ finely grated zest and juice of 3 limes
+ 2 large egg yolks
+ 1/2 garlic clove
+ 80 ml (2 1/2 fl oz/1/3 cup) extra-virgin olive oil
+ sea salt to taste

KALE CHIPS

+ 100 g (3 1/2 oz) (about 1/2 bunch) baby kale leaves, stripped from the stem
+ olive oil for drizzling
+ sea salt to taste

SALAD

+ 150 g (5 1/2 oz) baby corn
+ olive oil for brushing
+ 6 thick round slices or wedges of baby iceberg or baby cos (romaine) lettuce
+ 2 large handfuls of picked watercress leaves
+ 2 large handfuls of baby kale, purslane or wood sorrel
+ 150 g (5 1/2 oz) assorted radishes, quartered
+ 100 g (3 1/2 oz) jicama, thinly sliced (see Glossary)
+ 100 g (3 1/2 oz) assorted cherry and mini roma (plum) tomatoes, halved
+ 1 large handful of flat-leaf parsley
+ 1 avocado, sliced
+ 50 g (1 3/4 oz) fried masa corn (tortilla) strips or chips
+ 70 g (2 1/2 oz) piece salted ricotta, grated

SERVES 4

It's a little known fact that an Italian immigrant living in Mexico could be responsible for the caesar salad. I've added this whimsical recipe to the collection so it can be enjoyed with a little less guilt than the traditional rich version. The kale chips are breathtakingly easy to make and add crunch and colour. The dressing here is key and the salt/acid balance is very important! For me bacon, anchovies and eggs aren't needed as the dressing is rich enough. Avocado, radishes, jicama, corn and other leaves like watercress and iceberg lettuce are a big YES. Croutons if you must, but masa corn (tortilla) chips please! This salad is quirky and delicious.

Preheat the oven to 160°C (320°F).

Line a large baking tray with baking paper.

To make the dressing, place the sour cream, feta, lime zest and juice, egg yolks and garlic in a food processor and blend to combine. Gradually add the oil, blending to combine. Season with salt. Strain through a fine-mesh sieve and refrigerate.

To make the kale chips, place the kale in a medium bowl, drizzle with oil and toss to coat. Lightly season with salt. Spread the kale out onto the prepared tray and bake in the oven for 10–15 minutes, until crisp.

Meanwhile, heat a barbecue chargrill or overhead grill (broiler) to high. Lightly brush the corn with oil and grill, turning occasionally, until charred all over. Bake in the oven for 10 minutes, or until tender.

Thin the dressing down to a coating consistency, adding a little lime juice or water as necessary.

Pour a little of the dressing into a medium bowl, add the lettuce and toss to coat.

To assemble, arrange the lettuce on a serving platter. Toss the watercress, mixed leaves, radish, jicama, tomato and parsley all separately in the dressing, adding a little more as required and arrange on top of the lettuce. Lastly, lightly dress the avocado and arrange on top. Scatter with kale and corn chips and the salted ricotta over the top. Serve immediately.

NECTARINE & SWEET POTATO SALAD WITH GOAT'S CHEESE & REPOSADO VINAIGRETTE

~~~~~~~~~~

+ 125 ml (4 fl oz/½ cup) Latin vinaigrette, using tequila (page 36)
+ 200 g (7 oz) firm, mature Spanish-style goat's cheese, shaved

PICKLED NECTARINES

+ 3 nectarines, thinly sliced
+ Mexican pickle solution (see page 53)

SWEET POTATO CHIPS

+ 1 large sweet potato
+ rice bran oil for deep-frying
+ sea salt

SALAD

+ a combination of the following varied and textured leaves below (6 large handfuls in total):
+ dandelion
+ radicchio, witlof (Belgian endive/chicory)
+ purslane, red vein sorrel
+ flat-leaf parsley
+ green and red oak lettuce
+ rocket (arugula), baby gem lettuce
+ upland cress or watercress
+ frisée lettuce hearts
+ green and red elk lettuce, miner's lettuce
+ lamb's lettuce (mâche/corn salad)

SERVES 4

Simple salads rely on the best seasonal ingredients and this recipe is a good case in point. Selecting the appropriate ingredients that work as a whole will please every time, so consider texture and the bitter/sweet/savoury balance. The choice of lettuce is important, as a sharp dressing will destroy delicate leaves. Wild, bitter leaves full of flavour and texture will stand up beautifully! This salad is great with any salty complex cheese like Valdeón, Monte Enebro, Manchego or full-flavoured goat's cheeses like Ibores. I particularly like this salad with a grilled Saint-Marcellin - it's not very Latin but it's delicious all the same.

To prepare the pickled nectarines, place the sliced nectarines in a medium bowl and pour over the cooled pickling solution. Cover and set aside to pickle for 1 hour.

To prepare the sweet potato chips, peel and thinly slice the sweet potato using a mandoline.

Half-fill a large heavy-based saucepan with rice bran oil and heat it over medium–low heat to 140°C (275°F).

Fry the sweet potato in batches, for 2–3 minutes, until crisp. Remove using a slotted spoon and transfer to paper towel to drain.

Increase the heat of the oil to 180°C (350°F).

Refry the chips in batches for 1 minute, or until golden brown. Drain again on paper towel. Season with salt.

Drain the pickled nectarines.

Place the leaves in a medium bowl and lightly dress. Arrange the leaves, nectarines, cheese shavings and sweet potato chips in layers in a rustic-looking salad bowl. Drizzle with a little more dressing and serve.

SIKIL PAK WITH ASPARAGUS, GOAT'S FETA, ORANGE & AVOCADO

SIKIL PAK

+ 300 g (10½ oz/2 cups) pepitas (pumpkin seeds)
+ 60 ml (2 fl oz/¼ cup) extra-virgin olive oil
+ 4 eschalots, finely chopped
+ 4 garlic cloves, finely chopped
+ 1 jalapeño, finely chopped
+ 1 large handful of flat-leaf parsley
+ 1 large handful of coriander (cilantro) leaves
+ juice of 2 limes
+ finely grated zest of ½ orange

+ 50 ml (1¾ fl oz) tahini
+ ½ teaspoon smoked paprika
+ 125 ml (4 fl oz/½ cup) boiling water
+ sea salt to taste

SALAD

+ sea salt to taste
+ 500 g (1 lb 2 oz) (about 4 bunches) fresh green or white asparagus, woody stalks trimmed
+ Mexican pickle solution (see page 53)
+ 4 oranges, segmented

+ 1 red onion, thinly sliced
+ 1 jalapeño, thinly sliced
+ 2 avocados, sliced
+ 155 g (5½ oz/1¼ cups) pitted black olives, roughly chopped
+ 200 g (7 oz) goat's feta, crumbled
+ 30 g (1 oz/¼ cup) sunflower seeds, toasted
+ 2 large handfuls of purslane or watercress leaves

SERVES 4–6

For the salad, bring a large saucepan of water to the boil. Season with salt. Blanch the asparagus for 20 seconds, or until just tender. Drain and refresh in a bowl of iced water. Drain.

Place the asparagus in a bowl, pour over the pickling solution, cover and refrigerate for 1 hour.

Preheat the oven to 140°C (275°F).

Meanwhile to make the sikil pak, spread the pepitas out on a large baking tray and bake for 10–15 minutes, until lightly toasted.

Heat 1 tablespoon of the olive oil in a small frying pan over low heat. Cook the eschalot, garlic and jalapeño until softened. Transfer to a food processor or blender. Add the pepitas, parsley, coriander, lime juice, remaining oil and orange zest and blend with the tahini and smoked paprika, gradually adding the boiling water as required to make a smooth paste. Season with salt. Transfer to a bowl and set aside. Pass the sikil pak through a fine-mesh sieve, if desired, to create a very fine silky relish. (This step is not necessary but it's how we do it at the restaurant.)

To serve, drain the asparagus. Spread a large spoonful of sikil pak onto the serving plates. Arrange the asparagus, orange segments, red onion, jalapeño, avocado, olives, feta, sunflower seeds and leaves over the top.

PAUL'S TIP Sikil pak can be served simply with corn (tortilla) chips and spears of vinaigrette-tossed asparagus.

This is more beach food than street food and is from the Yucatán Peninsula, where colourful salads of pickled vegetables are common. Sikil pak is best described as a type of Mexican hummus, an ancient Mayan relish from Campeche. Made from toasted pepitas (pumpkin seeds), this sweet nutty relish is much more delicate and aromatic than its Mediterranean cousin. It's perfect with simply cooked or raw pickled vegetables like broccoli, asparagus and breakfast radishes. Serve alongside grilled fish or as an appetiser.

HEIRLOOM TOMATO ESCABECHE WITH FINGER LIME GOAT'S CREMA

~~~~~~~~~~~~

+ 1 kg (2 lb 3 oz) mixed heirloom tomatoes, cored and cut decoratively
+ Mexican pickle solution (see page 53)
+ 2 jicamas (see Glossary)
+ 200 g (7 oz) (about 1 bunch) black radishes
+ 125 ml (4 fl oz oz/1/2 cup) Pasilla chilli relish (page 25)
+ vinegar, honey and salt to season relish, if desired
+ 50 ml (1 3/4 fl oz) fruity olive oil
+ 2 hass avocados, sliced
+ 2-3 jalapeños, thinly sliced, or to taste
+ 1 large handful of micro coriander (cilantro)
+ 1 large handful of apple mint
+ blue corn (tortilla) chips, smashed, to serve

FINGER LIME GOAT'S CREMA

+ 250 g (9 oz/1 cup) goat's curd
+ 125 g (4 1/2 oz/1/2 cup) sour cream
+ 100 g (3 1/2 oz) finger lime flesh (see Glossary) or finely grated zest and juice of 2 limes
+ 1 large handful of oregano leaves, roughly chopped
+ 1 garlic clove, finely grated
+ pinch of ground cumin
+ sea salt to taste

SERVES 6

Avocados are as diverse as tomatoes, and also originated in Latin America. The word tomato comes from the Aztec word 'xitomatl' meaning 'small plump thing with a navel'. There are over 70 varieties of avocados that we know about. This salad is a sort of deconstructed guacamole using hass avocados and sweet marinated heirloom tomatoes which, thanks to farmers' markets, are becoming increasingly available. The goat's crema adds some comfort to the smoky pasilla chilli relish and is perfectly paired with the zingy tomato escabeche. Sprinkle with smashed corn (tortilla) chips and you have a Mexican panzanella. This makes a perfect summer salad.

Place the cut tomatoes on a tray, dress generously with the Mexican pickle solution, cover and refrigerate for at least 2 hours.

To prepare the finger lime and goat's crema, combine the goat's curd, sour cream, finger lime, oregano, garlic and cumin in a bowl and mix to a smooth sauce. Season with salt. Refrigerate until required.

Slice the jicama and radishes, using a mandoline or a very sharp knife, into thin sheets. Then cut the jicama into matchsticks.

Mix the pasilla chilli relish with a little warm water, to make it a drizzling consistency. Adjust the seasoning with a little vinegar, honey and salt, if required.

Remove the tomatoes from the pickling solution and drain on paper towel. Place the tomatoes in a medium bowl. Drizzle with oil and toss to coat.

To assemble, spoon a very generous amount of crema onto each serving plate spread into a neat round. Arrange the tomatoes on the crema and spoon the pasilla relish over and around the tomatoes. Arrange the jicama, radish, avocado, jalapeño and herbs over the top. Sprinkle with the smashed corn chips.

PADRÓN PEPPERS WITH SESAME PIPIAN

~~~~~~~~~~~

+ 30 g (1 oz/¼ cup) pepitas (pumpkin seeds)
+ 30 g (1 oz/¼ cup) sunflower seeds
+ 2 tablespoons sesame seeds
+ 2 tablespoons olive oil
+ 16 padrón peppers (see Glossary)
+ pinch of sea salt
+ pinch of smoked paprika
+ 200 ml (7 fl oz) Sesame pipian (page 31)
+ 1 small handful of mint leaves, roughly chopped
+ lime wedges to serve

FRIED GARLIC CHIPS

+ 6 garlic cloves
+ vegetable oil for frying

SERVES 4

Padrón peppers look like diminutive capsicums (bell peppers) and are sold fried or grilled in snack bars throughout Spain. Although they share the same herbaceous flavours as capsicums, padróns are more intense, thinner-skinned and sweeter. Roughly 10 per cent of padróns are overwhelmingly hot, making them perfect for a game of chilli roulette! The peppers, with their earthy nutty sauce, are a revelation hot or cold. Be careful, though, as they can be very hot despite the cooling sauce. Serve with all meats and robust seafood.

Combine the pepitas and sunflower and sesame seeds in a small dry frying pan and cook over medium–low heat for 3–4 minutes, until lightly toasted. Transfer to a small bowl and set aside.

To make the fried garlic chips, peel and thinly slice the garlic cloves and place in a frying pan. Cover with vegetable oil and gently heat over medium–low heat until the oil is hot and begins to bubble around the garlic. Fry, turning frequently, for 30 seconds, or until golden. Remove using a slotted spoon and set aside to drain on paper towel.

To cook the padrón peppers, preheat a large frying pan over high heat until very hot. Pour in the olive oil, add the peppers and stir-fry for 1 minute. Season with salt and smoked paprika and stir-fry for a further minute, until they begin to collapse and slightly char. Add the sesame pipian and heat until simmering, tossing to coat. Add a dash of water to thin down the sauce to a coating consistency.

Transfer the sauce-coated peppers to a serving dish and sprinkle with the toasted seed mixture, mint and fried garlic chips. Serve with lime wedges and toothpicks.

PAUL'S TIP If sesame pipian seems like a daunting sauce to make, a quick alternative is a blend of tahini and yoghurt with garlic, coriander (cilantro) leaves, lime juice, hot sauce and seasoning to taste.

CHORIZO POTATOES

~~~~~~~~~~~~~~~

+ 500 g (1 lb 2 oz) potatoes, such as russet, kipfler (fingerling), desiree or blue chipper
+ 2 rosemary sprigs plus extra to garnish
+ sea salt
+ oil for shallow-frying
+ 2 garlic cloves, thinly sliced
+ 50 g (1¾ oz) unsalted butter, melted
+ 2 tablespoons finely chopped oregano leaves

CHORIZO-FLAVOURED MINCED (GROUND) PORK

+ 2 tablespoons olive oil
+ 4 garlic cloves, finely chopped
+ 200 g (7 oz) coarsely minced (ground) pork
+ 1 tablespoon smoked paprika
+ 2 teaspoons ground cumin
+ ¼ teaspoon chilli powder
+ sea salt to taste

SERVES 4

I love the way Mexicans serve their chorizo loosely minced (ground). It makes a great addition to a pan of roasting potatoes or vegetables like mushrooms or green beans. I have recreated it here by using pork mince and adding that strong chorizo flavour with spices and caramelised onions. Pork or lamb mince would also work well in this recipe.

Preheat the oven to 200°C (400°F).

Peel and cut the potatoes into bite-sized pieces. Place the potatoes and rosemary in a large saucepan and cover with cold water. Season with salt. Bring to the boil and, once boiling, cook for a further 5–7 minutes, until tender. If they crack don't be concerned – it helps the crunchy frying process. Drain and scatter the potatoes onto a clean tea towel (dish towel) and set aside to dry out.

Pour enough oil for shallow-frying in a medium frying pan and heat over medium–high heat. Fry the potatoes, stirring occasionally, for 3–4 minutes, until they begin to colour all over.

Using a slotted spoon, transfer the potatoes to a baking tray, allowing the excess oil to drain as you go. Add the garlic and butter to the tray and toss to coat. Place in the oven and roast for 10 minutes, or until crisp and golden.

Meanwhile to prepare the chorizo-flavoured mince, heat the oil in a medium frying pan over low heat. Cook the garlic until softened. Increase the heat to medium, add the mince and spices and cook, stirring frequently, for 5 minutes or until browned. Season with salt.

Add the cooked chorizo mince to the roasted potatoes and garlic and toss to combine. Sprinkle with oregano and rosemary and transfer to a serving plate.

CRUSHED PURPLE CONGOES

~~~~~~~~~~

+ 500 g (1 lb 2 oz) congo or other purple-skinned potatoes
+ 6 garlic cloves, thinly sliced
+ sea salt
+ 200 ml (7 fl oz) extra-virgin olive oil
+ 155 g (5½ oz/1¼ cups) pitted black olives, finely chopped
+ 2 large handfuls of oregano leaves, roughly chopped
+ 50 g (1¾ oz) finely chopped drained chipotle in adobo (see Glossary) or 2 jalapeños
+ 100 g (3½ oz) salted ricotta, finely chopped

SERVES 4

Purple potatoes are available from gourmet grocers. They are not just attractive but have a lovely flavour too. I would serve these with fish before meat and make sure to use a nice fruity olive oil.

Peel and quarter the potatoes and cut them into bite-sized pieces. Place the potatoes and garlic in a large saucepan and cover with cold water. Season with salt. Bring to the boil and, once boiling, cook for a further 5–7 minutes, until tender. Drain and leave in the pan to dry out over low heat.

Crush the potatoes with a fork, gradually adding the olive oil to moisten.

Add the olives, oregano and chilli and mix to combine.

Transfer to a serving dish and sprinkle with the ricotta.

GREEN RICE WITH BLACK CABBAGE

~~~~~~~~~~~~~~~

+ 200 g (7 oz/1 cup) long-grain white rice
+ 75 g (2¾ oz) unsalted butter
+ 2 bunches of spring onions (scallions), finely chopped
+ 375 ml (12½ fl oz/1½ cups) chicken stock
+ 50 g (1¾ oz) chipotle in adobo sauce (see Glossary)
+ sea salt to taste

+ 150 ml (5 fl oz) Mexican salsa verde (page 20)
+ 100 g (3½ oz) (about ½ bunch) Tuscan cabbage or kale, stripped from the stem, blanched and roughly chopped
+ 90 g (3 oz/½ cup) broad (fava) beans, blanched and skinned
+ 100 g (3½ oz) salted ricotta, roughly chopped

SERVES 4

Green rice is a popular celebration dish in Mexico. I've added some Tuscan cabbage as well as the obligatory salsa verde, but you can add any green vegetable. This is a nice partner with all foods and provides a refreshing tasty rice dish to serve with the strong flavours in Mexican food.

Place the rice in a fine-mesh sieve and rinse under cold running water, until the water runs clear. Drain.

Melt 50 g (1¾ oz) of the butter in a medium saucepan over low heat. Cook the spring onions for 2 minutes, or until softened. Add the chicken stock and chipotle and bring to the boil for 1 minute. Process using a hand-held blender.

Add the rice and bring to the boil. Reduce the heat to the lowest setting, cover, and cook for 12 minutes. Remove from the heat and set aside, with the lid on, for 5–10 minutes to finish cooking.

Fluff the rice with a fork. Add the remaining butter and stir to combine. Season with salt.

Heat the salsa verde in a large saucepan over low heat. Add the cabbage, broad beans and a little water and heat through, stirring to combine. Add the rice and mix until just combined. Do not overmix or the rice will become mushy.

Serve sprinkled with the salted ricotta.

ZUCCHINI FLOWERS VERACRUZ-STYLE

~~~~~~~~~~~~~~~

+ 12 baby zucchini (courgettes) with flowers attached
+ 80 ml (2½ fl oz/⅓ cup) extra-virgin olive oil
+ 4 eschalots, finely chopped
+ 2 jalapeños, finely chopped
+ 6 garlic cloves, thinly sliced
+ 2 large handfuls of oregano leaves, roughly chopped
+ finely grated zest and juice of 2 oranges
+ 200 ml (7 fl oz) Veracruz sauce (page 41)

SALAD

+ 2 large handfuls of yellow frisée lettuce hearts
+ 4 breakfast radishes, thinly sliced
+ 1 small handful of tarragon leaves
+ extra-virgin olive oil for drizzling

SERVES 4

Traditionally a sauce served with seafood, here Veracruz sauce is used to braise baby zucchini (courgettes) and their flowers. This rich and creamy tomato-based sauce, with flavours of the Mediterranean - capers, olives and herbs - makes a lovely accompaniment to fish and seafood.

Slice the baby zucchini into 1 cm (½ in) rounds and cut the flowers into quarters lengthways.

Heat the oil in a large frying pan over medium–low heat. Cook the eschalot, jalapeño, garlic and oregano until softened.

Add the sliced zucchini and flowers to the pan and cook for 1 minute.

Add the orange zest and juice and simmer until reduced to a syrup. Add the Veracruz sauce and cook for 2–3 minutes, until the zucchini is tender.

Transfer to a large serving plate. Combine the salad ingredients in a medium bowl, drizzle with a little olive oil and toss to dress. Scatter the salad around the zucchini mixture to serve.

CHARRED BROCCOLI WITH SALSA MEXICANA

~~~~~~~~~~

+ sea salt
+ 1 kg (2 lb 3 oz) (about 2 medium heads) broccoli
+ olive oil for drizzling
+ 500 g (1 lb 2 oz/2 cups) Salsa mexicana (page 36)
+ 250 g (9 oz) pecorino or sharp Monterey Jack, shaved
+ 1 large handful of coriander (cilantro) leaves, roughly chopped
+ 1 large handful of mint leaves, roughly chopped
+ 200 g (7 oz/1¼ cups) macadamia nuts, toasted and roughly chopped
+ 70 g (2½ oz/½ cup) pepitas (pumpkin seeds), toasted
+ 1 red onion, thinly sliced

SERVES 4-6

Charred broccoli sounds odd but broccoli is a vegetable that works well with other flavours, and the grilling adds smokiness and a more savoury character. It's also good used as a mop for salsa and sauces.

Bring a large saucepan of water to the boil and season with salt.

Trim and discard 1 cm (½ in) from the broccoli base and cut the heads in half lengthways. Par-boil for 2 minutes. Drain.

Preheat a barbecue chargrill to high.

Drizzle the broccoli with olive oil and rub to coat. Grill, turning occasionally, for 5 minutes, or until lightly charred all over. Set aside to cool slightly.

Cut the broccoli into bite-sized pieces and place in a bowl. Add the salsa, cheese, coriander and mint and toss to combine.

Serve sprinkled with the macadamia nuts, pepitas and onion.

PAUL'S TIP Cut charred broccoli into small dipping pieces and serve with guacamole and corn (tortilla) chips as well, if you like.

WILD MUSHROOMS IN MEXICAN SALSA VERDE

~~~~~~~~~~~~~~~~~

+ 80 ml (2$^{1}/_{2}$ fl oz/$^{1}/_{3}$ cup) olive oil
+ 500 g (1 lb 2 oz) pine or slippery jack mushrooms
+ 300 ml (10 fl oz) Mexican salsa verde (page 20)
+ juice of 1 lime
+ sea salt to taste
+ 150 g (5$^{1}/_{2}$ oz/1 cup) pistachio nuts, toasted and roughly chopped
+ 100 g (3$^{1}/_{2}$ oz) salted ricotta, finely chopped

SERVES 4

Mexico has a great variety of wild mushrooms and there are many dishes with mushrooms to be found around the country. Mushrooms are delicious simply sautéed with poblano chillies, and mole and adobo sauce are also good partners - perfect for a vegetarian meal. Here I've used the versatile salsa verde and added finely chopped pistachio nuts for extra colour and crunch.

Heat the oil in a large frying pan over medium-low heat. Cook the mushrooms for 2-3 minutes, until just tender.

Add the salsa verde, lime juice and a little water to make a pesto-like consistency and heat through, tossing to coat. Season with salt.

Serve sprinkled with the pistachio nuts and salted ricotta.

PEA & FARRO SALAD

~~~~~~~~~~~~~~

+ sea salt to taste
+ 500 g (1 lb 2 oz/2½ cups) farro, rinsed (see Glossary)
+ 465 g (1 lb/3 cups) frozen or fresh peas
+ 2 celery stalks
+ ½ red onion
+ 2 jalapeños, seeded and finely chopped
+ 2 large handfuls of mint leaves, roughly chopped
+ 1 large handful of oregano leaves, roughly chopped
+ 200 ml (7 fl oz) Latin vinaigrette (page 36)
+ sea salt and freshly ground black pepper to taste
+ 100 g (3½ oz) hard goat's cheese, crumbled or grated

SERVES 6

Farro is a very healthy grain and just as versatile as rice. Be patient as it takes a while to cook well. A pinch of bicarbonate of soda (baking soda) helps to soften the grains. This salad is great served with white meat and seafood.

Bring a large saucepan of water to the boil. Season with salt. Cook the farro for 18–20 minutes, until tender. Drain and rinse. Set aside.

Blanch the peas in a saucepan of boiling salted water. Drain. Refresh in a bowl of iced water.

Finely chop the celery and onion.

Combine the farro, peas, celery, onion, jalapeño and herbs in a large bowl. Add the dressing and toss to combine. Season with salt and pepper.

Transfer to a large serving bowl and top with the grated goat's cheese.

TABLE-SIDE GUACAMOLE WITH SUPER GRAINS

~~~~~~~~~~~~~~~

+ 200 g (7 oz) (about 1 bunch) broccolini tops, roughly chopped
+ 200 g (7 oz) (about 1 medium) baby (pattypan) squash, diced
+ 70 g (2¹/2 oz/¹/2 cup) pepitas (pumpkin seeds)
+ 60 g (2 oz/¹/2 cup) sunflower seeds
+ 55 g (2 oz) chia seeds
+ 1 kg (2 lb 3 oz) (about 4-5) ripe hass avocados
+ 150 g (5¹/2 oz) cherry tomatoes, quartered
+ ¹/2 red onion, finely chopped
+ 2 jalapeños, thinly sliced
+ 150 g (5¹/2 oz/¹/2 cup) diced jicama (see Glossary)
+ 2 large handfuls of coriander (cilantro) leaves, roughly chopped
+ 90 g (3 oz) puffed farro (see Glossary)
+ juice of 6 limes, or to taste
+ 170 ml (5¹/2 fl oz/²/3 cup) avocado oil
+ ¹/2 teaspoon ground cumin
+ ¹/2 teaspoon ground allspice
+ 1 teaspoon sea salt
+ 200 g (7 oz) salted ricotta, finely chopped
+ 150 g (5¹/2 oz/1 cup) pistachio nuts, roughly chopped
+ micro coriander (cilantro) leaves to serve

SERVES 6-8

People have strong feelings about guacamole and can get very sensitive if you alter the recipe. The purist may argue about the logic of creating another fancy version but, for me, it's about making something old and familiar new and interesting, without losing its charm. By adding some healthy Aztec grains and nutritious vegetables I have created a more fulfilling and satisfying side dish. In good restaurants they make guacamole in front of the guests. Serve with Taro chips (page 39) or corn (tortilla) chips.

Bring a medium saucepan of water to the boil. Season with salt.

Blanch the broccolini and squash for 30 seconds, or until just tender. Drain and refresh in a bowl of iced water. Drain.

Combine the pepitas and sunflower and chia seeds in a small dry frying pan and cook over medium–low heat for 2–3 minutes, until lightly toasted.

Cut the avocados in half lengthways, remove the stone and scoop out the flesh using a large spoon. Arrange the avocado in an attractive mixing bowl.

Transfer the broccolini, squash, tomato, onion, jalapeño, jicama and puffed farro into separate colourful bowls, garnished with some of the seed mix or coriander, and present these on the table in front of your guests.

At the table, begin to crush the avocados with a large fork, adding the lime juice and avocado oil as required to moisten. Season with the cumin, allspice and salt and invite your guests to taste and check the seasoning.

Serve the guacamole in individual bowls. Sprinkle with a few toasted seeds, ricotta, pistachio nuts and micro coriander. Drizzle with more avocado oil and serve with taro and/or corn (tortilla) chips, if desired.

PAUL'S TIP Create your own superfood seed mix. Make a large batch with your favourites, then bake, season and store in an airtight container. They are great for sprinkling over salads or as a snack.

PUMPKIN MOLE WITH PISTACHIO SALSA PICANTE

~~~~~~~~~~~~~~~~~~~~~~

+ goat's crema (see page 120) to taste
+ micro coriander (cilantro) to garnish

PUMPKIN MOLE

+ 500 g (1 lb 2 oz) butternut pumpkin (squash), peeled and cut into 3 cm (1¼ in) cubes
+ 100 ml (3½ fl oz) agave syrup (see Glossary) or honey
+ 80 ml (2½ fl oz/⅓ cup) plus 1½ tablespoons freshly squeezed lime juice
+ 70 ml (2¼ fl oz) olive oil
+ 2 teaspoons ground cumin
+ 1 teaspoon smoked paprika
+ 1 teaspoon ground cinnamon
+ ½ teaspoon ground allspice
+ sea salt to taste
+ 65 g (2¼ oz/¼ cup) tahini
+ 1 red onion, finely chopped
+ 1 handful of coriander (cilantro) leaves, chopped
+ 1 jalapeño, finely chopped
+ habanero hot sauce to taste

PISTACHIO SALSA PICANTE

+ 100 g (3½ oz/⅔ cup) pistachio nuts
+ 80 ml (2½ fl oz/⅓ cup) olive oil
+ ½ teaspoon ground cumin
+ sea salt to taste
+ ¼ jicama, finely diced (see Glossary)
+ ½ small red onion, finely diced
+ 1-2 jalapeños, finely chopped
+ 1 small handful of oregano leaves, finely chopped
+ 1 small handful of tarragon leaves, finely chopped
+ 80 ml (2½ fl oz/⅓ cup) freshly squeezed lime juice
+ 2 teaspoons pistachio paste (see Glossary)
+ 1 garlic clove, finely grated
+ habanero hot sauce to taste

SERVES 4-6

Avocados are seasonal and at certain times of the year they skyrocket in price. So this recipe thinks outside the box of the traditional approach to guacamole, celebrating the eternally popular pumpkin (winter squash). Thanks to a growing interest in farmers' markets there are more heirloom varieties popping up to choose from. Butternuts are a favourite of mine because of their flavour and open, moist texture. They make a perfect filling for enchiladas or quesadillas too. The pistachio salsa adds a tart element and helps cut through the sweetness of the pumpkin. Serve with blue corn (tortilla) chips.

Preheat the oven to 190°C (375°F).

To prepare the pistachio salsa, spread the pistachio nuts on a baking tray, drizzle with a little of the oil and sprinkle with the cumin and salt. Roast for 5 minutes, or until lightly toasted. Allow to cool slightly then roughly smash using a mortar and pestle.

Combine the toasted pistachio nuts with the jicama, onion, jalapeño, oregano and tarragon in a small bowl. In a separate bowl, whisk the remaining oil, lime juice, pistachio paste and garlic together. Pour over the pistachio mixture and stir to combine. Season with habanero sauce and salt. Set aside.

To prepare the pumpkin mole, place the pumpkin in a large bowl. Add the honey, the 80 ml (2½ fl oz/⅓ cup) lime juice, 1½ tablespoons of the oil, the spices and salt and toss to combine. Transfer to a baking tray and cover with aluminium foil. Bake for 30-40 minutes, until tender.

Transfer half of the pumpkin to a medium bowl and coarsely mash. Place the remaining pumpkin and its marinade in a blender or food processor and purée.

Combine the 2 pumpkin mixtures, add the tahini, the second measure of lime juice and the remaining oil and mix well. Add the onion, coriander and jalapeño and stir to combine. Season with habanero sauce and salt. Set aside.

To serve, transfer the pumpkin mole into a serving dish, top with the pistachio salsa and and serve with goat's crema. Sprinkle with micro coriander to garnish. Serve with corn chips, if desired.

PAUL'S TIPS You can simply boil the pumpkin in salted water until soft. Drain and mash with a fork. Season with honey, lime juice and spices and top with your favourite salsa. Or simply marinate, roast, crush and blend pumpkin with lime juice, chilli and coriander (cilantro) leaves.

08

DESSERTS

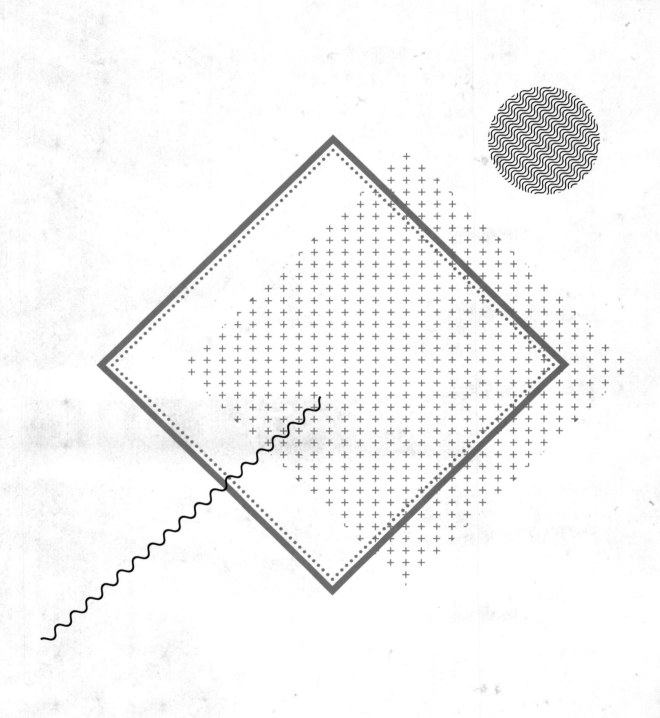

A myriad of sweet
treats exist in Mexico, often
created for religious and patriotic
celebrations. Marvelling at the ancient
grandeur of the dulcerias in Mexico City, it
reminded me of Paris with its pâtisseries.

There's less pastry but no less effort in drawing flavour from sour fruit, caramel, chocolate, exotic spices, nuts and goat's and coconut milk. Chocolate is treated with respect, bespokely ground and flavoured to your taste. Tequila and chocolate dance on your palate while cazuelas and capirotada remind us who first discovered the pleasures of sugar and spice. Dulce de leche reigns supreme until you try cajeta, a goat's milk version that will silence any rowdy table! These sweet treats will hopefully lure you back into the kitchen.

SESAME TUILLES

~~~~~~~~~~~~~~~~

+ 25 g (1 oz) butter
+ 80 g (2¾ oz/⅓ cup) caster (superfine) sugar
+ 1½ tablespoons liquid glucose
+ 1½ tablespoons milk
+ 155 g (5½ oz/1 cup) sesame seeds
+ 50 g (1¾ oz/⅓ cup) poppy seeds

MAKES 8-10

These crunchy, sugary tuilles can be served either whole, curved, flat or broken into shards to accompany creamy desserts for a textural difference.

Preheat the oven to 180°C (350°F).

Lightly grease and line 2 large baking trays with baking paper.

Combine the butter, sugar, glucose and milk in a small saucepan and bring to the boil over medium heat. Add the sesame and poppy seeds and stir to combine. Remove from the heat and allow to cool.

Once cooled, whisk together to combine. Roll the mixture into chestnut-sized balls and arrange 10 cm (4 in) apart on the prepared trays. Press to flatten slightly.

Bake for 10 minutes, or until golden brown. Remove from the oven and allow to cool for 1 minute, or until cool enough to handle but still warm enough to be pliable. Carefully remove with a palette knife and roll over the handle of a wooden spoon to create a curved shape, or leave flat and allow to cool.

Store in an airtight container for up to 1 week.

NUT PRALINE

~~~~~~~~~

+ 125 g (4$^{1/2}$ oz) hazelnuts, pistachio nuts or blanched almonds
+ 45 g (1$^{1/2}$ oz/$^{1/2}$ cup) flaked almonds
+ 140 g (5 oz/$^{2/3}$ cup) sugar
+ 2$^{1/2}$ tablespoons liquid glucose

MAKES 300 G (10$^{1/2}$ OZ/1$^{1/2}$ CUPS)

Any nuts can be used to make this praline. It adds a sweet, welcome crunch to many desserts. Take care when working with toffee as it gets very hot! Resist the temptation to taste-test before it has set and cooled.

Preheat the oven to 180°C (350°F).

Spread the hazelnuts and the flaked almonds over separate trays. Roast the hazelnuts for 5–8 minutes and the flaked almonds for 3–5 minutes, until golden.

Place the hazelnuts in a clean tea towel (dish towel) and rub to remove the skins.

Lightly grease a small baking tray with cooking spray.

Place the sugar and glucose in a medium heavy-based saucepan. Gently heat over low heat until the sugar begins to caramelise. Swirl the sugar mixture to help create an even caramel. Add the nuts, stirring constantly, to combine.

Pour the nutty caramel onto the greased tray and allow to cool.

Once cool, crush the praline into rough pieces with a rolling pin. Transfer to a food processor and coarsely blend.

Store in an airtight container in the freezer for up to 3 months.

PAUL'S TIP By blending the praline finely to a powder, then passing it through a sieve, you can create delicate nutty-flavoured wafers. Simply use a stencil, such as a cookie cutter, in your desired shape and place it on a lightly greased tray or silicone baking mat. Sprinkle the dust over the stencil and bake until the praline dust becomes liquid. Allow to cool slightly, then cut out once more with the cookie cutter for a more precise finish. Store in an airtight container in the freezer for up to 3 months.

DULCE DE LECHE ICE CREAM

~~~~~~~~~~~~~

+ 12 large egg yolks
+ 40 g (1½ oz) caster (superfine) sugar
+ 310 ml (10½ fl oz/1¼ cups) pouring (single/light) cream
+ 250 ml (8½ fl oz/1 cup) full-cream (whole) milk
+ 2 vanilla beans, split and seeds scraped
+ 150 g (5½ oz) dulce de leche

> MAKES APPROXIMATELY
> 1 LITRE (34 FL OZ/4 CUPS)

Dulce de leche is the classic caramel sauce of Latin cooking. It's incredibly popular and used in a range of recipes from cookies and cakes to a sauce or a condiment to spread on toast! Here is a simple dulce de leche ice cream recipe that I guarantee you will want in your freezer.

Combine the egg yolks and sugar in the bowl of an electric mixer fitted with a whisk attachment. Whisk until pale and creamy.

Combine the cream, milk and vanilla beans and seeds in a medium saucepan. Set over low heat and allow to simmer gently for 5 minutes. Add the dulce de leche and stir to combine.

Gradually pour the hot cream mixture into the egg yolk mixture, stirring continuously to combine.

Transfer to a clean saucepan and warm gently over low heat, stirring continuously, until the mixture thickens enough to coat the back of a spoon, or the temperature reaches 85°C (185°F) on a sugar thermometer.

Pour the custard into a stainless steel bowl and set it over a larger bowl of iced water, stirring, to chill rapidly. Refrigerate for 30 minutes.

Once chilled, remove the vanilla beans, pour the dulce de leche custard into an ice cream machine and churn as per the manufacturer's instructions.

Transfer to an airtight container and freeze for at least 4 hours, or until firm, before use. Store in an airtight container in the freezer for up to 6 months.

PAUL'S TIP Here's the recipe for a simple dulce de leche-style caramel. Pierce the top of a tin of condensed milk. Place the tin in a small saucepan and pour in enough water to come three-quarters of the way up the side of the tin. Simmer over low heat, topping up the water occasionally, for 3 hours. After 3 hours, remove the tin from the water and set aside to cool slightly. Open the tin and pour into a suitable container. The result is caramelised milk jam.

SWEETCORN ICE CREAM

〰〰〰〰〰〰〰

+ 12 large egg yolks
+ 55 g (2 oz/¼ cup) caster (superfine) sugar
+ 4 corn cobs, kernels removed and husks retained
+ 310 ml (10½ fl oz/1¼ cups) pouring (single/light) cream
+ 250 ml (8½ fl oz/1 cup) full-cream (whole) milk
+ 50 ml (1¾ fl oz) liquid glucose
+ 2 teaspoons vanilla extract
+ pinch of sea salt
+ 1 vanilla bean, split and seeds scraped

MAKES APPROXIMATELY
1 LITRE (34 FL OZ/4 CUPS)

The natural sweetness of corn is delicate and lovely. Here it makes a delicious ice cream that you could serve on its own or with stewed fruits. It goes very well with Rhubarb & corn cobbler (page 287).

Combine the egg yolks and sugar in the bowl of an electric mixer fitted with a whisk attachment. Whisk until pale and creamy.

Combine the corn kernels and husks with the cream, milk, glucose, vanilla extract, salt and vanilla bean and seeds in a medium saucepan. Set over low heat and allow to simmer gently for 10 minutes.

Remove the husks and vanilla bean. Transfer the mixture to a food processor or blender and process until smooth.

Strain through a fine-mesh sieve.

Gradually pour the hot corn liquid into the egg yolk mixture, stirring continuously to combine.

Transfer to a clean saucepan and gently warm over low heat, stirring continuously, until the mixture thickens enough to coat the back of a spoon, or the temperature reaches 85°C (185°F) on a sugar thermometer.

Pour the custard into a stainless steel bowl and set it over a larger bowl of iced water, stirring, to chill rapidly. Refrigerate for 30 minutes.

Once chilled, pour the corn custard into an ice cream machine and churn as per the manufacturer's instructions.

Transfer to an airtight container and freeze for at least 4 hours, or until firm, before use. Store in an airtight container in the freezer for up to 6 months.

CHOCOLATE SORBET

~~~~~~~~~~~~~~~

+ 500 ml (17 fl oz/2 cups) Sorbet syrup (page 56)
+ 250 ml (8 1/2 fl oz/1 cup) full-cream (whole) milk
+ 100 g (3 1/2 oz) best-quality unsweetened (Dutch) cocoa powder
+ 75 g (2 3/4 oz) best-quality bitter dark chocolate, minimum 50% cocoa solids

MAKES APPROXIMATELY
1 LITRE (34 FL OZ/4 CUPS)

A rich, smooth, double chocolate sorbet that can stand alone or pair with the Chocolate, cherry & chilli tart (page 272) as a decadent dessert.

Combine the sorbet syrup, milk, cocoa and chocolate in a medium heavy-based saucepan. Set over medium–low heat and bring to the boil, stirring occasionally, until the sugar dissolves and the chocolate melts. Remove from the heat and set aside to cool. Refrigerate to chill for at least 3 hours or until firm.

Once chilled, pour the chocolate mixture into an ice cream machine and churn as per the manufacturer's instructions.

Transfer to an airtight container and freeze for at least 4 hours, or until firm, before use. Store in an airtight container in the freezer for up to 6 months.

YOGHURT SORBET

~~~~~~~~~~~~~~~

+ 590 g (1 lb 5 oz/2 1/3 cups) Greek-style yoghurt
+ 500 ml (17 fl oz/2 cups) Sorbet syrup (page 56)
+ 60 ml (2 fl oz/1/4 cup) freshly squeezed lemon juice
+ 1/2 vanilla bean, split and seeds scraped

MAKES APPROXIMATELY
1 LITRE (34 FL OZ/4 CUPS)

A lighter-style sorbet, milky and slightly sour, this makes a great alternative to ice cream.

Combine the yoghurt, sorbet syrup, lemon juice and vanilla seeds in a medium bowl and mix well.

Pour into an ice cream machine and churn as per the manufacturer's instructions.

Transfer to an airtight container and freeze for at least 4 hours, or until firm, before use. Store in an airtight container in the freezer for up to 6 months.

LEMON SORBET

~~~~~~~~~

+ 7 lemons
+ 500 ml (17 fl oz/2 cups) Sorbet
  syrup (page 56)
+ 1 large egg white
+ pinch of sea salt

MAKES APPROXIMATELY
1 LITRE (34 FL OZ/4 CUPS)

A fresh and zingy sorbet made with lemon juice and infused with zest.

Wash the lemons and peel off the zest, removing any pith.

Place the zest and sorbet syrup in a medium saucepan and bring to the boil over medium heat. Set aside to cool.

Juice the lemons. Strain.

Add the lemon juice and 150 ml (5 fl oz) water to the cooled sorbet syrup. Cover and chill overnight.

Strain the syrup and pour into an ice cream machine.

Whisk the egg white and salt together until soft peaks form. Add the egg white mixture to the syrup and churn in the ice cream machine as per the manufacturer's instructions.

Transfer to an airtight container and freeze for at least 4 hours, or until firm, before use. Store in an airtight container in the freezer for up to 6 months.

BRANDY SNAP FLAUTAS WITH GOAT'S CHEESE & SALTED CARAMEL

~~~~~~~~~~~~~

+ 1 quantity Salted caramel sauce (page 56)
+ fresh figs, quartered, to garnish
+ raspberries and tart blackberries, halved, to garnish

GOAT'S CHEESE PARFAIT

+ 100 g (3½ oz) caster (superfine) sugar
+ 4 large egg yolks
+ 125 ml (4 fl oz/½ cup) cream with at least 35% fat content
+ ½ teaspoon vanilla extract
+ 1 vanilla bean, split and seeds scraped
+ 125 g (4½ oz/½ cup) goat's curd

BRANDY SNAP FLAUTAS

+ 90 g (3 oz) plain (all-purpose) flour
+ 90 g (3 oz) butter, softened
+ 100 ml (3½ fl oz) golden syrup (light corn syrup)
+ 220 g (8 oz) icing (confectioners') sugar, plus extra for dusting

SERVES 6

Goat's milk is very popular in Latin American gastronomy. Cajeta is a form of caramelised goat's milk. Here a goat's cheese parfait is layered with salted caramel to recreate the cajeta flavours. Flautas are traditionally rolled and fried tortillas, and are commonly filled with prawns (shrimp) and bathed in chipotle sauce. Here they inspire a dessert version of brandy snap flutes filled with rich parfait.

Lightly grease and line a shallow 20 cm (8 in) square tray with a double layer of plastic wrap.

To prepare the goat's cheese parfait, heat the sugar and 2 tablespoons water together in a small saucepan over low heat, until the sugar dissolves. Bring to the boil then set aside.

Whisk the egg yolks using an electric mixer until pale and creamy and doubled in size. Gradually pour the hot sugar syrup into the yolks, whisking continuously until combined, thick and cooled.

Whisk the cream, vanilla extract and vanilla seeds together in a medium bowl until soft peaks form. Add a spoonful of the cream to the goat's curd and stir to combine. Fold the goat's curd mixture into the remaining cream. Fold a large spoonful of the goat's curd cream mixture into the yolk mixture. Add the remaining cream and fold to combine.

Pour half of the mixture onto the prepared tray. Cover and freeze for 1–2 hours, until firm. Pour over enough salted caramel sauce, approximately 190 ml (6½ fl oz/¾ cup), to make a thin layer and top with the remaining parfait mixture. Cover and freeze for at least 2 hours, or until set.

Preheat the oven to 180°C (350°F).

Lightly grease and line a large baking tray with baking paper.

To prepare the brandy snap flautas, place the flour and butter in the bowl of an electric mixer fitted with a paddle attachment. Beat until white and creamy. Add the golden syrup and beat to combine. Sift in the icing sugar and beat to make a dough.

Divide the dough into walnut-sized balls. You should be able to make 14 but only require 12 for this recipe. The 2 extras cover you for any mishaps when shaping, or extra for tasting.

Place 3 dough balls on the prepared tray, leaving ample space between each, as they will spread to approximately 12 cm (4¾ in) in diameter. Press the balls to flatten slightly. Bake for 5 minutes, or until spread out flat, lacy and golden brown. Remove from the oven and leave for 1 minute to cool and set slightly. Working quickly, so that the discs don't harden and become unpliable, using a cookie cutter, cut out 10 cm (4 in) rounds. Roll the discs into wide cigar shapes. Set aside to cool. Repeat with the remaining dough to make 12 cigars.

To assemble, using a warm knife, cut the parfait into thin rectangles, slightly smaller than the cigars. Pack the parfait into the cigars, flattening the edges with a warm palette knife. Refreeze briefly.

To serve, place 2 cigars on each serving plate, dust with icing sugar. Garnish with fresh fig slices and berries and drizzle with the remaining salted caramel sauce.

BRANDY SNAP FLAUTAS WITH
GOAT'S CHEESE & SALTED CARAMEL
(pages 268–9)

CHOCOLATE, CHERRY & CHILLI TART

- + melted butter for greasing
- + flour for dusting
- + 1/2 quantity Macadamia pastry (page 54)
- + Chocolate sorbet (page 266) to serve

FILLING

- + 350 g (12 1/2 oz) dark chocolate, minimum 50% cocoa solids
- + 250 ml (8 1/2 fl oz/1 cup) double (heavy) cream

SERVES 16

- + 100 ml (3 1/2 fl oz) milk
- + 50 ml (1 3/4 fl oz) chilled espresso
- + 1 teaspoon ancho chilli powder (see Glossary) or 1/2 teaspoon regular chilli powder
- + 2 large eggs, lightly beaten
- + 55 g (2 oz/1/4 cup) caster (superfine) sugar
- + 200 g (7 oz/1 cup) liqueur-soaked cherries, drained, plus extra for garnish

CHOCOLATE GLAZE

- + 60 g (2 oz) bitter dark couverture chocolate, or good-quality dark cooking chocolate, minimum 50% cocoa solids
- + 125 ml (4 fl oz/1/2 cup) Sorbet syrup (page 56)
- + 2 tablespoons unsweetened (Dutch) cocoa powder

TOPPING

- + smashed amaretti cookies to garnish
- + flaked almonds or hazelnut praline (see Nut praline, page 263)

This decadent tart is perfect with a strong cup of coffee. Why not take the opportunity to try a single origin blend, or try something new? There are so many types of coffee available. When served with chocolate sorbet this dish is elevated to new heights of delectability.

Lightly butter and flour a 30 cm (12 in) tart (flan) tin that has a removable base.

Roll out the pastry between 2 pieces of baking paper, to make a disc large enough to line the prepared tin. Lay the disc in the tin and use your fingers to press and mould the pastry up the side of the tin. Trim off the excess pastry. Rest in the refrigerator for 30 minutes.

Preheat the oven to 180°C (350°F).

Cover the pastry shell with baking paper and fill with baking beans. Blind bake for 15 minutes. Remove the baking beans and paper and bake uncovered for a further 5 minutes, or until the pastry is just cooked through. Set aside to cool.

Reduce the oven temperature to 150°C (300°F).

To prepare the filling, place the chocolate in a heatproof bowl and set over a saucepan of barely simmering water, ensuring the base of the bowl is not touching the water. Stir occasionally until melted.

Brush the base of the cooled pastry shell with some of the melted chocolate and set aside.

Combine the cream and milk in a small saucepan and bring to the boil over medium–low heat. Remove from the heat and add the remaining melted chocolate, espresso and chilli powder and stir to combine.

Whisk the eggs and sugar together using an electric mixer until pale and creamy. Gradually pour in the hot cream mixture, stirring continuously, to combine.

Place the tart base on a baking tray. Scatter with the cherries and pour in the filling. Bake for 40 minutes, or until just set. Allow to cool to room temperature.

To prepare the chocolate glaze, place the chocolate in a heatproof bowl and set over a saucepan of barely simmering water, ensuring the base of the bowl is not touching the water. Stir occasionally, until melted and the chocolate reaches 40°C (104°F) on a sugar thermometer.

Warm the sorbet syrup in a small saucepan over medium heat but do not boil. Whisk the cocoa powder into the syrup and warm to 50–55°C (122–131°F). Gradually pour the sorbet syrup into the chocolate, stirring continuously, until the chocolate becomes liquid and shiny. Pour over the tart to cover. Scatter with the smashed amaretti cookies and the flaked almonds or praline, and add a few extra cherries. Set aside for 15 minutes, to set slightly. Slice and serve with the chocolate sorbet.

CARAMEL CHOCOLATE & PEAR CAZUELA WITH SALTED CARAMEL SAUCE

~~~~~~~~~

+ melted butter for brushing
+ unsweetened (Dutch) cocoa powder for dusting
+ 90 g (3 oz) dark chocolate melts (buttons)
+ 65 g (2¼ oz/¾ cup) flaked almonds
+ sesame seeds for sprinkling
+ vanilla ice cream to serve
+ 200 ml (7 fl oz) Salted caramel sauce (page 56)

POACHED PEARS

+ 4 packham pears, peeled
+ 500 ml (17 fl oz/2 cups) Stock syrup (page 57)
+ 1 cinnamon stick
+ 1 star anise

TEQUILA BATTER

+ 4 large eggs
+ 80 g (2¾ oz/⅓ cup) caster (superfine) sugar
+ 1 tablespoon añejo or dark reposado tequila (see Glossary)
+ 50 g (1¾ oz/⅓ cup) plain (all-purpose) flour
+ 375 ml (12½ fl oz/1½ cups) milk

CHOCOLATE BATTER

+ 400 g (14 oz) caramel-flavoured chocolate
+ 200 g (7 oz) unsalted butter
+ 4 large eggs
+ 55 g (2 oz/¼ cup) caster (superfine) sugar
+ 2 tablespoons cornflour (cornstarch)
+ 1 tablespoon plain (all-purpose) flour

SERVES 6

This comforting crowd-pleaser was born out of a new chocolate, flavoured with caramel, that made its way to the restaurant. We all agreed it would make a great pudding. Cazuela is the name given to a cooking pot or dish in Spanish cooking, and this dish is made in a similar style of pot. The batter is made in two stages as the alcohol tends to affect the mixture if combined too early. Serve with ice cream and salted caramel sauce. Hot, cold and sweet!

Preheat the oven to 180°C (350°F).

Brush a deep ovenproof dish approximately 25 cm (10 in) square or six 250 ml (8½ fl oz/1 cup) capacity ramekins with butter and dust with cocoa powder.

To poach the pears, place the pears in a medium saucepan, cover with stock syrup, add the cinnamon stick and star anise and bring to the simmer over low heat. Cover with a circle of baking paper, to help keep the pears submerged and gently simmer for 15 minutes. Remove from the heat and leave to cool in the stock. Once cooled remove the pears from the stock, core and quarter them and slice each quarter lengthways into 3.

To prepare the tequila batter, whisk the eggs, sugar, tequila and flour together in a medium bowl, until smooth. Strain through a fine-mesh sieve and set aside for 15 minutes, to rest.

To prepare the chocolate batter, place the chocolate and butter in a medium heatproof bowl and set over a saucepan of barely simmering water, ensuring the base of the bowl does not touch the water. Stir occasionally, until melted. Remove from the heat and set aside to cool slightly.

Place the eggs and sugar in the bowl of an electric mixer and whisk, until very thick and almost doubled in size. Sift the cornflour and plain flour over the top and gently fold to combine. Fold in the chocolate and butter mixture.

Add the milk to the tequila batter and stir to combine.

Gently fold the tequila and the chocolate batters together.

Spoon some of the batter into the prepared dish, scatter with some of the pear, spoon on more batter and repeat until you have used all the batter and pears. Scatter with chocolate melts and flaked almonds.

Bake for 20–30 minutes, or until just set.

Sprinkle with sesame seeds and serve immediately with vanilla ice cream and a generous amount of salted caramel sauce poured at the table.

COCONUT PANNA COTTA WITH NAPA-STYLE STRAWBERRY & MANGO SALAD

~~~~~~~~~~

+ almond praline to garnish (see Nut praline, page 263)

POACHED STRAWBERRIES

+ 500 ml (17 fl oz/2 cups) pinot
+ 80 g (2¾ oz/⅓ cup) caster (superfine) sugar
+ 50 ml (1¾ fl oz) reduced balsamic vinegar
+ 1 small handful of mint leaves
+ 1 small handful of basil leaves
+ 1 vanilla bean, split and seeds scraped
+ 500 g (1 lb 2 oz/3⅓ cups) strawberries, hulled

COCONUT PANNA COTTA

+ 500 ml (17 fl oz/2 cups) coconut milk
+ 250 ml (8½ fl oz/1 cup) full-cream (whole) milk
+ 125 ml (4 fl oz/½ cup) pouring (single/light) cream
+ 115 g (4 oz/½ cup) caster (superfine) sugar
+ 40 g (1½ oz) freeze-dried strawberries, lightly crushed
+ 1 vanilla bean, split and seeds scraped
+ very small pinch of sea salt
+ 4 gelatine leaves

STRAWBERRY & MANGO SALAD

+ quarters or perfect slices of poached strawberry (see above)
+ perfect cubes or slices of mango

SERVES 4

This dessert celebrates summer in Australia, which reminds me of visiting the Napa Valley in California. Both places have access to some wonderful local produce. Incredible local strawberries from the Mornington Peninsula in Victoria are as big as tomatoes and full of flavour. Here they are steeped in local pinot and infused with vanilla and fresh herbs. Set this dessert in a large glass so there is ample room for plenty of fruit and pinot syrup!

To prepare the poached strawberries, combine the pinot, sugar, balsamic reduction, mint, basil and vanilla bean and seeds and simmer over medium–low heat for 20 minutes. Set aside to cool. Drain the strawberries, straining the liquid into a small saucepan. Pour the cooled pinot liquid over the strawberries, cover and refrigerate for 1 day to infuse.

To prepare the panna cotta, combine the coconut cream, milk, cream, sugar, dried strawberries, vanilla bean and seeds and salt in a medium saucepan and cook over low heat until warm. Set aside for 20 minutes to infuse.

Blend the infused cream using a hand-held or stand blender until smooth. Strain through a fine-mesh sieve. Return 250 ml (8½ fl oz/1 cup) to the saucepan and warm over low heat.

Soak the gelatine leaves in cold water for 5–10 minutes, until softened. Squeeze out the excess water and add to the warm cream mixture. Stir to dissolve. Add the mixture to the remaining infused cream and stir to combine. Transfer the mixture to a pitcher.

Pour the infused cream into 4 large glasses, to fill just under halfway. Cover the glasses with plastic wrap and refrigerate overnight until set.

Simmer the liquid over medium–low heat, until reduced by half to become a more full-flavoured liquid. Cool and chill.

To serve, place neat layers of the poached strawberries and mango on the set panna cottas and top with the chilled strawberry liquor. Garnish with the praline.

COFFEE & TEQUILA CRÈME CARAMEL

~~~~~~~~~

CARAMEL

+ almond or rice bran oil for greasing
+ 110 g (4 oz/1/2 cup) sugar
+ 1 tablespoon corn syrup or golden syrup
+ splash of Patrón XO Café tequila (see Glossary)

CUSTARD

+ 190 ml (6 1/2 fl oz/3/4 cup) pouring (single/light) cream
+ 125 ml (4 fl oz/1/2 cup) full-cream (whole) milk
+ 1 cinnamon stick
+ 1/2 vanilla bean, split and seeds scraped
+ 50 ml (1 3/4 fl oz) espresso
+ 25 g (1 oz) dark chocolate, minimum 50% cocoa solids
+ 2 large eggs
+ 1 large egg yolk
+ 75 g (2 3/4 oz/1/3 cup) sugar

GARNISH

+ Chocolate sauce (page 55)
+ splash of Patrón XO Café tequila (see Glossary)
+ 1 tablespoon sesame seeds, lightly toasted (optional)
+ 100 g (3 1/2 oz) Sesame tuilles (page 262) (optional)

SERVES 4

Coffee and tequila might seem like an odd combination but aged tequila tastes like a fine liqueur and marries beautifully with coffee and cinnamon. A Mexican twist on a classic dessert, this version is darker and more adult than the sickly sweet varieties you can sometimes be served. Enjoy it spoonful by spoonful.

Preheat the oven to 150°C (300°F).

Lightly grease four 125 ml (4 fl oz/1/2 cup) capacity ovenproof moulds with the almond oil.

To make the caramel, combine the sugar, corn syrup and tequila in a small saucepan and set over low heat. Gently heat until the sugar begins to caramelise. Swirl the sugar mixture to help create an even caramel. Pour the caramel into the bases of the prepared moulds.

To prepare the custard, combine the cream, milk, cinnamon stick and vanilla bean and seeds in a medium saucepan and bring to a simmer. Add the espresso and chocolate and stir to melt the chocolate and combine. Set aside to infuse and cool slightly.

Whisk the eggs, egg yolk and sugar together in a medium bowl, until pale, creamy and all the sugar has dissolved. Gradually pour in the coffee cream, stirring with a wooden spoon to combine. Strain through a fine-mesh sieve. Pour into the caramel-lined moulds, to fill.

Line a small deep baking tray with a clean tea towel (dish towel) or a few layers of paper towel. Arrange the moulds in the tray and pour in enough boiling water to come halfway up the sides of the moulds.

Carefully place the tray in the oven and cook for 20 minutes, or until the crème caramels are just set and firm to the touch.

Remove the moulds from the tray and set aside to cool.

Refrigerate overnight before serving.

To serve, using your fingers, gently press the set custard around the inner edge, to break the seal of the mould. Invert onto shallow serving dishes and garnish with chocolate sauce, a splash of the tequila and a sprinkle of sesame seeds and shards of sesame tuilles.

PISTACHIO & CHOCOLATE SOUFFLÉ WITH DULCE DE LECHE ICE CREAM

~~~~~~~~~~

+ unsalted butter, softened, for greasing
+ 50 g (1¾ oz) dark cooking chocolate, minimum 50% cocoa solids, finely grated
+ 8 very ripe small green figs, or small figs in syrup
+ 50 g (1¾ oz/¼ cup) pistachio praline (see Nut praline, page 263) or pistachio nuts, toasted and roughly chopped
+ icing (confectioners') sugar for dusting

+ 200 ml (7 fl oz) Chocolate sauce (page 55), warmed
+ Dulce de leche ice cream (page 264)

CHOCOLATE SOUFFLÉ

+ 3 large egg yolks
+ 55 g (2 oz/¼ cup) caster (superfine) sugar
+ 2 tablespoons plain (all-purpose) flour

+ 250 ml (8½ fl oz/1 cup) milk
+ 75 g (2¾ oz) pistachio paste (see Glossary)
+ 30 g (1 oz/¼ cup) unsweetened (Dutch) cocoa powder
+ 5 large egg whites
+ 80 g (2¾ oz/⅓ cup) caster (superfine) sugar

| SERVES 4 |

Everyone is impressed by the theatre of a good soufflé. I love the hidden fig in this one. This is an exotic Latin variation of the traditional soufflé served with, of course, dulce de leche ice cream.

Preheat the oven to 190°C (375°F). Place a baking tray in the oven to heat.

Grease four 250 ml (8½ fl oz/1 cup) capacity ovenproof soufflé dishes or ramekins with softened butter, using upward strokes for the sides. Place a tablespoon of finely grated chocolate into each dish. Rotate to coat the sides, tipping out any excess as you go. Set aside.

To prepare the soufflés, whisk the egg yolks, sugar and flour together in a medium bowl.

Place the milk and pistachio paste in a small saucepan and bring to the boil over medium–low heat.

Gradually pour the hot milk into the egg yolk mixture, stirring continuously to combine. Return to the pan and bring to the boil over medium–low heat, whisking constantly, until thickened. Sift in the cocoa powder and stir to combine. Transfer to a medium bowl and set aside to cool.

Place the egg whites in the bowl of an electric mixer fitted with a whisk attachment. Whisk the eggs until frothy. Continue whisking, gradually adding the caster sugar, until soft peaks form. Fold one third of the egg whites into the pistachio and chocolate cream. Add the remaining egg whites and gently fold to combine.

Place 2 figs in each soufflé dish and pour the soufflé mixture over the top. Smooth the top of each soufflé with the back of a knife, to create a flat surface. Run the handle of a teaspoon around the edge of the dishes to ease the mixture away from the sides. Sprinkle the tops with crushed praline and bake on the preheated tray for 15 minutes, or until well risen and cooked through.

Dust with icing sugar and serve immediately with the warm chocolate sauce and dulce de leche ice cream.

FLAMING FINGER LIME & TEQUILA TART

~~~~~~~~~~~~~~~~~

+ melted butter for greasing
+ flour for dusting
+ ½ quantity Macadamia pastry (page 54)
+ sea salt for sprinkling
+ Yoghurt sorbet (page 266) to serve

FILLING

+ 2 whole eggs
+ 4 egg yolks
+ 25 ml (¾ fl oz) añejo tequila (see Glossary)
+ finely grated zest and juice of 6 limes
+ 400 ml (14 fl oz) tin condensed milk

MERINGUE

+ 5 large egg whites
+ 285 g (10 oz/1¼ cups) caster (superfine) sugar
+ 1 teaspoon vinegar
+ ½ teaspoon cornflour (cornstarch)

GARNISH

+ 6 finger limes (see Glossary) fleshed, or key limes or dessert limes, thinly sliced
+ 60 ml (2 fl oz/¼ cup) tequila

> SERVES 10-12

This tart takes its inspiration from the classic American key lime pie. Here it's prepared with a youthful Mexican twist by adding tequila and combined with some very Australian ingredients in macadamia nuts and finger limes. Tequila and lime is a combination that will make you smile and it adds a lovely warmth to the dish. The delicate and delicious pastry is made from macadamia nuts sprinkled with sea salt, for further enjoyment of that sweet-and-sour margarita combination.

Lightly butter and flour a 26 cm (10¼ in) deep flan (tart) tin with a removable base. Chill for at least 15 minutes prior to lining with pastry.

To prepare the pastry shell, use your fingertips to press the chilled pastry evenly over the base and up the side of the tin. Evenly trim off any excess dough.

Preheat the oven to 180°C (350°F).

Cover the pastry shell with baking paper and fill with baking beans. Blind bake for 15 minutes. Remove the baking beans and paper and bake, uncovered, for a further 5 minutes, or until the pastry is just cooked through. Set aside to cool.

Reduce the oven temperature to 140°C (275°F).

To prepare the filling, combine the eggs, egg yolks and tequila in a medium heatproof bowl and set over a saucepan of barely simmering water, ensuring the base of the bowl does not touch the water. Whisk the eggs continuously over the hot water, for 2 minutes, or until thick and foamy. Gradually add the lime zest and juice, a little at a time, whisking after each addition until the mixture is thick and foamy. This process will take approximately 10 minutes. Remove from the heat and gradually whisk in the condensed milk.

Sprinkle the tart base with sea salt and pour in the filling.

Bake for 10 minutes, or until the filling is just set. Set aside to cool. Refrigerate for 30 minutes, or until completely set.

Reduce the oven temperature to 90°C (195°F).

To prepare the meringue, draw a circle on some baking paper that is exactly the same size as the pastry tart shell.

Place the egg whites in the bowl of an electric mixer and whisk until foamy. Gradually add the sugar, continuously whisking, until stiff peaks form. Add the vinegar and cornflour and whisk until thick and glossy.

Spoon the meringue into a piping (icing) bag fitted with a large plain nozzle. Pipe the meringue on top of the circle on the baking paper as if you were piping onto the tart itself, to create a large pavlova-type lid. Bake for 40 minutes, or until the meringue is set but not coloured. Set aside to cool to room temperature. Once cool, place the meringue lid on the cooked lime tart.

To serve, lightly sprinkle with sea salt flakes and finger lime flesh or lime slices. For some retro flambé action, warm the tequila in a small frying pan over low heat. Carefully pour the liquid over the meringue and then immediately ignite the liquid to flame in front of your guests as you serve the tart.

LEMON ASPEN & LIME SLICE WITH MESCAL-ROASTED PINEAPPLE

~~~~~~~~~~

- + Lemon sorbet (page 267) to serve
- + Dried vanilla beans (page 54) to garnish

LEMON CAKE

- + 145 g (5 oz/^{2}/$_3$ cup) caster (superfine) sugar
- + 4 large eggs, separated
- + 1 teaspoon vanilla extract
- + finely grated zest of 1 lemon
- + 85 g (3 oz) plain (all-purpose) flour
- + 1 tablespoon cornflour (cornstarch)
- + 1 teaspoon baking powder
- + pinch of salt
- + 1 teaspoon cream of tartar
- + 1 tablespoon vegetable oil

SERVES 12

LEMON SYRUP

- + 100 ml (3^1/$_2$ fl oz) lemon juice
- + 100 g (3^1/$_2$ oz) sugar

MOUSSE

- + 250 ml (8^1/$_2$ fl oz/1 cup) freshly squeezed lime juice
- + 100 g (3^1/$_2$ oz) lemon aspen (see Glossary) or yuzu flesh
- + 170 ml (5^1/$_2$ fl oz/^{2}/$_3$ cup) full-cream (whole) milk
- + 75 g (2^3/$_4$ oz/^{1}/$_3$ cup) sugar
- + 2 large egg yolks
- + 4 gelatine leaves
- + 300 ml (10 fl oz) pouring (single/light) cream

MESCAL-ROASTED PINEAPPLE

- + 1 baby pineapple
- + 115 g (4 oz/^{1}/$_2$ cup) brown sugar
- + 50 g (1^3/$_4$ oz) unsalted butter
- + 80 ml (2^1/$_2$ fl oz/^{1}/$_3$ cup) mescal (see Glossary)
- + 1 cinnamon stick
- + 1 vanilla bean, split and seeds scraped

LIME CURD GLAZE

- + 1^1/$_2$ gelatine leaves
- + 60 ml (2 fl oz/^{1}/$_4$ cup) freshly squeezed lime juice
- + 55 g (2 oz/^{1}/$_4$ cup) sugar
- + 1 tablespoon tequila (see Glossary)
- + 100 ml (3^1/$_2$ fl oz) homemade Lime curd (page 57) or store-bought lime curd

Lemon aspen is a very unique flavoured native Australian fruit, found in Northern Queensland. They are available frozen through the internet from outback or gourmet food suppliers. The bitter-sweet flavour of the yuzu, available from Asian grocers, would make a good substitute. Mescal should be used sparingly in this dish, otherwise its smokiness can overpower the delicate citrus flavours. You can make this dessert any shape you like or layer it in a glass like a trifle.

Preheat the oven to 180°C (350°F).

Lightly grease and line a 23 cm (9 in) square cake tin with baking paper.

To prepare the lemon cake, place the sugar, egg yolks, vanilla and lemon zest in the bowl of an electric mixer and whisk until pale, creamy and doubled in size. Add 2 tablespoons water, sift in the flour, cornflour and baking powder and fold to combine.

In a clean bowl, whisk the egg whites and salt, until frothy. Add the cream of tartar and whisk until firm peaks form. Add a large tablespoon of whites to the egg yolk mixture and stir to combine. Gently fold the remaining whites into the batter. Pour the vegetable oil down the side of the bowl into the batter and gently fold to combine.

Pour the batter into the prepared cake tin and bake for 15–20 minutes, until golden and a skewer comes out clean when tested. Leave in the tin to cool for 10 minutes. Turn out onto a rack, remove the baking paper and allow to cool completely.

To make the lemon syrup, combine the lemon juice and sugar in a small saucepan and simmer over low heat for 5 minutes, until reduced to a light syrup.

Lightly grease and line a 23 cm (9 in) square baking tin with plastic wrap.

Cut the cake in half crossways, creating 2 even layers. Trim if necessary. Brush both sides of the cake layers with lemon syrup to moisten. Place the top layer of the cake, coloured side down, into the base of the prepared pan.

To prepare the mousse, combine the lime juice and lemon aspen in a small saucepan and boil for 4 minutes. Transfer to a food processor or blender and process until smooth. Strain through a fine-mesh sieve.

Bring the milk and sugar to the boil in a small saucepan over medium–low heat. Set aside.

Whisk the egg yolks in a medium bowl, until pale. Gradually pour the hot milk into the yolks, whisking continuously, until combined. Return to the pan and cook, stirring continuously with a wooden spoon, over low heat, until thickened enough to coat the back of the spoon.

Soak the gelatine leaves in cold water for 5–10 minutes, until softened.

Whisk the cream in a medium bowl, until soft peaks form. Set aside.

Squeeze the excess water out of the softened gelatine and add to the hot custard. Stir to dissolve and combine. Strain the custard through a fine-mesh sieve into a medium bowl. Set the bowl over a larger bowl of iced water and whisk until cold. Add

the lime and lemon aspen juice and whisk until thickened. Add a large spoonful of the whipped cream and stir to combine. Fold in the remaining cream. Pour the mousse into the cake-lined tin. Top with the remaining cake layer, coloured side up, pressing down gently to secure. Cover and refrigerate for 2 hours, or until set.

Meanwhile to prepare the pineapple, peel it retaining the natural pineapple shape, cut the pineapple into 4 wedges lengthways and remove any excess core. Heat a large frying pan over medium–high heat and cook the pineapple until a dark brown caramelised colour on all sides. Add the sugar and caramelise further. Add the butter, mescal, cinnamon stick and vanilla bean and seeds and simmer for 10 minutes, or until reduced to a rich caramel. Set aside and leave the pineapple to cool in the caramel.

To make the lime curd glaze, soak the gelatine leaves in cold water for 5–10 minutes, until softened.

Simmer the lime juice, sugar and tequila together in a small saucepan, stirring occasionally, until the sugar dissolves. Remove from the heat. Squeeze the excess water out of the softened gelatine and add to the liquid, stirring to dissolve and combine. Set aside to cool to room temperature. Add the lime curd and stir to combine.

Pour the glaze over the cake. Refrigerate for 15 minutes, or until set.

To serve, using a hot knife, slice the cake in half and then across to make 12 even-sized 12.5 cm (5 in) long rectangles.

Warm the pineapple pieces basting in the caramel until warm and glazed. Transfer them to a chopping board and cut into thin slices. Arrange the pineapple decoratively, dress the plate with the pineapple, mescal and caramel sauce. Top the cake with the lemon syrup and garnish with dried vanilla beans. Serve immediately with a scoop of lemon sorbet.

CAPIROTADA WITH TAMARIND & PEARS

~~~~~~~~~~~~~~~~~~~~

+ 50 g (1³/4 oz) butter, softened
+ 300 g (10¹/2 oz) cinnamon fruit loaf or fruit brioche, cut into 2 cm (³/4 in) slices
+ 60 g (2 oz/¹/3 cup) dried apricots, finely chopped
+ 40 g (1¹/2 oz/¹/3 cup) sultanas (golden raisins), soaked in boiling water for 10 minutes, drained
+ 125 g (4¹/2 oz/1 cup) finely grated salty cheddar
+ 55 g (2 oz/¹/4 cup) stem ginger, finely chopped
+ 45 g (1¹/2 oz/¹/2 cup) flaked almonds
+ 50 g (1³/4 oz/¹/3 cup) chocolate melts (buttons)
+ Yoghurt sorbet (page 266) to serve

POACHED PEARS

+ 4 packham pears, peeled
+ 500 ml (17 fl oz/2 cups) Stock syrup (page 57)

CUSTARD

+ 200 ml (7 fl oz) full-cream (whole) milk
+ 200 ml (7 fl oz) double (heavy) cream
+ 1 vanilla bean, split and seeds scraped
+ finely grated zest of 1 orange
+ 2 teaspoons ground cinnamon
+ 1 teaspoon freshly grated nutmeg
+ ¹/8 teaspoon ground cloves
+ 2 large eggs
+ 2 large egg yolks
+ 80 g (2³/4 oz/¹/3 cup) brown sugar, plus extra to sprinkle on top

TAMARIND SAUCE

+ 125 g (4¹/2 oz/¹/2 cup) tamarind pulp
+ 125 ml (4 fl oz/¹/2 cup) freshly squeezed lime juice
+ 250 g (9 oz) brown sugar
+ 1 cinnamon stick
+ 120 g (4¹/2 oz/²/3 cup) pitted dates
+ 1 vanilla bean, split and seeds scraped
+ 1 tablespoon pouring (single/light) cream

SERVES 6

Capirotada is basically Mexican bread pudding. It's a big call but I firmly believe that my mum makes the best bread pudding! I know I'm biased, and sorry to all the beautiful mamas out there, but it was a neighbourhood favourite in my North London home and all the kids loved hanging around our house when Mum was cooking it. This recipe may seem wild but the pudding has received rave reviews from our restaurant customers. Cook it with or without the tamarind sauce and serve with yoghurt sorbet.

Preheat the oven to 180°C (350°F).

To poach the pears, place them in a medium saucepan, cover with stock syrup and cook over low heat until simmering. Cover with a circle of baking paper, to help keep the pears submerged, and gently simmer for 15 minutes. Remove from the heat and leave to cool in the stock.

To prepare the custard, combine the milk, cream, vanilla bean and seeds, orange zest and spices and allow to simmer over medium–low heat for about 5 minutes.

Place the eggs, egg yolks and sugar in the bowl of an electric mixer and whisk until pale and creamy. Gradually pour in the hot milk mixture, whisking continuously on low, until combined. Set aside to infuse.

Butter the bread and cut it into cubes.

To assemble the pudding, create a layer of fruit and cheese, scattering half of the apricots, sultanas, cheese and ginger in the base of a medium ovenproof casserole or pie dish. Top with the buttered bread cubes and pour over the infused custard. Sprinkle with the remaining fruit and cheese, the almonds, chocolate and the extra brown sugar.

Bake for 30–40 minutes, until the pudding is firm to the touch. Allow to cool slightly.

To make the tamarind sauce, combine all the ingredients, except the cream, in a medium saucepan and cook over low heat for 15 minutes, until the tamarind has dissolved and the dates have softened to a pulp. Transfer to a food processor and blend to make a smooth sauce. Strain through a fine-mesh sieve. Add the cream and stir to combine. Keep warm.

Cut the poached pears into quarters and then slice each quarter lengthways into 4 slices.

To serve, present the pudding in its cooking dish or cut into individual portions. Serve the pears alongside or scatter the pudding with pear slices, top with yoghurt sorbet and serve with the warm tamarind sauce. Garnish with cinnamon sticks and vanilla beans, if desired.

RHUBARB & CORN COBBLER

~~~~~~~~~~

+ icing (confectioners') sugar for dusting
+ toasted pepitas (pumpkin seeds) for garnish
+ toasted black and white sesame seeds for garnish
+ Sweetcorn ice cream (page 265) to serve

RHUBARB COMPOTE

+ 750 ml (25 1/2 fl oz/3 cups) moscato
+ 110 g (4 oz/1/2 cup) sugar
+ 100 g (3 1/2 oz) split frozen rosella (wild hibiscus) (see Glossary) or 50 ml (1 3/4 fl oz) pomegranate molasses
+ finely grated zest and juice of 1 lemon
+ 2 cinnamon sticks
+ 1 vanilla bean, split and seeds scraped
+ 500 g (1 lb 2 oz) rhubarb, peeled and cut into 2 cm (3/4 in) lengths

TOPPING

+ 150 g (5 1/2 oz/1 1/2 cups) masa harina PAN flour (see Glossary)
+ 100 g (3 1/2 oz) sugar, plus extra for sprinkling
+ 1/2 teaspoon baking powder
+ 1/2 teaspoon bicarbonate of soda (baking soda)
+ 80 g (2 3/4 oz) unsalted butter, at room temperature
+ 125 ml (4 fl oz/1/2 cup) buttermilk
+ 2 large eggs, lightly beaten
+ 1/2 teaspoon vanilla extract

SERVES 4

Cobbler is an English dessert that has been embraced by our American cousins. Here it's given a Latin twist by making the dumplings with masa harina flour which adds a nice sweetcorn note and it's gluten-free! The sweetness of the corn complements the sourness of the rhubarb but you could use any sour fruit.

Preheat the oven to 180°C (350°F).

To prepare the compote, combine the moscato, sugar, rosella, lemon zest and juice, cinnamon sticks and vanilla bean and seeds in a medium saucepan and bring to the boil. Reduce the heat and simmer for 10 minutes. Strain.

Place the rhubarb in a medium ovenproof casserole or pie dish and pour in enough of the infused wine to cover. Bake for 10 minutes, or until tender.

Place the remaining cooking liquid in a small saucepan and simmer over low heat, until reduced to make a rich glaze. Pour over the tender rhubarb.

To prepare the topping, combine the flour, sugar, baking powder and bicarbonate of soda in a food processor and blend to combine. Add the butter and blend to resemble coarse crumbs. Add the buttermilk, eggs and vanilla extract and blend to form a rough dough. Turn out onto a clean work surface and shape into golf ball-sized balls.

Arrange the balls on top of the rhubarb compote, leaving space for the dumplings to expand. Sprinkle with the extra sugar. Bake for 20 minutes or until the dumplings are golden brown and the filling is bubbling up around the sides.

Dust with icing sugar, sprinkle with the pepitas and sesame seeds and serve hot with the sweetcorn ice cream.

SALTED CARAMEL ICE CREAM CHURROS TACOS

~~~~~~~~~

+ rice bran oil for frying
+ cinnamon sugar for dusting
+ Salted caramel sauce (page 56) to serve
+ hazelnut praline to serve (see Nut praline, page 263)

SALTED CARAMEL ICE CREAM (MAKES 1 LITRE/34 FL OZ/4 CUPS)

+ 8 large egg yolks
+ 500 ml (17 fl oz/2 cups) pouring (single/light) cream
+ 500 ml (17 fl oz/2 cups) full-cream (whole) milk
+ 1/2 vanilla bean, split and seeds scraped
+ 165 g (6 oz/3/4 cup) sugar
+ 1 1/2 teaspoons sea salt

CHURROS TACOS

+ 100 g (3 1/2 oz) butter
+ finely grated zest of 1 orange
+ 150 g (5 1/2 oz/1 cup) plain (all-purpose) flour
+ 1 teaspoon ground cinnamon
+ 1/4 teaspoon sea salt
+ 3 large eggs

SERVES 4

For a new venture I introduced chef-inspired daily delicious ice cream, made from all natural seasonal ingredients, available to take home from the restaurant. To promote this offer I created a fun spin on the classic tubular churros. We piped them flat like tacos so you can eat your ice cream and churros together, rather than dipping them. The churros can be either fried or baked. Both elements in the dish can be made in advance so you can have a delicious dessert at a moment's notice.

To prepare the ice cream, place the egg yolks in a medium bowl and whisk until pale. Combine the cream, milk and vanilla bean and seeds in a medium saucepan and heat until simmering. Set aside.

Combine the sugar and 125 ml (4 fl oz/1/2 cup) water in a medium heavy-based saucepan set over medium–low heat and cook until the sugar begins to caramelise. Swirl the sugar to help create an even caramel.

Gradually pour in the hot cream mixture, stirring continuously to combine. Take care it doesn't splatter. Add the salt and cook over low heat until all the caramel is melted.

Gradually pour the hot cream mixture into the egg yolks, stirring to combine. Return the mixture to the pan and cook over low heat, stirring continuously, until the mixture thickens enough to coat the back of a spoon, or the temperature reaches 85°C (185°F) on a sugar thermometer.

Pour the custard into a stainless steel bowl and set it over a larger bowl of iced water, stirring, to chill rapidly. Refrigerate for 30 minutes.

Once chilled, remove the vanilla bean, pour the salted caramel custard into an ice cream machine and churn as per the manufacturer's instructions. Transfer to an airtight container and freeze for at least 4 hours, or until firm, before use.

To prepare the churros tacos, combine 250 ml (8½ fl oz/1 cup) water with the butter and orange zest in a medium saucepan and bring to the boil over medium heat.

Combine the flour, cinnamon and salt in a small bowl.

Add the flour mixture to the boiling water and stir to come together to make a dough. Cook over medium heat, stirring continuously, until the dough forms a ball and comes away from the side of the pan.

Transfer the dough to the bowl of an electric mixer fitted with a paddle attachment. Beat the dough, adding the eggs, one at a time, beating well after each addition, to incorporate and make a smooth and glossy paste. Set the dough aside to rest for 10 minutes.

Cut four 10 cm (4 in) squares of baking paper.

Spoon the dough into a piping (icing) bag fitted with a large star nozzle. Pipe the mixture onto the paper squares in a spiral, circular fashion, working from the inside out, to form approximately 10 cm (4 in) diameter discs. Store in the freezer until required.

To cook, pour enough rice bran oil into a large deep frying pan to fill it 4 cm (1½ in) deep. Heat the oil to 180°C (350°F).

Carefully slide the piped papers of churros into the oil, 2 at a time. Fry for 2 minutes on each side, until golden brown and cooked through. Remove using a slotted spoon and drain on paper towel. Dust with cinnamon sugar.

Serve the churros tacos on plates while still warm, top with a scoop of ice cream, drizzle generously with salted caramel sauce and sprinkle with praline.

PAUL'S TIPS Churros dough can be made and piped into shape in advance. Store in an airtight container in the freezer for up to a month.

Store salted caramel ice cream in an airtight container in the freezer for up to 6 months.

SALTED CARAMEL ICE
CREAM CHURROS TACOS
(pages 288–9)

DRINKS

09

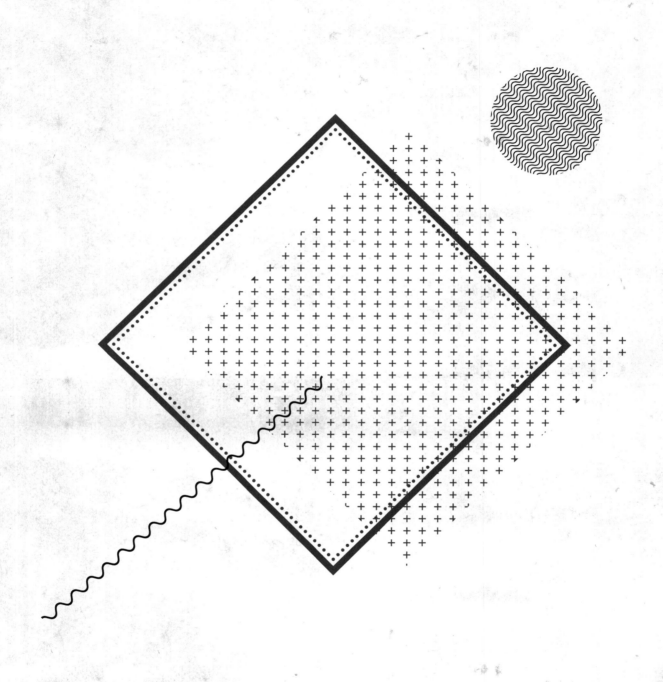

Celebrated as much as
the exotic foods of Mexico, the
unique spirits and distilled elixirs
from the native agave plant are considered
a national treasure.

~~~~~~~~~~~~

Note that mescal is not the same as tequila. Technically, tequila
is a form of mescal and most Mexicans regard some tequila
brands as created only for tourists. Mescal can be made from
11 types of agave native to the state of Oaxaca. The flavours are
as diverse as grapes in wine-making. Our excitement for Latin
culture has led us to the creation of many wonderful cocktails.
In this chapter I have taken a less typical approach, and
have used exotic fruits and flavours designed to
highlight the flavours of Mexico with abandon.
Let your hair down and turn up the
music. It's fiesta time!

ROSELLA ROYALE

~~~~~~~~~~~~~~~~~~

+ 30 ml (1 fl oz) blanco tequila (see Glossary)
+ 30 ml (1 fl oz) rosella tea (see below)
+ 10 ml (¼ fl oz) pulque (see Glossary)
+ French Champagne, chilled
+ riberry (see Glossary) or blackberry to garnish

ROSELLA TEA

+ 250 g (9 oz) sugar
+ 250 ml (8½ fl oz/1 cup) water
+ 125 g (4½ oz) split rosella (wild hibiscus) flowers (see Glossary)
+ 125 g (4½ oz) riberries or frozen blackberries
+ 1 cinnamon stick
+ 2 cm (¾ in) piece fresh ginger, peeled and sliced

SERVES 1

In Mexico the rosella, also known as the wild hibiscus flower, is referred to as the flor de Jamaica. The growing interest in foraged foods has reminded us that there are so many new and interesting wild foods. The Australian riberry, also known as lilly pilly, is one of these. Red currants would make a great substitute. This refreshing aperitif is a great way to start an evening. Made with tequila blanco, homemade rosella tea and crowned with Champagne and native berries this is the perfect summer drink!

To make the rosella tea, combine all of the ingredients in a medium saucepan and cook over low heat until simmering, stirring occasionally until the sugar dissolves. Gently simmer for 20 minutes. Set aside to cool. Strain through a fine-mesh sieve, pressing to extract as much flavour from the fruit as possible.

Pour the blanco tequila, 30 ml (1 fl oz) of the rosella tea and the pulque into a chilled Champagne flute. Top up with Champagne and garnish with a fresh riberry or blackberry.

PAUL'S TIPS Store any remaining rosella tea in an airtight container in the refrigerator for up to 3 months.
  Riberries, also known as lilly pillies, are native to Australia and can be sourced frozen from specialty stores or fresh from a bush, if you have access to one.
  Rosella (wild hibiscus) flowers are available frozen or dried from gourmet food stores.

SMOKY COLD MEDINA

~~~~~~~~~~~~~~~~~

+ smoked sea salt to serve
+ 10 ml (1/4 fl oz) reposado tequila (see Glossary)
+ 10 ml (1/4 fl oz) mescal (see Glossary)
+ 10 ml (1/4 fl oz) jalapeño-infused blanco tequila (see below)
+ 1 lime
+ ice cubes to serve
+ dash of angostura bitters to serve
+ jalapeño slices to serve (optional)

JALAPEÑO-INFUSED TEQUILA

+ 750 ml (25½ fl oz/3 cups) blanco tequila (see Glossary)
+ 2-3 jalapeños

SERVES 1

This takes its name from the classic 1980s rap song 'Funky Cold Medina' by Tone-Lōc. It has become compulsory to listen to the tune while making this cocktail! Like the song, this cocktail is great for getting a party started. Made with two types of tequila along with mescal, angostura bitters and lime, it's served in a smoked salt-rimmed glass. This cocktail packs a punch!

To make the jalapeño-infused tequila, pour the tequila into a 1 litre (34 fl oz/4 cup) jar with a lid. Split the jalapeños lengthways and add them to the tequila. Seal and set aside for 2–3 days, depending on how hot you like it. Strain, returning the liquid to the original bottle.

To coat the rim of the glass, sprinkle enough smoked salt over a small plate to roughly cover. Run half a lime around the rim of a whiskey glass and dip it into the salt.

Pour the reposado tequila, mescal and jalapeño-infused tequila into a cocktail shaker. Add a squeeze of lime and a few cubes of ice. Shake to combine.

Strain into the prepared whiskey glass and top up with ice. Add a dash of bitters and serve. Add some sliced jalapeño to the glass if desired.

MEXICAN MANHATTAN

~~~~~~~~~

+ 60 ml (2 fl oz/1/4 cup) añejo tequila (see Glossary)
+ 30 ml (1 fl oz) Heering cherry liqueur
+ 30 ml (1 fl oz) sweet vermouth
+ 1 large chunk of ice to serve
+ maraschino cherry to garnish

SERVES 1

This Mexican twist on the classic New York City cocktail, the Manhattan, is classy and smooth with an edge. Made with aged tequila, cherry liqueur and sweet vermouth, this cocktail oozes sweet sophistication. It's best served with a single large chunk of ice and garnished with a maraschino cherry.

Pour the tequila, cherry liqueur and sweet vermouth into a mixing glass and gently stir. Place the chunk of ice in a chilled highball or martini glass. Pour the cocktail over the ice and garnish with a cherry.

SANGRITA

~~~~~~~~~

+ 25 ml (3/4 fl oz) pomegranate molasses
+ 10 ml (1/4 fl oz) freshly squeezed orange juice
+ squeeze of lime juice
+ pinch of chilli powder
+ ice for shaking
+ shot glass of Herradura tequila

SERVES 1

This cocktail is the house cocktail of the famous Rosa Mexicano restaurants in the United States. I am always reminded of being in New York when I make this. A lovely sweet and sour drink, it is served in a long shot glass with a matching shot of tequila. To drink, alternate sips between both shots and savour the unique contrasts provided.

Combine the pomegranate molasses, orange juice, lime juice and chilli powder in a cocktail shaker with a few cubes of ice. Shake to combine. Strain into a tall shot glass. Serve with a matching shot of Herradura tequila.

TIJUANA SUNSET

~~~~~~~~~~

+ 30 ml (1 fl oz) blanco tequila (see Glossary)
+ 20 ml (3/4 fl oz) freshly squeezed lime juice
+ pinch of salt
+ ice cubes to serve
+ 90 ml (3 fl oz) freshly squeezed blood orange juice
+ 90 ml (3 fl oz) soda water (club soda)
+ lime wedge to garnish

SERVES 1

A sophisticated take on the tequila sunrise, this refreshing drink is great served after a long day in the sun. Made with tequila blanco, blood orange juice and soda water (club soda), sip this while the sun goes down. It's also a great pick-me-up after a night on the town!

Combine the tequila, lime juice and salt in a chilled highball glass. Add ice and top up with blood orange juice and soda water. Garnish with a lime wedge and serve.

CHERRY MARGARITA

~~~~~~~~~~

+ 125 ml (4 fl oz/1/2 cup) merlot
+ 60 ml (2 fl oz/1/4 cup) reposado tequila (see Glossary)
+ 60 ml (2 fl oz/1/4 cup) freshly squeezed orange juice
+ 60 ml (2 fl oz/1/4 cup) freshly squeezed lime juice
+ 60 ml (2 fl oz/1/4 cup) agave syrup (see Glossary)
+ 100 g (3 1/2 oz) fresh pitted cherries
+ dash of cherry brandy
+ 150 g (5 1/2 oz/1 cup) crushed ice

SERVES 6

The combination of sweet and sour in this recipe balances perfectly to create a delicious and refreshing drink that will have you coming back for more. Made with fresh cherries, this cocktail really shines.

Pour the merlot, tequila, orange juice, lime juice and agave syrup into a mixing pitcher and stir to combine.

Separately muddle the cherries with a dash of cherry brandy, to extract most of the juice.

Strain the cherry juice into a blender. Add the wine mixture and crushed ice and blend to combine.

Pour into chilled margarita glasses to serve.

WATERMELON MARGARITA

~~~~~~~~~~~~~~~~

Sometimes all you need is a margarita and this watermelon-based version is a great summer alternative to the classic citrus-based drink. This recipe needs to be started a couple of days in advance to give the tequila and watermelon time to infuse. It's a refreshingly sweet, but not too sweet, drink with the bitter lemon balancing the sweetness without overpowering the delicate flavour of the melon.

+ 125 ml (4 fl oz/1/2 cup) watermelon-infused tequila (see below)
+ 150 g (5 1/2 oz/1 cup) crushed ice
+ 60 ml (2 fl oz/1/4 cup) bitter lemon
+ 30 ml (1 fl oz) Cointreau
+ 3–4 cubes tequila-marinated watermelon (reserved from the watermelon-infused tequila, see below)
+ small watermelon wedges to garnish

WATERMELON-INFUSED TEQUILA

+ 750 ml (25 1/2 fl oz/3 cups) blanco tequila (see Glossary)
+ 1 kg (2 lb 3 oz) seedless watermelon, cubed

SERVES 2

To make the watermelon-infused tequila, pour the tequila into a 2 litre (68 fl oz/8 cup) jar with a lid. Top up with watermelon cubes. Seal and set aside, gently shaking occasionally, for at least 2 days or up to a week. Strain, returning the liquid to the original bottle. Reserve the tequila-infused watermelon for making the cocktail.

Combine the watermelon-infused tequila with crushed ice, bitter lemon, Cointreau and marinated watermelon in a blender and process until smooth.

Pour into chilled margarita glasses and garnish with the watermelon wedges.

FROZEN FINGER LIME MARGARITA

~~~~~~~~~~~~

+ 125 ml (4 fl oz/1/2 cup) blanco tequila
+ 90 ml (3 fl oz) juice and finely grated zest of 2 limes
+ 30 ml (1 fl oz) Cointreau
+ 300 g (10 1/2 oz/2 cups) crushed ice
+ 2 finger limes to garnish
+ agave syrup to taste (see Glossary)

SERVES 4

Australia has unique finger-shaped limes with caviar-like flesh. These are exported all over the world. Once squeezed out, the flesh makes a great topping for this classic margarita. Made with fresh lime and lots of ice this cocktail is great on a hot day and adds that cooling chill of crushed ice. It's a grown-up slushy of sorts!

Combine the tequila, lime juice and zest, Cointreau and crushed ice in a blender and purée until slushy. Slice 1 finger lime thinly and place in the bottom of the glasses, if desired. Sweeten the cocktail with agave syrup and pour it into chilled margarita glasses.

Cut the remaining finger lime in half and squeeze the flesh out on top of the margarita to garnish.

FROZEN LYCHEE MARGARITA

~~~~~~~~~~~~

+ 125 ml (4 fl oz/1/2 cup) blanco tequila
+ 125 ml (4 fl oz/1/2 cup) freshly squeezed lime juice and finely grated zest
+ 100 g (3 1/2 oz) strained tinned lychees
+ 30 ml (1 fl oz) Cointreau
+ 30 ml (1 fl oz) lychee liqueur
+ 300 g (10 1/2 oz/2 cups) crushed ice
+ lime slices to garnish

SERVES 4

This is a sweeter alternative to the Frozen finger lime margarita (see left). The fragrant taste of lychees is either liked or disliked passionately, but this cocktail is a must for any fan!

Combine the tequila, lime juice and zest, lychees, Cointreau, lychee liqueur and ice in a blender and purée until slushy. Pour into chilled margarita glasses and garnish with slices of lime.

MICHELADA

~~~~~~~~~~~~~~~~~~~~~

+ 1 teaspoon sea salt
+ 1 teaspoon chilli powder
+ 1 lime wedge
+ 60 ml (2 fl oz/¼ cup) tomato juice
+ 30 ml (1 fl oz) freshly squeezed lime juice
+ 1 teaspoon worcestershire sauce
+ dash of hot sauce
+ pinch of ground cumin
+ pinch of freshly ground black pepper
+ pinch of celery salt
+ 1 small chilled bottle of Mexican beer
+ 1 radish, sliced, to garnish

SERVES 1

Big night? The michelada will come to your rescue. Essentially a spicy bloody mary made with beer, this drink is bound to get you going. Made with chilli, lime and hot sauce – just to name a few ingredients – and garnished with a jalapeño, this is a pick-me-up, morning-after drink. It's topped with Mexican beer with the rest of the beer offered as a chaser.

To coat the rim of the glass, combine the salt and chilli powder and sprinkle over a small plate to roughly cover. Run the lime wedge around the rim of a tall beer glass and dip the rim into the spiced salt.

Combine the tomato juice, lime juice and worcestershire sauce in the glass and stir to combine. Add hot sauce, cumin, pepper and celery salt, to taste. Top up with beer and garnish with radish slices.

BUENOS NOCHES

~~~~~~~~~~

+ 60 ml (2 fl oz/1/4 cup) hot espresso infused with cinnamon (see below)
+ 60 ml (2 fl oz/1/4 cup) chipotle-infused reposado tequila (see below)
+ 15 ml (1/2 fl oz) Patrón XO Café tequila
+ whipped cream to serve
+ finely shredded candied orange peel to garnish

CHIPOTLE-INFUSED TEQUILA

+ 750 ml (25 1/2 fl oz/3 cups) reposado tequila
+ 1 dried chipotle chilli

CINNAMON-INFUSED ESPRESSO

+ 60 ml (2 fl oz/1/4 cup) espresso coffee, hot
+ 1 cinnamon stick

SERVES 1

We all love a nightcap but this one won't send you to sleep, that's for sure. This warm, comforting drink is my Mexican twist on an Irish-style coffee. Made with reposado tequila, coffee tequila, hot coffee and infused with cinnamon and chipotle, this is a warming drink to end the night. For a non-caffeinated version you can substitute your favourite drinking chocolate for the coffee.

To make the chipotle-infused tequila, pour the tequila into a 1 litre (34 fl oz/4 cup) jar with a lid. Split the chipotle lengthways and add it to the tequila. Seal and set aside for 2–3 days, depending on how hot you like it. Strain, returning the liquid to the original bottle.

For the cinnamon-infused espresso, transfer the hot espresso into a small saucepan, add the cinnamon stick and set aside to cool. Gently warm the coffee back up and remove the cinnamon stick.

Combine the infused espresso with the chipotle-infused tequila and Patrón XO Café in a glass. Top with whipped cream and sprinkle with candied orange peel to garnish.

PAUL'S TIP Instead of infusing the tequila with chipotle (which may not be to everyone's taste) you can simply add a 3 cm (1 1/4 in) piece of chipotle to the coffee with the cinnamon.

GLOSSARY

~~~~~~~~~

GENERAL NOTE: If you have trouble finding ingredients, try mail-order through online stores.

achiote paste Also known as recada rojo, this is a blend of achiote (annatto) seeds, Mexican oregano, cumin, allspice, black pepper, salt and garlic, which is used in Mexican food, particularly from the Yucatán region. The paste is available from Mexican grocery stores.

adobo sauce A dark red, piquant sauce, made from ground chillies, herbs and vinegar, used in Mexican and Latin dishes. The sauce is available from Mexican grocery stores. See also chipotle in adobo.

agave syrup Also known as honey water, this sweet syrup is extracted from the same succulent plant that mescal and tequila come from, which grows in the southwestern United States, Mexico and Central America. It is available from supermarkets, gourmet suppliers and Mexican grocery stores.

amaranth The seeds and greens of the amaranth plant are both edible. The seeds are often used as a cereal or ground into flour, and are similar to quinoa. In Mexico the seeds are used to make a popular candy called alegria. Amaranth seeds and flour can be found in health food stores and some supermarkets.

cactus Cactus 'paddles' are the leaves of the prickly pear, or nopal. The outer spiny skin is first peeled and then the leaves are cooked before using in Mexican dishes. The flavour is similar to green beans and asparagus. If you are unable to find the leaves fresh, they are available tinned, either pickled or packed in water, from Mexican grocery stores and some gourmet suppliers. Prickly pear juice is also available.

chipotle in adobo Dried smoked jalapeños in adobo sauce. These are available tinned from Mexican grocery stores. See also chillies and peppers.

farro A type of grain that is composed from the grains of members of the wheat family. It has a nutty flavour and chewy texture and is available from health food stores and gourmet delis.

finger lime The finger lime is a gourmet bush food native to Australia and is sometimes known as lime caviar due to its caviar-like flesh. It has a citrus flavour similar to lime. Available from bush food specialists and some gourmet grocery stores.

garlic, black This is a type of caramelised garlic prepared through a process of fermentation that takes about three weeks. The end result is garlic with a flavour reminiscent of caramelised balsamic vinegar. It is often used in Asian cuisine and is available from Asian grocery stores and gourmet greengrocers.

hominy A type of corn that is treated by a process called nixtamalisation so the germ and hull are removed. It is often served as a side dish, similar to rice. It's sold tinned, dried or ground (grits) and is available from gourmet and Mexican grocery stores.

huitlacoche Also known as cuitlachoche, corn smut or maize mushroom, this is a type of fungus that forms in the ear of corn. It has been prized as a food since the time of the Aztecs. It has a smoky-sweet flavour somewhere between mushroom and corn. It makes an unusual alternative to mushrooms. It is available tinned from Mexican grocery stores.

jicama Sometimes called the 'Mexican potato', this tuber has crispy white flesh with a nutty flavour, somewhat like a water chestnut. It can be eaten raw or cooked. It is available from some supermarkets and gourmet greengrocers.

lemon aspen A small pale yellow fruit, native to Australia, with a lemon flavour and aroma and spongy flesh. It is good for desserts, drinks and sweets. It is available from bush food specialists and some gourmet greengrocers.

masa This is the dough that is made from masa harina flour, used for making tortillas. See also masa harina and masa PAN flour.

masa harina A finely ground flour made from hominy (nixtamalised corn). It is used for making masa dough. It is available from some supermarkets, health food stores and gourmet or Mexican grocery stores. See also masa and masa PAN flour.

masa PAN flour Also known as harina PAN, this is a type of masa harina flour from Venezuela. It is available from South American grocery stores. See also masa and masa harina.

mescal Mescal is an alcoholic liquor distilled from the agave plant, a succulent native to the southwestern United States, Mexico and Central America. Mescal, or mezcal, has a smoky flavour and is one of Mexico's most traditional beverages. It is often sold in bottles containing an agave worm. See also tequila.

morcilla A type of Spanish blood sausage usually made from pig's blood, onion, spices and other flavourings. Look for it at Spanish grocery stores and butchers.

mushroom, trompet Also known as trumpet mushroom, this is a type of wild mushroom available from gourmet greengrocers.

pistachio paste With a consistency rather like tahini, this paste is made from ground and puréed pistachio nuts. It is often used to make desserts and is available from gourmet suppliers.

pulque A milky white alcoholic beverage made from fermented agave sap. It is available from some bottle shops and Spanish or Mexican grocery stores.

riberry Also known as lilly pilly, this is the berry of a tropical plant often used for jam. It is available fresh or frozen from gourmet suppliers.

rosella Also known as the wild hibiscus or flor de Jamaica, in Mexico this flower is used to make sweet-and-sour drinks and preserves. The flowers are available in syrup, frozen or dried from Mexican grocery stores and spice shops.

tequila Tequila is an alcoholic liquor distilled from the agave plant, and it is actually a type of mescal. There are various types of tequila, and the ones I have called for in this book are: tequila añejo (an amber-coloured tequila, aged for at least 1 year); tequila blanco (unaged tequila from the blue agave where you can really taste the sweet flavour of the plant); tequila reposado (tequila at its first stage of resting and ageing, usually between 2 and 11 months old).

tomatillo Also known as Mexican green tomato, this small, green tomato-like fruit is a staple in Mexican cooking and can be found at some supermarkets and greengrocers.

CHILLIES AND PEPPERS

There are more than 200 varieties of chillies and peppers and, amazingly, more than 100 of them are native to Mexico. Chillies and peppers vary from mild to scorchingly hot, and the heat is measured on the 'Scoville Scale'. In this book I have used or mentioned the following types:

amarillo or aji amarillo A medium-hot chilli very popular in Peru. It starts off green but matures to a yellowish-orange and has a fruity flavour. The amarillo is sold either fresh, pickled and tinned, or ground, and is available from Mexican and South American grocery stores.

ancho This is a poblano chilli that has been dried to form a large, flat, reddish-brown chilli with a sweet and medium-hot flavour. It is used regularly in Mexican cooking, especially in tamales. It is often sold ground and is available from gourmet suppliers and at Mexican grocers.

bullhorn Also known as chile de agua, this is a long, narrow green chilli with a fairly mild and sweet flavour. It is often used in salsas. It is sold fresh, dried or tinned at Mexican grocery stores and some supermarkets.

chipotle This is a dried, smoked jalapeño that is often used in Mexican cooking. It is dark brown and wrinkled in appearance and has a sweet and smoky, almost chocolatey, flavour. It is available both dried and tinned from Mexican grocery stores. See also chipotle in adobo.

guajillo This long dried mirasol chilli is a shiny dark red and has a green tea-like flavour with berry notes. It must be soaked for longer than other dried chillies. Look for it in Mexican grocery stores.

habanero These very hot chillies, used in Mexican, Caribbean and South American cooking, are small and lantern-shaped and range from green to bright orange. They are available fresh and dried from Mexican grocery stores and gourmet greengrocers.

mulato This type of dried poblano chilli is mild to medium-hot with a fruity, smoky flavour with chocolate and licorice notes. The mulato is part of the famous Mexican 'holy trinity' of chillies, along with ancho and pasilla, used in mole as well as other Mexican sauces and stews. It is available from Mexican grocery stores.

padrón pepper A small fiery green pepper from Spain, green or yellowish green in colour.

pasilla This is a dried chilaca chilli, blackish-brown in colour and raisin-like in flavour. It is very popular in Oaxaca in Mexico. Look for it both whole and ground in Mexican grocery stores.

poblano A large chilli with a mild to medium-hot flavour that is often stuffed, such as in the classic dish chillies rellenos. When roasted the flavour intensifies. Look for it in some Mexican grocery stores or gourmet greengrocers.

serrano A small hot chilli that starts off green but matures to red. It is available fresh, pickled or dried (chile seco). It is often used in hot sauces and is available in Mexican grocery stores.

INDEX

Entries with an initial capital letter are recipes; lower case entries are general topics.

THANK YOU

~~~~~~~~~~~~~~~~~~~~~~~~~~~~~~~~

It's been an incredible period developing this book. I would like to sincerely thank all the dedicated and talented chefs, front of house, providores, farmers, customers, clients, journalists, restaurateurs and advisors with whom I have had the pleasure of collaborating and corresponding during the production of this book. In no particular order: Wayne Manney, Julian Peroudin, Andrew Logan, Jake Nicholson, the team at El Cielo, Cameron Denning, Stephen O'Connell, Kestrel, Ashley Hicks, John Demitrious, Hassim Sulficar, Reg Lodewyke, Lyndon Tyers, Dan Hawkins, Michelle Payne, Jean Slattery, Jess Harker, Ted Rubira, Paul Lew, Krystal Marshall and Vaj, Amy Sutherland, Mitchell Townrow, Madeline Morgan, Sarah James, Stephen Burke, Daannen Nootenboom, Sally Humble, the entire team at Icebergs, Julian Gurner, Tom Walker, Andrew and Gerry Ryan, Marino Angelini for the opportunity to relaunch so many businesses with all the attendant challenges - it has been an invaluable experience. A special thank you to Tony Bourdain for being the man he is and enriching the culinary world.

This publication's most influential food suppliers: Nick Mirikilis, Vegetable Connection; Anthony Puharich, Vics Meats; Maria Tsihlakis, The Essential Ingredient; Con and James Andronis, Clamms Seafood's; Paul de Silva, Casa Iberica; Steve Watson; Tony Mann; Pick of the bunch; Ken King, Horizon farms.

My passion for food is only equalled by my love and gratitude to all my family and friends who always support my endeavours. In particular I would like to thank: Andy and Josie; Matt and Sally; Sean and Natalie; Clyde and Simone; Ben and Kirsten; Lee and Meagan; Zoe; Sarah; Fiona and Damon; Kirsty; Georgina and Kamahl; Tony and Gab; Andrew and Maria; Ernst and Petra; Cindy and Michael; Maurice and Lucy; Damien and Genevieve; my personal trainer, Myles Kelly, for keeping me fit; Marco and Ilona; Sheridan and Karlose; Geoff and Jane; Virginia and Clinton; Helen and Dane; Anna and Renato; George and Helen; my extraordinary parents, Robert and Eileen, and my brothers, Clive and Mark, who are my inspiration, as well as their wonderful families Les, Wendy, Emma, Conor and Gemma for continuous love and support; my Australian family, Christine, Peter, Fiona, Tom, Fred, Johnson, Karen and Chris; my mentor, Armando, who is always in my thoughts (RIP); and finally my beautiful wife, Bec, for her undying love and friendship.

Thanks also to the entire team at Hardie Grant, in particular Paul McNally for his patience and Lucy Heaver and Murray Batten, whose talent and enthusiasm have enriched this book.

Published in 2014 by Hardie Grant Books

Hardie Grant Books (Australia)
Ground Floor, Building 1
658 Church Street
Richmond, Victoria 3121
www.hardiegrant.com.au

Hardie Grant Books (UK)
5th & 6th Floor
52 54 Southwark Street
London SE1 1RU
www.hardiegrant.co.uk

A Cataloguing-in-Publication entry is available from the catalogue
of the National Library of Australia at www.nla.gov.au

Cantina
ISBN 978 1 74270 399 2

Publishing Director: Paul McNally
Managing Editor: Lucy Heaver
Editor: Ariana Klepac
Design Manager: Mark Campbell
Design Concept: Murray Batten
Typesetter: Susanne Geppert
Photographer: Chris Middleton
Stylist: Vicki Valsamis
Production Manager: Todd Rechner
Production Coordinator: Carly Milroy

Colour reproduction by Splitting Image Colour Studio
Printed in China by 1010 Printing International Limited

Find this book on **Cooked.**
www.cooked.com.au
www.cooked.co.uk